Korea's

TWENTIETH-CENTURY ODYSSEY

Korea's
TWENTIETH-CENTURY ODYSSEY

Michael E. Robinson

University of Hawai'i Press
Honolulu

12 11 10 09   6 5 4 3

Library of Congress Cataloging-in-Publication Data
Robinson, Michael Edson.
    Korea's twentieth-century odyssey : a short history /
Michael E. Robinson.
        p. cm.
    Includes bibliographical references and index.
    ISBN-13: 978-0-8248-3080-9 (hardcover : alk. paper)
    ISBN-13: 978-0-8248-3174-5 (pbk. : alk. paper)
        1. Korea—History—20th century—Textbooks.
    2. Korea (South)—History—20th century—Textbooks.
    3. Korea (North)—History—20th century—Textbooks.
    I. Title.
        DS916.R63 2007
        941.904—dc22
                                2006038995

Designed by Dianna Little

Printed by Edwards Brothers Inc.

In Memory of James B. Palais

. . . . . .

CONTENTS

· · · · · ·

PREFACE AND ACKNOWLEDGMENTS

• • • • • •

I HAVE RELIED ON MY OWN RESEARCH, teaching experience, and a large body of secondary literature on Korea to write this book. In addition, I owe a heavy debt to my colleagues in Korean Studies from a number of different fields. Without their work, a synthetic narrative such as this would be impossible to write. To cite exact references throughout the text would be at cross-purposes with my desire to shape a simple and reader-friendly narrative, one that can be used in college-level courses as well as by the general reader. Many of the analytical observations that appear in this book are not mine, but I have brought them together with my own understanding of how the narrative of modern Korean history should be shaped. Where I use another scholar's ideas, where I paraphrase, analyze, or otherwise owe a substantial debt to the work of others in shaping a paragraph, I have cited the author and year of publication at the end of the sentence. Where I have quoted directly, I cite author, date of publication, and page numbers. Readers need only consult the references at the back of this volume to find publication titles. Of course I am solely responsible for all mistakes of fact and my thematic shaping of this short narrative.

This project was made possible by a timely Korea Foundation Advanced Research Grant. I am grateful to the Korea Foundation for their support throughout the years. Very simply, this grant and the encouragement and commitment of Patricia Crosby at the University of Hawai'i Press made this project possible. I must also acknowledge the invaluable help and inspiration provided by close colleagues. Special thanks go to my fellow traveler in the recent Korean past, Carter Eckert, whose friendship and good humor have always sustained me. John Duncan also provided encouragement and advice at crucial moments as well as a critical reading of the manuscript. A further debt is owed to two anonymous readers for the University of Hawai'i Press for their honest, sometimes brutal, but enormously helpful criticism. Of course no project emerges half as well without expert and meticulous copyediting; for this I wish to thank Margaret Black. And my thanks as well to Norman Thorpe, who by sharing his enormous collection of historical photographs, some published herein, helped enliven my imagination and hopefully my prose.

Over the years my interaction with and the work of a wonderful group of Koreanists inspired the writing of this book. The writing and consultations with

Bruce Cumings, Gari Ledyard, Donald Clark, Vipan Chandra, Gi-Wook Shin, Clark Sorensen, Roger Janelli, Linda Lewis, Laurel Kendall, Edward Shultz, Kenneth Wells, Eun Mee Kim, Wayne Patterson, Andrew Nahm, Chae Jin Lee, Han Kyo Kim, Roger Janelli, Chŏng Chinsŏk, Choi Jang Jip, Kim Min Hwan, Lew Young Ick, Donald Baker, Katie Oh, Park Chung-shin, Nancy Ablemann, Alan Delissan, Koen De Ceuster, Boudewijn Walraven, Andre Schmid, Hwang Kyung Moon, Charles Armstrong, Yoo Sun-Young, Ch'oe Kyong Hee, Hong Kal, Chiho Sawada, were all indispensable in the crafting of this book. Where I have used their ideas, I hope I have represented them accurately.

As every author knows well, friends and family play crucial roles in our often lonely pursuit. To my siblings Jim, Mary, and Sue, I can only continue to offer my gratitude for a lifetime of support and love. Special friends Carolyn and Jim Moore and Ellen Brennan also eased my labors by being willing to listen endlessly to my laments. And Sue Hathaway and Scott O'Bryan provided hours of companionship and encouragement at particularly difficult times in the writing of this book. I am profoundly grateful for their understanding and caring. I have dedicated this book to the memory of my graduate school mentor, Jim Palais. If the past is a foreign country, he urged me to travel there and taught me how to decipher its language. I only wish he was still here to take credit for whatever contributions this book makes to the field.

KOREA'S TURBULENT TWENTIETH CENTURY

머 릿 말

HE PEOPLE OF THE KOREAN PENINSULA, now divided into northern and southern nation-states, have had a turbulent twentieth century. In relation to the size of its population and breadth of its territory, Korea has also played a disproportionately important role in the last hundred years of world history. There is considerable irony in this statement because as late as 1876 Korea existed on the margins of the world system, recognizing only one primary interstate relationship—with China—and maintaining only infrequent and highly circumscribed contacts with Japan. Of the West and the expanding capitalist world system Korea knew very little. In the late nineteenth century the Chosŏn dynasty had ruled the people of the peninsula for the astonishingly lengthy tenure of 500 years. Chosŏn's isolation had obscured from the view of the rest of the world a people who possessed a historical lineage of great antiquity and who had made considerable contributions to East Asian civilization. Written history traces the early states on the peninsula to the fourth century B.C. and since the late seventh century large portions of Korea's present territory have been ruled by unified state systems: the Unified Silla state (668–918), the Koryŏ dynasty (918–1392), and finally the Chosŏn dynasty (1392–1910).

In spite of its ancient lineage and long history of autonomy in East Asia, Korea is often thought of as a mere appendage to the great Chinese empire on its northeast border. Korea is no larger than a middle-sized province of China, and it was always in peril of Chinese military aggression. At several times in its history the peninsula or portions thereof have been directly subjugated by Chinese power. But relatively speaking, Korea maintained its political and cultural integrity in the face of its colossal neighbor. It did so through careful attention to power relations along its northern border. And from 1392 until the late nineteenth century, the Chosŏn dynasty maintained a peaceful relationship with the Celestial Empire that was marred only by the disruptions attending the replacement of the Ming by the Qing dynasty during the 1630s and 1640s.

Western observers have often mistakenly interpreted this long relationship as one of vassalage. Indeed, this perception was furthered by the ritual subordination that characterized Korea's formal relationship with China. Korea was, however, an independent state; its society, politics, and culture had evolved separately for over a millennium. While the trappings and administrative structure of the Chosŏn

1

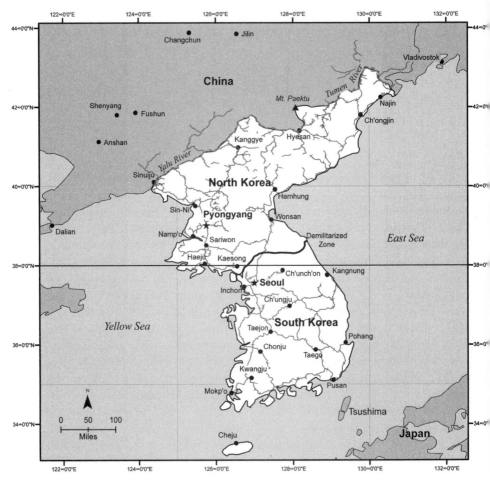

*Korea. Source: Made at the University of Indiana Libraries with data from Environmental Systems
Research Institute (ESRI) and the National Geospatial Intelligence Agency.*

dynastic system seemed to mirror those of the Ming (1368–1644), these surface *[handwritten margin note]* features obscured an intricate assimilation of Chinese ideas and institutions with *[handwritten: CHINESE]* indigenous Korean patterns that had a far more ancient provenance. Korea had *[handwritten: INFLUENCES]* absorbed influences from China from the time its first state structures emerged; it *[handwritten: BUT KOREA IS UNIQUE]* used Classical Chinese as the official writing system of government and elite inter- *[handwritten: IND. + UNIQUE]* course. But it is more important to recognize what was expressed in this admittedly foreign writing system. Korean state structures may have mirrored those of the Chinese, but their operation reflected earlier Korean patterns of aristocratic hierarchy and stratification. Not until the Chosŏn period did Neo-Confucianism become established as state orthodoxy, and even then its values and language were melded into the indigenous political culture of Korea. Given the commonalities, however, it is not surprising that many still view Korea as an offshoot of Chinese civilization. It was indeed a part of the East Asian civilization defined in many ways by Chinese cultural norms. But Chinese influences account for only a portion of Korea's own unique civilization.

This book seeks to explore Korea's historical experience over the last hun- *[handwritten: "EAST ASIA" =]* dred years. It is an experience shaped by foreign intrusion, occupation, war, and *[handwritten: CHINA + JAPAN]* often violent social and economic upheaval. If such experience were a journey, it *[handwritten: WHAT ABOUT]* would be an odyssey in the true sense of the metaphor. In order to make sense *[handwritten: KOREA?]* of its twists and turns, we must sort misconceptions from realities. This is all the more important because of the significant role Korea has played in the evolution of modern East Asia. From the beginning of the process that forced Korea into the world system in the late nineteenth century, outsiders were perplexed by Korea's responses to the threats and opportunities it faced. Their bafflement was, perhaps, in direct proportion to their ignorance of Korean culture and society. Surprisingly, outsiders today exhibit the same kind of ignorance when news of Korea hits the front pages of Western newspapers or is flashed around the Internet. This book is designed to provide a short analytical narrative of Korea's twentieth century that will provide a better understanding of the experiences and forces that have shaped politics and society on the peninsula and a clearer understanding of the behaviors and interests that drive the two Korean states in the complex regional politics of East Asia today.

Chapter One deals with traditional Korea, the Korea encountered by Western and Japanese diplomats and traders in the last quarter of the nineteenth century. It gives a concise account of the political culture, economy, and international relations of Chosŏn Korea. Many have decried Chosŏn's reluctance to accept the new world order as it was emerging in the nineteenth century in East Asia, but much of this criticism ignores the sources of this resistance. In terms of its stability, durability, and cultural accomplishments, Chosŏn Korea was a successful system. It had already lasted almost 500 years, so it stands to reason that its leaders would not easily discard policies that had worked so well for so long. The chapter discusses the difficult path taken by the Chosŏn dynasty as it attempted to maintain its autonomy and identity in the face of imperialism. Ultimately, the traditional Korean state was unable to defend itself, the Japanese annexed Korea as their formal colony, and the dynasty ended in 1910. But this did not happen until after the intrusion of capitalist market forces and new ideas from the West and Japan had begun a transformation of Korean society. It was in these last decades of Chosŏn that both the Korean nationalist movement and the economic and cultural modernization of Korea began. Indeed, this book takes the explicit stance that the origins of Korea's modernity should be traced to the late nineteenth century, not the era following World War II, as the vast bulk of literature on Korean development so ahistorically insists. Already in the decline and ultimate failure of Korea's ancient regime we can find the seeds of its modern transformation.

Chapters Two, Three, and Four recount the turbulent history of Korea's colonial experience under Japanese rule. This is a difficult history to write because the memory of this period still generates passionate feelings in both countries. Moreover, the colonial legacy figured heavily in the ideological warfare between North and South Korea after the division of the peninsula. The complexity and nuance of these critical decades is often lost in the polemical wars between the two Koreas, and concepts are frozen within highly politicized, state-sponsored historical narratives in each country.

Chapter Two outlines the structures of the Japanese colonial state and the institutions that framed Korea's social, cultural, and economic transformation from 1910 to 1945. Understanding how such structures affected Korea's early modernity does not imply that the evolution of modernity in Korea was strictly a Japanese affair. The colonial period set a Japanese agenda, and the colonial state's policies skewed development toward the broader interests of the empire, but even so, Korean agency was still evident, most apparently in the emergence of Korea's national independence movement after the Japanese takeover. While this narrative recognizes how brutal, discriminatory colonial policies made life miserable for the Korean people, it also attempts to present a nuanced view of how Koreans were implicated in and became part of the colonial system. Understanding the colonial period consists neither in cataloguing Japanese abuses and exploitation, nor in focusing solely on heroic Korean resistance. Its goal is to understand how the entire colonial experience produced the contradictions that in combination with the unique circumstances of its demise contributed to the complex evolution of two Korean nation-states on the peninsula.

Chapter Three analyzes the intellectual underpinnings of a conservative reform-based cultural nationalism that emerged in the 1920s and how it was challenged by radical nationalists influenced by the growing popularity of social revolutionary thought. Ultimately these two poles of thought, cultural reformism and socialist radicalism, became the vortices upon which Korean nationalist movement divided itself. This ideological division festered during the colonial period and then emerged quite openly in the post-Liberation era, when it was further complicated by the conflict between exiled nationalist and socialist leaders who had returned. At the end of World War II in the Pacific, the joint Soviet and US occupation created polarizing forces that intensified this original schism, leaving little space for the evolution of a middle ground in postwar nationalist politics. The tragedy of Korea's subsequent division, therefore, claims a portion of its genesis in the colonial period.

Chapter Four recounts the burgeoning modernity that emerged during the thirty-five years of Japanese rule. It is important to note how colonialism structured the early modernity of Korea because it established patterns that informed later developments in post-colonial Korea. Many antecedents of contemporary Korean life were directly or indirectly shaped by forms that evolved within what I refer to as Korea's colonial modernity. After a colonial experience, nations are driven by the desire to excise the remnants of colonialism and to resurrect agency and self-respect for their formerly subjugated people. But as post-colonial studies have shown, one of the most insidious legacies of colonialism is how it colonizes the consciousness of the subjugated political and social elites. Similarly, the form and operation of modern institutions developed within a colonial setting are often the antecedents for later modernization. In Korea, the structure and functioning of state bureaucracies, modern companies, public infrastructures (transport, sanitation, media, etc.) first emerged in the last decades of Chosŏn rule, and they continued to evolve in the colonial setting. Much from this beginning carried over in the post-colonial setting out of sheer convenience. But even more difficult to excise was the habitus of modernity. It is no accident, then, that modern forms of organization in Korea often continue to resemble, at least on the exterior, Japanese forms, even though their function was quickly adapted to Korean control and leadership. Finally, because modernity evolved in a colonial setting, the relationship of the Korean people to modernity was skewed by Japanese political and economic power. Therefore understanding Korea's colonial modernity is crucial to appreciating the point from which subsequent Korean social and economic development began.

Chapter Four concludes with a detailed description of the last decade of colonial rule and the tumultuous aftermath of Liberation in the period from 1945 to 1950, a period that ends with the Korean War. It is important, here, to balance our discussion of colonial modernity with an appreciation of the bleakness of the last years of Japanese rule. The worst Japanese depredations have decisively influenced the memory of colonialism in the present, particularly the Japanese policy of forced assimilation. The attempts to force Japanese cultural practices on Koreans after 1935—Japanized names, family law, Shinto worship, and obligatory Japanese language use—were particularly galling. And these policies were enforced during a period of total war mobilization that wrought enormous hardship on the Korean people.

Chapter Five narrates events of the immediate postwar period. Its purpose is to sort out the colonial legacy and to determine how it affected the intricate political struggles that emerged during the joint American-Russian occupation of the peninsula. In order to understand the Korean War, it is necessary to detail the circumstances that inhibited Korean attempts to produce a unified political leadership. Indeed, the combination of a legacy of colonial contradictions—class conflict, collaboration issues, population upheaval, etc.—and the presence of two superpowers destined to become the major vortices of the bipolar Cold War world order prevented the emergence of a unified middle ground from which a single nation-state might have evolved. Unfortunately, in the West an understanding of the origins of the war remains captive to a Cold War narrative of the struggle between communism and democracy. The story ends with the outbreak of the Korean War, a civil war compounded by and decisively driven by international intervention. Perhaps the Korean War was inevitable, given the implacable positions of the warring factions within post-Liberation Korean politics. But a more comprehensive narrative must show how the United States and USSR were implicated in the original division and how their policy choices in the early months after August 15, 1945, supported various sides within the Korean political game. This complex narrative closes with the battle lines freezing into a no-man's land tracing the current Demilitarized Zone (DMZ) that still divides Korea today.

The emergence of the Republic of Korea (ROK) after 1948 is the subject of Chapter Six. It is a story of the ROK's struggle to evolve a pluralist democracy despite enormous economic and social problems, the threat from North Korea, and Cold War politics. Without question, ROK presidents used the imperatives of national security and economic development to justify authoritarian abuses; the struggle between pluralist forces and authoritarian leadership played out dramatically for nearly forty years. This chapter also details the emergence and fruition of the economic development programs initiated in South Korea in the early 1960s. The nation's astonishingly successful economic development led to social and political changes that undermined all arguments for continuing authoritarian controls. This part of the story culminates with the emergence of a coalition of opposition forces in 1987 that forced democratic reforms and inaugurated a new era of democratization in South Korean politics.

Chapter Seven provides a contrasting picture of nation-building in North Korea, known formally as the Democratic People's Republic of Korea (DPRK). The purpose of the chapter, however, is not to highlight the contemporary contrasts between a postmodern and globalized South and the international isolation and economic failure of the North at the beginning of the twenty-first century. Rather, it attempts to describe both the DPRK's unique genesis and its early social and economic strengths—strengths that in the early decades outstripped the lesser achievements of the South. From there, however, it is necessary to uncover the sources of the senescence of the North Korean economy and the unique political formations that have led to the emergence of contemporary North Korea as one of the most isolated, totalitarian, and enigmatic nation-states in the world today, a nation whose nuclear ambitions threaten the East Asian region as well as the global nonproliferation movement.

We return to South Korea in Chapter Eight, where the narrative highlights the halting course of democratization of South Korea since 1987, its successes as well as failures. While South Korea has democratized in terms of procedural democracy and individual rights, its political system remains captive to elitist and highly personalized political parties. How the system will evolve to include the voice of all major interest groups in society is still a work in progress. Since the late 1980s South Korea has also emerged as an increasingly wealthy consumer society, and this development has generated a host of new problems. The South Koreans have begun to question what was lost in the pell-mell drive to modernize. As South Korea approached the new century, it was consumed by a number of new debates that considered how to reconstitute itself as an affluent consumer society with open global connections to the postmodern world.

Finally, the Epilogue examines some of the contemporary issues now facing the Korean peninsula. It is difficult, perhaps impossible, to provide a definitive narrative of more contemporary events. The two Koreas are important actors in a region of the world that has been rocked by recent dramatic changes the ultimate meaning of which can only be assessed in the years to come. The protracted recession in Japan during the 1990s, the Asian financial crisis of 1997–1998, the meteoric rise of the Chinese economy, the North Korean famine of 1995–1997, and the seemingly endless crisis provoked by the DPRK's nuclear ambitions have all destabilized the fifty-year-long regional political consensus built at the beginning of the now long-gone Cold War. What happens on the Korean peninsula in the next decade will have a decisive effect on how the entire region will realign itself to the realities of the twenty-first century. Thus just as they did at the beginning of the last century, the inhabitants of the Korean peninsula will again bear witness to and affect the future of the region. What more reason is needed for a close reexamination of the historical antecedents of the two states that now divide these people?

Chapter One

A NEW CENTURY
AND THE END OF AN ERA

일

ON APRIL 10, 1900, officials in Seoul ceremoniously threw a switch that turned on the first electric streetlights in Korea. In the following days journalists trotted out numerous metaphors of light to note the event's significance as further evidence of progress and enlightenment on the Korean peninsula. The lighting of Seoul's streets was one of many "firsts" marked at the turn of the century for the then-named Taehan Empire. Many of these noted the inaugurals of various modern transportation and communications technologies such as railroads, telephones, and telegraph. In fact as the new century dawned, Korea seemed on a trajectory that was integrating its economy, politics, and culture into the rapidly developing regional ties between Japan, coastal China, and by extension, the global economy of the early twentieth century. The vast majority of the Korean people had not yet seen those streetlights, but transnational forces were increasingly affecting their lives.

In the fall of 1900, trains began running on the new Seoul-Inch'ŏn rail line. This was the first fruit of what would become a railroad-building boom between 1900 and 1910. Completion of the Seoul-Pusan (1904) and Seoul-Sinŭiju (1906) segments of a north-south trunk line made it possible to travel the length of the peninsula, more than 500 miles from the straits of Tsushima to the Yalu River, in a single day. Moreover, by the end of the decade, the connection of this trunk line to the Southern Manchurian rail system made possible overland travel from Korea to Europe via the trans-Siberian railroad. Travel of such speed and convenience in Korea had been scarcely imaginable just thirty years before when a reluctant Chosŏn government signed its first Western-style commercial treaty, the Kanghwa Treaty, with the new Meiji Japanese state in 1876.

This new infrastructure was only part of the visible changes that had appeared on the peninsula since the advent of commercial and diplomatic relations with the outside world in 1876. In 1900 clusters of multistory Western-style buildings had begun to reshape vistas in the ancient city. Foreign embassies, a new central post office, and Japanese commercial buildings competed for attention with Chosŏn government compounds, the recently rebuilt (1867) Kyŏngbok palace, the great gates in the city walls, and the elaborate, tile-roofed mansions of the *yangban* aristocracy in the northeastern quadrant of the city that had heretofore defined the skyline. These tangible signs of change had been underway for a generation by the turn of the century, and they symbolized deeper currents of transformation in Korean society. In 1876 opponents of the Kanghwa Treaty feared that opening the country to foreign trade and diplomatic representation would destabilize rice markets (rice production being the basis of Confucian economics) and allow further introduction of heretical ideas and practices from without. They were right; the treaty opened a Pandora's box of economic, intellectual, political, and cultural forces that ultimately led to the fall of the Chosŏn dynasty.

Railroads, new buildings, streets, and streetlights were only superficial indications of change, but even so their meaning remained obscure to the overwhelming majority of the Korean population. Broader forces, however, had been at work over the last quarter of the nineteenth century. The 1876 opening signaled the beginning of capitalist market penetration of the Korean peninsula. Key provisions of the Kanghwa Treaty were of tremendous importance to Korea's future economic independence. While Korean negotiators had doggedly argued for restrictions on the rice trade, they allowed foreign currencies to become mediums of exchange inside the newly opened ports. The same negotiators ignored the potential state revenue that would come from customs and other commercial taxes while they obsessed about protocol and ritual language that might alter Korea's special relationship to China. In the end, the Koreans felt they had minimized the effects of opening the country, at the same time they had solved the foreign crisis of 1874–1876, but in reality they had seriously compromised Korea's sovereignty.

A view of the Great South Gate and the new trolley line circa 1900. Source: The Norman Thorpe Collection.

The Chosŏn Dynasty Exposed to Outside Forces

Exposed to international market forces, the Korean economy gradually reoriented itself. By 1900 the export market for rice had stimulated changes in the production and marketing of rice, particularly in areas served by the new international ports. Larger landlords who had heretofore reinvested rent surpluses in land began to recognize new opportunities for greater returns in rice milling or other enterprises related to the new export market in rice. Korean merchants also responded to opportunities as import-export brokers or middlemen to foreign trading companies in the ports. By 1920 an extensive railroad grid and growing network of motor roads served a transformed market for bulk grains heading for international markets.

Market penetration also opened the Korean domestic market to imported foreign manufactured goods. Beginning with inexpensive machine-produced household goods and extending quickly to inexpensive, superior-quality cotton textiles, foreign imports immediately challenged the traditional handicraft industry. As inexpensive, utilitarian imports gained a place in the domestic market, Korean consumers increasingly marketed their rice for cash in order to purchase goods they had previously bartered for or made within the household. By the 1920s traditional Korean handicraft industries were dying, and the largest handicraft industry, home weaving, had been severely compromised in competition with foreign machine-loomed threads and textiles.

The 1876 treaty permitted construction of foreign diplomatic compounds in Seoul, and these acted as a wedge opening the country to new intellectual and cultural influences. The Chosŏn government had originally restricted the movement of foreigners to the immediate hinterland of the new ports and the diplomatic residences in Seoul. But as more treaties were signed in the 1880s with the United States, France, Germany, Belgium, and the like, the early Kanghwa Treaty restrictions were undone. Even the Qing dynasty, not trusting that Korea would honor its avowed special relationship, signed a detailed commercial treaty with Korea at the end of the decade. Indeed, the general public was increasingly aware of the presence of traders, missionaries, and foreign troops, and they directly connected the foreign presence with deteriorating conditions in the countryside. In the early 1890s antiforeign statements were prominent in the new Tonghak movement's protests over the dynasty's continuing persecution of them and their beliefs.[1] Interestingly, the great rebellion of 1894 led by the Tonghak movement broke out in Chŏlla province in the southwest—the most productive agricultural region of Korea and an area of early and intensive foreign presence related to the rice market.

The opening of the country also forced the dynasty to tolerate the presence of Christian missionaries, a reversal of the government's long-standing policy of rooting out this heretical influence in society. Unlike traders, soldiers, or diplomats, Western missionaries penetrated Korean society directly to establish their evangelical missions, and they not only founded churches but also built hospitals and schools as important adjuncts for serving the citizenry and attracting new converts. Missionaries became the first Westerners to systematically study Korean history, culture, and language; their work formed a growing Orientalist literature on Korea, with its curious mixture of exotica, condescension, critique, and praise that subsequently shaped attitudes about Korea in the West for several generations. Mission schools were active in the 1890s and became models for the establishment of secular Korean schools devoted to a nontraditional, Western-studies curriculum, which also appeared in the 1890s. The missionary schools and hospitals attracted Koreans interested in new ideas and institutions. Initially, the church grew slowly, but in the early 1900s there was an explosion in the number of converts, making Korea the one great success story of Christian missions in Asia. Exactly why Koreans embraced Christianity in such numbers remains subject to debate. Some analysts point to a particular affinity between Christian monotheism and Korean folk belief; others assert that deteriorating rural conditions drew Koreans to Christian relief efforts. It was clear, however, that ambitious Koreans associated the church with Western knowledge and education, and the church schools produced many of the first generation of modern Korean intellectual and political leaders.

A general intellectual revolution was underway by the first decade of the twentieth century. A group of men trained in the 1880s in traditional Confucian studies, but increasingly interested in the new Western learning that emerged after the 1894 abolition of the traditional examination system, began to participate in reform debates both inside and out of government. These transitional intellectuals translated many of the first Japanese and Chinese books on Western philosophy, history, and politics; shortly thereafter Korean translations of Western works supplemented this early body of knowledge and circulated among intellectuals. By 1910 the trickle of students returning from travel and study abroad increased to a steady stream. Many found jobs in the Chosŏn government on the basis of their new credentials; an equal number, however, discouraged by the enervating politics at the center, went to work in the private sector, in the new schools and in publishing, journalism, and commerce.

In fact, the real locus for progressive change within Korea had already fallen to the private sector by 1900. In retrospect, it is clear that those changes in the Chosŏn system that might have helped maintain Korean independence threatened the system itself; vested interests at the center fought to maintain their political hold on governance by fighting change and to buttress their traditional monopoly of social and economic power in the society. The monarch tolerated reform debate only insofar as it did not threaten his traditional prerogatives. The predominately conservative officialdom fought changes that might erode their political power. As a consequence, the motive force for change in society fell to private organizations, study clubs, schools, and newspapers. After the 1890s there were plenty of new ideas and progressive patriots willing to work for a new Korea. They lacked, how-ever, entrée into the inner circles of political decision-making and power. More-over, by 1900 foreign interests were so entrenched and state resources so depleted that it is hard to imagine the country could have righted its course, even with progressive policies emanating from a core of decisive and empowered leaders.

In the early 1900s the Chosŏn government was fighting the increasing Japa-nese intrusion in its affairs. Between 1896 and 1904, however, it had found breath-ing room by encouraging Russian interests as a counterweight to Japan. The Triple Intervention of 1895 in the aftermath of the Sino-Japanese War had curbed the Japanese advance temporarily, but unfortunately this lull in political and diplo-matic pressure only encouraged the Chosŏn leaders to continue their policy of try-ing to neutralize foreign power on the peninsula by pitting one imperialist against another.[2] Continuing conservative opposition to internal political, economic, and social reforms enervated any positive program to create sufficient national power to counter foreign intrusion and guarantee Korean sovereignty.

The changes in Korean society that heralded its entrance into the world order need to be placed in the context of late-nineteenth-century political, economic, and cultural imperialism. While one of the early pro-Korean experts, the mission-ary Homer Hulbert, might write eloquently about the "potential" of the Korean people and the great strides taken to begin the process of reform, there lingered a judgment that Korean culture and society were inferior. In a defense of Korea published after Japan's defeat of Russia in 1905 and the de facto beginning of its occupation of Korea, Hulbert still asserted that the Koreans had much to do before "they [could] prove themselves the equals of their conquerors and, by the very force of genuine manhood counteract the contempt which the Japanese feel [for them]" (Hulbert, 1906, p. 463). Even from the mouth of a friend such a statement contains the bigotry (not to mention sexism) common to that period and at the core of imperialist ideology. Hulbert was saying that if Korean society was too effeminate to defend itself from the predations of more masculine societies, then it deserved to fall under the tutelage of Japan. Judged on the basis of its worst political tendencies and its economic and military enervation, not upon its best aspirations and genuine achievements to create sufficient national power for sur-vival, Korea was disparaged as hopeless without outside guidance. As will become apparent, Korean intellectuals who savaged their own tradition as the cause of their country's formal loss of sovereignty in 1910 also absorbed this critique.

At the start of the century bright forecasts filled the condescending reports of Western missionaries to their home churches, but after 1902 the political situation for the Chosŏn government worsened by the month as Japan and Russia moved toward what seemed to be an inevitable showdown. And indeed, Japan's victory in the Russo-Japanese War in 1905 ultimately determined the fate of the dynasty. Thereafter the Taehan Empire became a Japanese diplomatic dependency with no rights of self-representation in the world system, and after the forced abdication of

King Kojong (1864–1907) in 1907, a Japanese resident general and his officials controlled Korea de facto. From an opening in the name of commerce and diplomatic intercourse with the new (to Korea) global system of nations as defined by the Western European powers, Korea had in only thirty years devolved into a colony of the only Asian power to join to the imperialist club. At the end of the dynasty in 1910, four sets of forces were working at different levels within Korea: there was the political and military aggression and rivalry of Korea's neighbors and the Western powers; there was the transforming action of global market forces; there was the halting political reform movement; and finally, there were many intellectual and cultural changes. All had combined with changes already underway in Korea in the last quarter of the nineteenth century. In the end the ancient regime failed to either deflect or direct these forces in ways that could ensure its survival.

Chosŏn Korea's Struggle for Survival: 1876–1895

This summary of the Chosŏn dynasty's demise vastly oversimplifies what happened, and it downplays Korean agency in the process. The thirty-year period after the signing of the Kanghwa Treaty witnessed the unfolding of an extraordinarily complex story of change at all levels of Korean society as well as the gradual break-up of the traditional sociopolitical order. The story is often cast as the interplay of foreign aggression and greed, corrupt officials, and the intransigent conservatism of Korea's landed aristocracy. This scenario provides villains aplenty, both outside and inside, upon whom to cast blame for the loss of Korean sovereignty. But it is not my purpose to assign responsibility for the failure of the Chosŏn system. There was no single element at the center of Korean politics and society that could be blamed for the country's mistakes and misguided decisions; nor were the Koreans innocent victims of foreign aggression. Actually, the problem at the end of the dynasty was the presence of too many agencies of power whose conflicting interests prevented any significant change in the status quo. Extraordinary pressures and new forces threatened the dynasty and Korea's efforts to reform itself in order to preserve its sovereignty.

That story unfolds in two parts. The first focuses on politics—international and domestic—and the attempts of the Chosŏn state to strengthen itself in face of a growing threat to its sovereignty. The second narrative examines the country's intellectual transformation. It examines how new ideas and cultural influences from outside Korea changed the worldview of Koreans, discredited the politics of the old regime, and laid the foundation of modern Korean nationalism. With the fall of the Chosŏn state in 1910, Korean nationalism, until then a reform movement, became the driving force in the effort to regain Korean independence.

Korea's second-to-last monarch, Kojong (1864–1907), attained his majority in 1874 and took the reins of power in the midst of the foreign policy crisis that led to the opening of Korea to foreign commercial contacts with the signing of the Kanghwa Treaty of 1876. The signing marked the beginning of a whole new era in foreign relations and the exposure of Korea to the vastly different international climate in East Asia. But perhaps more importantly, it signaled a gradual rupture of Korea's special relationship with China and a transformation of Korea's traditional worldview. The crisis had originated in Korea's refusal to recognize the restoration of the Japanese emperor to center place in the new Meiji state. Korea had always organized its foreign relations by recognizing the transcendent position of the Chinese emperor and by taking a ritually subordinate position to China. It refused to recognize any other emperor in East Asia. By 1873 Korea's haughty refusal to recognize the Meiji government led to a serious debate in Japan over

Portrait of last Chosŏn monarchs circa 1890, Kojong (seated) and his son Sunjong. Source: The Norman Thorpe Collection.

SMALL EGO OF JAPAN

whether to mount a punitive military action. At last the Koreans recognized the *KOREA* genuine threat of Japanese military power, having observed the effect of the Chi- *FOLLOWED* nese losses in wars with England over similar issues in 1842 (the Opium War) and *CHINA'S* 1860 (the Anglo-French War). The Chinese had taken the stance that the demands *LEAD* for trade could be controlled by enmeshing the Western powers in treaties and holding them to the letter of the agreements. In 1876 they counseled the Kore- *(CHINESE)* ans to end the crisis by negotiating a treaty with the Japanese that would at least limit Japanese access to trade on the coast. The Koreans took the Chinese counsel and signed a treaty with the Japanese in 1876. Although the decision was very unpopular with conservative forces within the bureaucracy, Kojong finally signed the treaty. It satisfied Japanese demands for recognition of its government, altered Korea's traditional diplomatic forms, and opened selected ports on the Korean coast to Japanese trade, providing precedent for a general opening of trade later.

The Kanghwa Treaty and subsequent treaties with the Western powers as well *TREATY* as its traditional Chinese mentors exposed Korea to unprecedented outside influ- *EXPOSED* ences. Initially it was useful for the Koreans to bring in all the various actors on the *KOREA TO* East Asian diplomatic stage in order to play them off against each other and thus *WORLD* create room for Korea itself to maneuver. In the last decades of the nineteenth century, Kojong and his government attempted to maintain neutrality by balancing the predatory interests of the many foreign powers now active on the peninsula. Such a policy was the logical outgrowth of Korea's dependence on Chinese power and influence during the early phase of its participation in the treaty system in East Asia. The fallacy of the policy was to think that foreign powers were more afraid of conflict with each other than they were on maintaining or developing a predominate position in Korea.

In terms of diplomatic maneuvering, the end of the nineteenth century can be divided into phases of dominant foreign influence in Korea: China between 1884–1894, Japan immediately following the Sino-Japanese War of 1894–1895, an interregnum of balanced Japanese-Russian rivalry between 1896–1904, and Japanese ascendancy after the Russo-Japanese War of 1904–1905. Although the Korean government intended to play one power off against another, more often than not the Koreans found themselves under the thumb of whatever power predominated at the moment. Immediately after signing the Kanghwa Treaty, the Koreans relied on the Chinese for advice and protection within the new treaty system, only to discover that the Chinese were abandoning their traditional policy of noninvolvement in Korean political affairs. The height of Chinese interference came after 1884, the year they used military force to put down the Kapsin Coup, a brief takeover of the Korean government by Korean progressives (see below). Later, railroad, mining, and timber concessions and other economic privileges were the price of keeping multiple Western interests engaged in Korea so that the Korean government could use them in their elaborate diplomatic balancing act. It was only later that the Koreans learned the "good offices" and "amity" in the treaty boilerplate with Western nations did not mean these powers would automatically align themselves against the rising power of Japan.

The lack of consensus in domestic politics about what course to take in the deepening crisis of sovereignty in the late nineteenth century also inhibited any program to gather resources and build up the power necessary for national survival. Multiple interest groups resided within the bureaucracy and even divided the royal house. The officialdom was generally conservative, and they were suspicious of all reforms that might prove inimical to their vested political and economic interests. In the early 1880s such entrenched officials were challenged by a group of younger, progressive appointees who had gained the support of Kojong. Some of this group had traveled abroad, and they returned with a number of ideas drawn from Western and Japanese political practice. The monarch remained an important actor in the political struggles of the 1880s and 1890s, and his voice was crucial in policy formation, but he was unable to unify the political forces within the bureaucracy that were fighting at cross-purposes to gain his support and vital legitimating seal. The Min family, consort clan to the king, represented another independent—and often nakedly self-interested—political force during this period. Having been muscled out of power by the surprising rise of Kojong's father, the Taewŏn'gun, during Kojong's minority (1864–1874), the Min family sought to take advantage of their connection to the throne after his retirement.[3] In addition, out-of-office *yangban* literati regularly chimed in with memorials supporting or opposing various policies, and finally, private pressure groups emerged in the 1890s as a force in a slowly opening public sphere in Korean society.

Early Reform Measures

In the aftermath of the debate over the opening, Koreans scrambled to gain information about the changing conditions around them. The monarch sent representatives to Japan, China, and the United States for reports on conditions abroad. Students were dispatched to the new schools in China that specialized in Western military technology and foreign language study. In the early 1880s the government established its own school for the training of foreign experts, and it accelerated the process of reorganizing and reequipping its small standing military. A new branch of government, the Office for Management of State Affairs (T'ongni kimu amun), established at the level of the State Council, oversaw the self-strengthening effort (Deuchler, *Confucian Gentlemen*, 1977). These were radical and unsettling changes for many key officials who had hoped to reaffirm the traditional ideology of ritual obeisance to China and isolation as the key elements of Korea's foreign policy. Conservatives within government argued that to incorporate foreign methods into policy threatened the Dao (Tao) of Confucian governance; they opposed proposals to revamp decision making at the highest levels of government, to establish new methods for the recruitment of officials, and to legislate social reforms.

There was considerable opposition to the policies and how rapidly the pro- *ANTI-FAST*
gressives were implementing them between 1880 and 1884. As long as Kojong *PROGRESS?*
continued to provide them with positions and resources, however limited, the
progressives could continue the modest reform program. In 1881 the military
reorganization created a new Special Skills Force intended as a demonstration
unit for military modernization. This force, however, created resentment within
the ranks of traditional units, whose own resources were being diverted to pay for
the model unit. In 1882 disaffected soldiers rioted in Seoul, demanding back pay.
Opponents of reform, including the retired Taewŏn'gun, seized upon the chaos
to regain power. When the chaos in Seoul extended to burning the Japanese legation and killing Japanese diplomats, Chinese troops arrived to quell the violence.
Thereafter, the Chinese increased their influence within the Korean government
by dispatching a "chief commissioner of diplomatic and commercial affairs" to
Korea. This marked the beginning of Chinese ascendancy in the Korean capital; by
1884 the entire progressive movement was in retreat in the face of increasing Chinese pressure and its support of conservatives within the Korean government.

In 1884 occurred one of the most important events of the 1880s, an abortive *KAPSIN*
seizure of the palace by progressive forces known as the Kapsin Coup. With the *COUP*
support of Japanese legation guards, the progressives, led by Kim Okkyun, (1851–
1894) and Pak Yŏnghyo (1861–1939), seized the palace and formed a reform government. In the next days they issued a series of edicts under the seal of the king
completely reorganizing the government and calling for a breathtaking series of
economic, social, and cultural reforms. The effort was stillborn. Within days the
palace was retaken by Chinese troops under the command of Yuan Shih-k'ai (Yuan
Shikai), who would later gain infamy for his failed attempt at dynastic restoration in China following the Republican Revolution of 1912. The Kapsin Coup, a
bloody attempt at top-down revolutionary change by the progressives, discredited
their cause because of its means and its association with Japanese military force. It *IMPORTANT*
strengthened the hand of the Chinese in Korea and brought conservative factions
back to the center of power. The 1884 coup not only marked a watershed for early
reform within the Korean government, it also marked the beginning of a decade-
long Chinese intrusion and a dangerous military rivalry with Japan over influence
on the peninsula.

Japanese Ascendancy on the Peninsula after 1895

In 1894–1895 the Sino-Japanese War ended the rivalry. The Japanese victory heralded the rise of Japan to the status of a regional power, and the victory so alarmed
the Western powers that they intervened to limit Japanese gains in Northeast Asia.
The casus belli for the war had been the simultaneous dispatching of Chinese and
Japanese troops to Korea following a major rebellion in Korea's southwest prov-

inces. The Tonghak rebellion began as a movement to protest corruption in local governance. It escalated into a full-scale rebellion in the wake of the government's military response. By the spring of 1894, the Tonghak rebels had captured the provincial capital of Chǒnju, and the rebellion had spread to the north and east. Kojong's ill-considered request for Chinese military aid to repress the rebellion set in motion a series of events that led to China's war with the Japanese.

The Japanese response to the unilateral dispatch of Chinese troops to Korea in 1894 was decisive. It sent its own expeditionary force in June of that year and after a month of futile negotiations engaged China in war that ended in a decisive, humiliating defeat of China in 1895. During this time the Japanese military occupied Seoul and imposed a number of concessions on the Korean government: the right to build railroads between Pusan and Seoul, the opening of the new port on the west coast (Kunsan), a military alliance with Japan, and more ominously, a vague agreement on the part of the Koreans to "accept" Japanese advice on internal reforms. This last took shape in a series of major governmental reforms known as the Kabo Reforms of 1894–1895.

The Japanese helped the Korean government create a new deliberative body that they packed with moderate reformers and pro-Japanese officials. They eventually brought back from exile the leaders of the failed Kapsin Coup, Pak Yǒnghyo, Sǒ Chaep'il, and Sǒ Kwangbǒm (1859–1897). What ensued was a sweeping set of changes in government structure, fiscal organization, methods of government recruitment, and traditional social norms. Much of the governmental reorganiza-

Japanese troops celebrating victory over the Chinese at Asan in 1894. Source: The Norman Thorpe Collection.

tion mimicked Japan's own recent adaptation of Western governmental structures. The idea was to realign bureaus and departments into eight ministries to reflect new government responsibilities and interests. Important reforms also diluted the monarch's relationship to government by characterizing his role as a reigning, not ruling, king; and additional provisions segregated royal financial assets from state assets within a department of Royal Household Affairs. Ministries of Finance, Agriculture and Commerce, and Industry consolidated all state economic functions. A reformed Ministry of Education became responsible for creating a new system of modern normal and primary schools, in addition to overseeing traditional educational institutions such as the Academy for Confucian Studies (Sŏnggyun'gwan). The Kabo Reforms abolished the traditional examination system that had been the means for recruiting officials as well as validating social status among the *yangban* class. This effectively diminished the value of Confucian studies as the major determinant of talent and stranded an entire generation of young scholars in the midst of their preparation for civil office. In its place the reforms created a recommendation system that privileged new skills learned in the growing number of schools that emphasized Westernized curricula. Many younger scholars caught in the switch of credentialing systems for government service, as well as a younger generation of officials already ensconced in the central bureaucracy, shifted their attention to the study of foreign languages, Western history and politics, or commerce. Some of these men, such as the well-known translator and journalist Chang Chiyŏn (1864–1921) or the historians Sin Ch'aeho (1880–1936) and Pak Ŭnsik (1859–1926), were important representatives of this generation.

The Kabo social legislation was also significant, but as with all attempts to legislate changes of long-entrenched social norms and mores, results were not immediate. The old, fixed class structure and the institution of slavery were abolished formally. And the long-standing prohibition of the remarriage of widows, most important perhaps among the upper classes, was eliminated. The removal of traditional status distinctions in society worked in tandem with the elimination of the civil examination system that had effectively been open only to *yangban*. It was now possible for anyone to serve in the government on the basis of education, skills, and recommendations. Other, more cosmetic, pronouncements, such as the encouragement of Western dress and hairstyles, followed the year after the initial Kabo legislation.

Less than a year after the announcement of the Kabo Reforms, the intervention of Russia, Germany, and France (the Triple Intervention of 1895) revised the Treaty of Shimonoseki that had concluded the Sino-Japanese War. This cancelled the Japanese lease of the strategic Liaodong peninsula and brought Russian influence back into Korea. A general reaction followed with another reshuffle of the Korean cabinet. The ensuing struggle between the Japanese and anti-Japanese forces led to a bizarre plot to assassinate Queen Min, the symbolic leader of the anti-Japanese reaction. Her horrible murder galvanized anti-Japanese forces and badly tarnished the Japanese image in East Asia. Following the assassination the Korean government leaned to the Russians for help. The viciousness of political struggles in Korea led to more rioting, rumors, and counterplots; ultimately, Kojong, fearing for his life, sought refuge at the Russian embassy in early 1896. The murder of the queen and the king's flight marked the nadir of Korean political agency and made a mockery of the last vestiges of royal prestige claimed by the Chosŏn monarchy.

No one could have foreseen the disastrous set of events that propelled Kojong to the Russian embassy in fear of his life in 1896. Moreover, it would be a mistake to assume this humiliation was the natural outcome of the Korean traditional leadership's indifference to the worsening fortunes of the country since 1876. Nor are reform ideas taken from Western or Japanese models the only ideas worthy of our discussion. During the twenty years after the opening, conservative and progressive Confucians alike had weighed in with suggestions for reform. There was sincere interest across the ideological spectrum in righting the system for its own protection, and a sincere patriotic response by officials and Confucian scholars out of government to shore up the system and preserve its sovereignty and values. These efforts were, of course, complicated by an additional mix of personal ambition, class interest, royal household politics, and patriotic reform proposals. The resulting lack of consensus, however, further eroded the already weak state's response to the overwhelmingly superior economic and military forces that were destroying the basis of the entire East Asian world order and legitimating new standards of civilization.

Western Civilization and a New World Order

Behind the political drama within the government and its struggle with the foreign powers encroaching on Korean sovereignty, there is another story to be told. This is the story of the gradual shift in how Koreans perceived the world around them and how they came to accept foreign ideas and culture. The same forces that threatened Korean sovereignty had already created a new system of international relations in East Asia as a whole. By 1896 Meiji Japan was emerging as an important player in this system. The new international system into which Korea had been pulled was based on the conception of a world order made up of individual nation-states that competed in a global economic and political order. Unlike the implicit scale of cultural affinity with a single set of cultural norms centered on Chinese civilization that formed the traditional hierarchy of East Asian peoples, the Western global system based itself on a hierarchy of economic and military power. While there had evolved a ritual equality within Western diplomatic protocol, treaties and alliances were negotiated on the basis of national interest and in full recognition of power relations within the world community. The great powers that led the imperialist expansion into Asia might struggle among themselves for economic advantage and control of territory, but as a collective they disparaged the technological backwardness, military weakness, "irrational" political institutions, "primitive" social arrangements, and religious "superstition" of the peoples that came under their domination.

The power that legitimated Western cultural superiority was organized within the nation-state form. Although it took some time for the East Asians to accept and then learn the lexicon and rituals of Western diplomatic behavior, by the time the Koreans were forced into Western-dominated global politics, both Japan and China were already acting like nations in the new system. By the 1880s China was enmeshed in a number of treaties with Western nations that regulated trade and various extraterritorial rights. These impinged on Chinese sovereignty, but had seemed a small price to pay for peace. Concurrently, having given up the idea of direct control in China, the Western powers found it convenient to support the ailing Qing dynasty so as to maintain their privileges within what was becoming a semicolonial system. The Japanese response was different. Accepting the new power realities foisted upon them, the new Meiji state proceeded to emulate the form and institutions of the Western nation-state as the means to protect its independence. Their nation-building program was based on economic development and military strength; it was calculated to equalize Japan's legal status within the nation-state system, that is, revise the unequal treaties. Accordingly the Japanese wanted to clarify the old ambiguous relationship that had upheld Korean autonomy vis-à-vis China while concurrently endowing the Chinese with special interests on the peninsula. This was the seed of the conflict between China and Japan that finally established Korea's independence within the nation-state system only to expose its inability to survive in the competition that ensued.

The progressive weakening of the Chinese empire in tandem with the imposition of an entirely new system of interstate relations began the process of decentering China within the Korean worldview (Schmid, 2002). If China was too weak to provide insulation from predatory imperialism, why bear the ignominy of ritual subordination in interstate relations? This question hung in abeyance during the period of Chinese ascendancy in Korea after the failed coup of 1884. But Japan's ᵁᴺᴰᴱᴿ victory in the Sino-Japanese War of 1894 decisively clarified the situation. It elimi- ᴶᴬᴾᴬᴺ? nated any Chinese claims to some special interest in Korea, and thereafter Korea was set adrift as a truly independent state within the imperialist politics of the period.

The decline of Chinese power and the progressively weakening fortunes of ᴸᵒᵒᵏ ᵀᵒ Korea encouraged reform-minded officials and intellectuals to seek inspiration ᵂᴱˢᵀ from the West. In the 1890s and early 1900s reformers, both in and out of government, began to see traditional institutions and values as the reason for Korea's enervation, not its salvation. Some, like the radical progressives of the 1884 coup, called for wholesale change toward a Western-style government. Others thought an evolutionary approach toward constitutional monarchy might be more fruitful.

Even conservatives hostile to any massive shift toward Western ideas and institutions conceded that major reforms were in order, but they began to focus on how to preserve at least the spiritual values of Korea's Confucian order.

Thus in the aftermath of the Sino-Japanese War there was a major shift in the tenor of Chosŏn politics. With the East Asian world order in shambles, China's power receding in Northeast Asia, and a growing set of bilateral relationships within the new order, Korea began to think of itself as a nation like others in the global order of things. Such thinking required a wholesale reexamination of Korea's collective identity as a society and led to new forms of imagining Korea's past and future as part of a global system made up of nation-states.

Modern Korean nationalism was born of such reflection; it was national survival that drove the political discourse over reform after 1894. There was still formidable conservative opposition to wholesale changes in the substance of Chosŏn political and social arrangements, but at the level of interstate relations the monarch and officialdom were using the language of national autonomy and prestige. Few disputed that the issue was how to develop enough national power to maintain Korean independence in the face of imperialist encroachment. And this led to further discussion about how the Western nation-state was able to mobilize and project such power. Opinions varied as to the reasons for Western wealth and power. Reformers focused on a number of elements: liberal democratic ideology, various forms of popular government, conscript armies, mass education systems, capitalist economics, or the support of a patriotic citizenry. Depending on their own experience, reform thinkers offered different national models for emulation: Japan, the United States, and England. Whatever model was under discussion, it was the ability of the nation-state to channel the economic, social, and political resources of its people and focus them in the service of the national collective that attracted the Korean reformers. Over the course of twenty years the debate shifted from Eastern versus Western civilization to modernity versus tradition—modernity being the future, tradition the past. By 1900 more Korean intellectuals were firmly associating the nation-state form with modernity itself, modernity with Western civilization writ large, and both with Korea's future.

For them, the road to modernization led through the construction of a modern nation-state. This meant that Chosŏn had to be transformed. How much change would be necessary, what models should be followed, and who would lead this effort remained open questions. And in the later half of the 1890s the debate engaged not only officials, former officials, rusticated scholars, and students newly returned from abroad, but also teachers in the new schools and journalists writing in the new press. By this time the schools, both government and private, that taught a Western curriculum were producing their first generation of graduates, and this had increased the audience for the first Korean vernacular newspapers, which began to appear after 1896. In short, the discussion about how to revitalize Korea had come a long way from the narrow confines of high Chosŏn officials in camera with the monarch. It was now a public discussion, and it quickly transformed into a broad intellectual movement known today as the Korean Enlightenment.

The Korean Enlightenment and the Origins of Korean Nationalism

During the Sino-Japanese War the Japanese took advantage of the chaotic situation to gain additional concessions (the most important being railroad-building rights) as well as to support the return of pro-Japanese officials into government. The Kabo Reforms were another result of this temporary surge of influence. Without knowing that the next ten years would bring much worse, many Koreans experienced the next few years as the nadir of dynastic prestige. After all, the lethal atmosphere of anti-Japanese reaction, the assassination of Queen Min, and the murder of prominent officials Kim Hongjip and Ŏ Yunjung had caused Kojong to seek foreign protection out of fear for his life. In the midst of these events, a group of moderate officials and reform-minded citizens established an organization that would inaugurate a new era in Korean intellectual and political life.

Formed in the spring of 1896, the Independence Club (Tongnip hyŏphoe) was the brainchild of Philip Jaesohn (Sŏ Chaep'il), a young man who had recently returned to Korea after finishing medical training in the United States (Chandra, 1988). Chartered with the blessing of King Kojong, the Independence Club was a private organization where officials and private citizens gathered to discuss policy issues and reform proposals. It broke the monopoly on political discussion by the Confucian elites, and it created precedents for the expansion of public life by holding public debates on government policy, publishing the first vernacular newspaper, the *Independent (Tongnip sinmun),* lobbying for ordinary citizen participation in government, and pushing the government to expand public education. Its three principal goals were to strengthen Korean independence, promote national "self-strengthening," and advocate democratic participation in government decisions (Chandra, 1988).

Initially the club focused on symbols. It began a campaign to petition the king to rename the kingdom the Empire of the Great Han (TaeHan Cheguk) in order to make more explicit Korea's independence from China; in addition, the club urged Kojong to adopt the title of emperor *(hwangje)* in place of king *(wang)* in order to assume equal nominal status with the Chinese and Japanese emperors. Kojong, who had left Russian protection in July 1897, granted their wish; he took the title emperor and declared the first year of his new reign era Kwangmu (Illustrious Strength) in a coronation ceremony in October of 1897. The club also raised funds to erect a monumental arch, Independence Gate (Tongnipmun), on the site of the Gate of Welcoming Imperial Grace (Yŏng'ŭnmun), where the Chosŏn kings had officially welcomed envoys from China. This project expanded to remake the former Chinese diplomatic residence, the Hall of Cherishing China (Mohwagwan), into a public meeting place renamed Independence Hall (Tongnipgwan), which they then surrounded with a public park. These were popular projects both at court and with the Seoul public, and they ended formally the usage of the now, in nationalist terms, humiliating tributary language of past Korea-China relations.

The club charted a course for a movement that encompassed public education, the creation of a national newspaper, and the beginning of language reform, all projects that anticipated the gradual emergence of a new public sphere in Korea. The club's newspaper was the vehicle for realizing, at least in part, all of these goals. The *Independent* used the vernacular script *han'gŭl*, which had been invented in the fifteenth century during the reign of one of Chosŏn's most revered monarchs, Sejong the Great.[4] From that time Classical Chinese had continued to be the official written language of the court and elite communication, but *han'gŭl* was used for didactic tracts published for the peasantry and for popular translations of Confucian and Buddhist texts. The proliferation of novels written in *han'gŭl* in the seventeenth and eighteenth centuries had solidified its nonofficial use in society.

The *Independent*'s use of *han'gŭl* was a deliberate statement about national cultural unity and linguistic identity. Editorials in the paper decried the use of Classical Chinese as the official language of government and literary language of the *yangban*. In a scathing editorial on the national language, Chu Sigyŏng (1876–1914), a young member who later became the founder of the modern vernacular movement, asserted that perfecting and spreading the use of *han'gŭl* was the principle means for "ending the habit of aristocratic cultural slavery to Chinese culture" (Robinson, *Cultural Nationalism*, 1988, p. 34). This widened the attack begun against symbolic arches and imperial nomenclature on what the club perceived to be a slavish subordination of Korean elites to Chinese culture in general. This nationalist attack against elite identification with China began the process of transforming the very language used to describe Korean-Chinese relations. The term *sadae* (to serve the great) had heretofore simply described the old ritual relationship between Korea and China. But Chu turned it into an epithet that denounced subservience or toadyism to foreign culture in general. Subsequently, *sadae* and its various forms, *sadaejuŭi* (the doctrine or "ism" of subservience) or *sadae ŭisik* (a consciousness or mentality of subservience) became a trope for antinational sentiments or subservience to things foreign. In post-colonial and divided Korea this terminology still lingers in political and cultural discourse.

The newspaper was the core of a nascent public sphere that the club helped to establish in late Chosŏn Korea. Although its circulation never exceeded 3,000, in relative terms it represented a radical departure from business as usual in the heretofore tightly closed political arena. The paper announced public debates, editorialized on national affairs, and was filled with announcements and news items. In short, it created a political agenda for discussion by previously disenfranchised people from outside of the narrow confines of the Chosŏn bureaucracy and state councils. Moreover, the public debates the club organized brought together individuals from a broad spectrum of status groups and class backgrounds. An open discussion of matters of state in which *yangban* officials mingled with members of secondary status groups *(chungin* and *hyangni* and *muban)* as well as commoners and low-status was unprecedented, and the common cause that overrode class and status barriers was the current crisis facing what was more frequently being called the Korean nation.

The club ultimately foundered because of its radical political program for reforming the government into a constitutional monarchy and its advocacy of representative democracy. It proposed the creation of a privy council made up of both *yangban* officials and "wise and erudite men" selected from outside the government. Conservatives within the government seized upon this issue and convinced the monarch that such ideas would ultimately lead to the destruction of royal authority. Thus there is little mystery as to why Kojong disbanded the Independence Club after barely a year and a half of existence. He had been pleased by the club's support and creation of national symbols that augmented his prestige, but he was still dependent on officials who owed their power to the traditional political system. In the end, Kojong opted to uphold the theory of royal authority, however limited it was in reality, rather than risk opening the political system to public participation.

The disbanding of the Independence Club ended the brief reform movement of 1896–1898, but it had had a galvanizing effect on the intellectual climate of Korea. In its short life it spearheaded the cause of intellectual inquiry into the fundamental sources of Western power and introduced important issues such as the role of the people in legitimating state power and the importance and potential power of public participation in government. Furthermore, it had linked political participation with social emancipation and public education in ways that forever changed the language of politics in Korea. Henceforth the concept of an inclusive nation of active citizens, not passive subjects, framed the debates over reform. Moreover, a number of former club members, such as Yun Ch'iho (1865–1946), Syngman Rhee (Yi Sŭngman) (1875–1965), Yi Sangje (1850–1927), An Ch'angho (1878–1938), and Chu Sigyŏng, subsequently became prominent leaders of various political or cultural movements.

The short-lived projects of the Independence Club established precedents for a burgeoning of organizations, schools, and publications. The *Capital Gazette* (*Hwangsŏng sinmun*, 1898–1910) and *Imperial Post* (*Cheguk sinmun*) hit the streets in 1898 before the lapse of the pioneering *Independent*. The *Capital Gazette* became the newspaper for moderate members of the Independence Club who were interested in retaining significant aspects of Korea's traditional culture as part of necessary reform. It was printed in mixed script, a combination of vernacular Korean and Chinese characters that appealed to more traditionally minded elites. The *Imperial Post,* published in pure *han'gŭl,* was reputed to be most widely read among women and the less educated. Like the *Independent,* both papers published in lots of 2,000 to 3,000. In 1904 the *Korea Daily News (Taehan maeil sinbo)* emerged in time to cover the Russo-Japanese war. Owned and operated by an Englishman, the *Korea Daily News* enjoyed extraterritorial protection and thus avoided censorship until the final Japanese takeover in 1910. It quickly became the most popular newspaper of the day, with the largest circulation, because of its uncompromising editorials and fearless reportage. The newly emergent Korean press is often regarded as insignificant because of its small circulation and poor financial situation. But it played an important role as the foundation of an expanding field of journalism, in which the Korean intelligentsia began to articulate a new collective Korean identity.

The newspapers reported on the activities of new national and regional educational and reform associations spawned by the energy of intellectuals both in Seoul and outside. Around the time of the Russo-Japanese war these organizations became very active, with dues-paying members often exceeding a thousand individuals. A study of one such association, the Northwest Education Association (Sŏbuk hakhoe), revealed that the membership included a range of status groups from *yangban* through the so-called secondary groups to commoners (Schmid, 2002, p. 48). This diversity resulted from occupation and education being the focus for membership, not class or status. Although based in Seoul, the association spoke for the region; local officials, teachers, school principals, magistrates, technicians, and businessmen were among its members. Such diversity indicated the increasing interaction between private citizens and officials in public forums, whether in the new press or face-to-face at association functions. The monthly journals of these groups revealed how the associations competed among themselves to be most advanced, most reform-minded, best organizers of new schools, and so forth. Regional journals and newspapers became the forum for a unique conversation among educated Koreans, and out of these disparate opinions and passionate outpourings emerged a new imagined community.

A New Universal Path and the Discovery of the Nation

The lively intellectual outpouring in the new press contrasted starkly with the siege mentality of the increasingly moribund government. As the Chosŏn government circled the wagons in their last defense of the realm, the new intelligentsia was producing and propagating knowledge drawn from Western thought and refocusing Korea's crisis. Theirs was an effort to understand the dilemma facing the nation as well as a prescription for its resuscitation. The diverse writings of the Enlightenment fell into three related sets of inquiry: discovery and elucidation of a new universal path of social and political development, a rethinking of Korean society as a nation within this developmental course, and a critique of Korean tradition as

[handwritten: TRADITION = BACKWARD / MODERN = FUTURE]

an obstacle to the nation's future development. This discourse found its common vocabulary under the rubric of "civilization and enlightenment" *(munmyŏng kaehwa);* taken as a whole, it represented an attempt to understand how Korea should take its place in a global political economy dominated by imperialist expansion. Concurrently, there was intense interest in what defined Korea as a nation within this world framework and what should be done to ensure its survival as a unique society.

The gradual decentering of China in the Korean worldview had begun the redefinition of Korea as a nation-state, but moving Korean cultural identity away from any reference to China was neither an easy nor happy task. While Korea's participation within the cosmopolitan East Asian world order had made sense in a Sino-centric world order, within the particularistic logic of nationalism it was an anathema. This logic assumed that nations were the building blocks of the global order, with each claiming a distinct culture, history, and identity as a society. In East Asia the neologism used to represent the concept of nation—*minjok* in Korean—had been in use for at least thirty years before Koreans actually began to think and write about their society in such particularistic terms. The Chinese characters for *minjok—min* (people) and *jok* (family)—lend a unique quality to the term itself; so combined, these characters carry strong racial/ethnic and genealogical connotations. To this day, because of American stress on legal citizenship, an identity potentially open to all races and ethnicities because the United States is a nation of immigrants, Americans are surprised by the racial/familial emphasis carried within Korean national identity. In the period between 1905 and 1910, the first explorations of the evolution and character of the Korean *minjok* began to appear in calls for the rethinking of Korea's history.

A young editorial writer for the *Korea Daily News,* a man now celebrated as Korea's pioneering nationalist historian, Sin Ch'aeho, became one of the first to advocate writing a new, *minjok*-centered history for the nation (Em, 1999). In "A New Reading of Korean History," a serialized essay published in 1908 by the *Korea Daily News,* Sin reread Korean history as a story of the Korean people *(minjok),* not its state *(kukka)* or its ruling family *(wangjok).* He attacked the tradition of Confucian historiography with its moral judgments of good and bad kings and its emphasis on the fortunes of the state. What was needed, according to Sin, was an account of the *minjok* from its earliest moments and of its contact and competition with its neighbors. In this view history became a story to bind together the people who comprised the national subject; the purpose of history was to celebrate the triumphs of the *minjok* and mourn its defeats, and to account for the evolution of its unique culture and identity into the present. Sin's "New Reading" emphasized the ethnic/racial difference of the Koreans from their neighbors by locating the origins of the Korean race in 2333 B.C. in the person of a mythological progenitor Tan'gun. Thus Sin reoriented Korean history as a story of a single people that was distinct from China or any other neighboring group. By locating the beginning

[handwritten margin notes: ☆ NEW KOREAN HISTORY - NEW CENTER INDEPENDENCE]

of Korean history with Tan'gun, Sin sought to invalidate the Sino-centric myth of Korea's civilization being founded by a migrating Chinese official, Kija, a tale that had been in favor during the Confucianized Chosŏn period.

Sin's historiography highlighted the call in many contemporary writings for exhuming a true, singular Korean culture. For Sin's older contemporary Pak Ŭnsik, another prominent early historian, history was a means of defining or capturing the national soul *(kukhon)* or essence *(kuksu)*. For the linguist Chu Sigyŏng, that spirit lived in the vernacular language that had evolved along with the *minjok*. And knowledge of both was vital to the project of instilling in the Korean people a strong sense of themselves as part of this unique construct. After the Japanese Protectorate (1905), Korean intellectuals were in the struggle of their lives to not only create a national history and produce textbooks for propagating the national narrative in the new schools, but also to ensure that Korean history was not colonized by competing Japanese versions. Japanese colonial control after 1910 brought Korean historians' worst fears to fruition in the form of Japanese-produced textbooks and the colonial state's massive historiographical project to write Korea into the story of Japan's rise to dominance in East Asia.

These new histories emerged at a time when Social Darwinist ideas were in vogue throughout Asia. The idea of applying natural selection to societies, perceived to be in a grand struggle for survival, was supported in the minds of its Western adherents by their presumed higher technical and social/political evolution. Indeed, the ideology of imperialism was rife with Social Darwinist justifications for doing to colonies what the colonial peoples could not do for themselves. Curiously, the doctrine was accepted in Korea as part of a universal law of social development, and, in tandem with the discovery of nation, it provided a way out of the political and cultural crisis. Accepting the idea of linear history and progressive development, Korean intellectuals began to reflect on how to redirect Korea's evolutionary path in order to develop the strength and power to survive. Ironically, this evolutionary construct allowed Koreans to see the failure of the current political system as having been imposed from without (by China) and a distortion from the true path of national development. Extending this logic, reformers began to advocate the removal of pernicious external influences in Korean society and the adoption of more progressive habits, institutions, ideas, and technologies that would bolster national power in the grand struggle of societies, the nation-state being the highest level of social evolution.

Throughout the last years of the Chosŏn dynasty, Korean reformers gradually accepted Western concepts of progressive history, social evolution, and the role and function of the nation-state. In this way, they reconfigured the knowledge about the West that had been pouring into Korea since the first study trips abroad in the early 1880s as the most highly evolved cultural and technical values that could be appropriated in the service of the nation. By 1900 Japanese and Chinese scholars had built an impressive body of knowledge about the West, and it was primarily from these secondary works that Koreans constructed their own [WEST BOOKS TRANSLATED INTO KOREAN] programs for action. Chang Chiyŏn's translations of the writings of the famous Chinese reformer and interpreter of Western society Liang Ch'i-chao indirectly transmitted the writings of Darwin, Huxley, and Spencer to Korea. Journals of the regional study societies and the new nationwide organizations such as the National Self-Strengthening Association (TaeHan chaganghoe, 1906–1910) and the New People's Association (Sinminhoe, 1907–1910) devoted considerable space to the Western scientific tradition and positivism, a tradition they believed underlay the success of Western political institutions.

Pak Ŭnsik continued the discussion of the Western liberal tradition as he attempted to reconcile the concepts of Rousseau and Locke with a reinterpretation of Confucianism. The writings of American-educated leaders like Philip Jaesohn (Sŏ Chaep'il) and Yun Ch'iho in the *Independent* examined the liberal tradition for insights into the relationship between the state and the people and the role of the individual in society. The idea of a social contract highlighted the weak connection, in the minds of some reformers, between the traditional state and the Korean masses. Thus, democratic institutions such as elections, representative bodies, free speech, and a popular press came to be viewed less as guarantees against state [CONFUCIANISM VS. DEMOCRACY] domination of free individuals than as important sources of encouragement for mass identification with the state, and hence a source of state power. The idea of free individuals joined together socially but preserving their autonomy conflicted directly with prevailing views about man and society. In Korea, individual identity was expressed as an element of the collective; the individual was enmeshed in a web of social relationships and played out prescribed roles within the group, whether the family, the lineage, one's occupation, one's status or class, or one's gender. In contrast Western individualism stressed inherent rights, autonomy, and freedom for the individual.

Simultaneously there was a growing attack on Korean tradition. This iconoclasm conflicted with the concurrent movement to celebrate indigenous Korean traditions and create an autonomous nation-subject within a new historiography. But if Western values of individual freedom were a source of dynamism, then perhaps Confucian social mores were the main obstacle to its realization in Korea. The [WEST CHURCH EDU. = ANTI- CONF THOUGHT] critique of the traditional social system fell principally on the Confucian concepts of filial piety, social harmony, and social relations. Ignoring Confucian values with a positive valence, early iconoclasts focused on the authoritarian aspects of ancestor worship, prohibition of widows' remarriage, obligations to parents and elders, subordination of women, and the excessively elaborate ritual protocols as destructive of individual initiative and free will. There was an echo of Protestantism in some of this writing, particularly its characterization of ancestor ritual as "wasteful ceremony" and support for freeing women from the worst excesses of Confucian patriarchy. This was, in part, a result of the importance of church schools and the prominence of Christian converts within the Enlightenment movement itself.

The women's movement in Korea was born of this early attack on traditional values and institutions. The Christian church and the Tonghak religion (later, Ch'ŏn-dogyo, see endnote 1) were instrumental in advancing for the first time the idea that improving women's position in society should be part and parcel of national strengthening. Early women's movement leaders attacked the traditional precept of *namjon yŏbi* (revere men, subordinate women) as the core concept of gender relations. The Ch'anyanghoe established by the wives of aristocrats affiliated with the Independence Club and later various Patriotic Women's Associations *(aeguk puinhoe)* became the genesis of a broader movement to educate women and to elevate their status in Korean society.

Another feature of Enlightenment iconoclasm was the attack on traditional Korean folk culture. Although the elite Confucian tradition had seeped down in Korean society and regulated family ritual, most notably with regard to ancestor worship, peasant society remained strongly influenced by coexistent indigenous folk beliefs and norms. Korean folk culture, with its shamanistic tradition, was a rich and regionally diverse mixture of customs and beliefs tied together with ritual, dance, music, and art. Although this folk tradition provided a rich repository of unique symbols of national identity, Enlightenment thinkers decried folk culture as antiscientific, superstitious, and fatalistic. In their minds, belief in spirits and the powers of shamans blocked acceptance of modern science, and dependence on fortune-tellers and geomancy encouraged fatalism and passivity. Interestingly, Korean attitudes toward their own folk traditions rose and fell throughout the twentieth century. Folk culture was "rediscovered" by Korean ethnographers of the 1920s and 1930s as part of a movement to revive and codify specifically Korean traditions in the face of Japanese cultural assimilation. Having again fallen into disrepute by the 1960s, folk culture flourished anew in the 1970s as part of both formal South Korean government policies for preserving folk tradition and as part of the *minjung* opposition movement's appropriation of folk culture during the 1980s (see Chapter Six).

Such ambivalence reveals the tension between Enlightenment rationality and the articulation of Korean nationalism. Early nationalists were simultaneously asserting a long historical evolution of the Korean people and celebrating its unique identity as a nation, while at the same time they were trying to excise selectively those elements of the tradition that had deflected Korea from the main stream of world development. Some nationalists stressed reforming Korea along the lines of successful Western nation-states and downplayed the inherent contradiction such Westernization might imply. Others, however, were skeptical of such wholesale adoption of foreign ideas within Korea.

After a hundred years, it is easy to overlook other responses to Korea's cultural and political crisis of the early years of the twentieth century. This is especially true given the post-Korean War emphasis on martial valor in nationalist histories. But particularly in the pages of the *Capital Gazette (Hwangsŏng sinmun)* progressive Confucians worked to preserve traditional values amidst a general enthusiasm for reform. They argued for preserving Confucian morality as the basis for social harmony. They offered the best of East Asian traditions as an alternate civilization to the West while admitting that Confucianism had fallen behind with regard to the general principles of world civilization. This was a curious turn because in creating an opposition between East and West, they were trying to seek an Eastern equivalence with the West using Western standards. Reform-minded Confucians selectively cast their gaze over the Eastern tradition to find equivalents to the West. Finding enlightened practices from the past meant that the East need not be judged inferior to the West. But the fact remained that regardless of plentiful evidence of past enlightened practices, many reformers viewed Korea's present social and political condition as abysmal and felt that major reforms would be required for Korea to regain its vitality.

A final strand of thought within Korean Enlightenment discourse was pan-Asianism (Schmid, 2002). This was another way to juxtapose East and West and to defy the universalist claims of Western superiority. In keeping with the thinking of the period with its strong emphasis on racial categories, Koreans joined others in Japan and China in speculating about a regional unity based on racial affinity as a means to resist the encroachment of the West. Pan-Asianist thinking ran the gamut from specific programs that supported Asian unity under Japanese leadership to vague speculation about the latent power of Asia's combined population. Indeed, because both Korea and China had failed in the face of imperialist pressure, Japan, as the only Asian nation to successfully oppose Western imperialism, loomed large for a leadership role. Such was the case with one rabidly pro-Japanese association in Korea, the Unity and Progress Society (Ilchinhoe, est. 1904), but more moderate pan-Asianists in Korea were careful to hold a special place for the Korean nation within their advocacy of regional, racial unity against white imperialism. While nothing came of the pan-Asianist movement at the turn of the century, it was revived with a vengeance when the Japanese attempted to mobilize Asian racial unity under the banner of the Greater Asian Co-prosperity Sphere during World War II.

A decade after the abolition of the old state examinations, the intellectual world of Korea was actively rethinking its history, social values, and political structures based on the growing acceptance of a new standard of civilization. The monarch had elevated himself to a position coequal with the Chinese and Japanese emperors, and the bureaucracy was using the vocabulary and rituals of a nation-state. But for those clinging to power, the state was still for the most part the old Korean kingdom; state bureaus may have been reorganized and renamed, diplomatic missions dispatched, postal stamps issued in the name of the new empire, and Korea's small army dressed in Western-style uniforms, but these and other national symbols had simply been patched over the shell of the ancien régime.

Within the small but growing public sphere, however, a process was underway that would lead to a reimagining of the old kingdom as a modern nation. This process was driven by private intellectuals of disparate political leanings and social backgrounds who were casting about in a wide pool of knowledge, some of ancient provenance and some newer ideas and models borrowed from the West. Unfortunately for Korea, there was never a melding of the private energy embodied in the schools, newspapers, study societies, historical studies, and public debates that made up the Korean Enlightenment with the leadership and resources of the Chosŏn state. Unlike its Meiji counterpart, the Chosŏn state did not initiate a purposeful program of nation-building from the top down. The interference of foreign powers, Chosŏn's lack of military resources, and the resistance of a core of conservative elites who believed that wholesale reform would lead to their own disenfranchisement inhibited a resolute response. The state dabbled in reform at the margin, but was unable to establish a consensus within government about any long-term program of revitalization.

The Korean Enlightenment combined a number of conversations, all focused on the issue of Korea's present political crisis and national future. "Enlightenment" may be a misnomer because the term links the movement in Korea too closely to the ideas—the discovery of science and reason—of its European namesake. Perhaps "awakening" would be more apt. The external and internal shocks to the Chosŏn system had provoked the discovery and discussion of new ideas as well as the reexamination and reformulation of traditional knowledge. Not since the Manchu invasions and its attendant identity crisis had Korean intellectuals spent such energy redefining their society and its position in the world.

Not only was the awakening at the turn of the century different in scale and urgency, it was part of a global phenomenon. As capitalism and imperialism spread into the last redoubts of the non-Western world, it provoked similar intellectual movements. By 1900 emergent national movements—the acceptance of the national model—marked a new stage in the spread of the modern. While the modern nation-state may have originated in Europe, its transplantation in Asia immediately mutated to form unique variations. If this was an early moment in the modernization project in Korea, then it was from the beginning an alternative modernity that folded newly discovered Western values, racial rediscovery, and defensive Confucianism into its foundations.

The End of the Chosŏn Dynasty

After the Russo-Japanese war, the "civilized world" that had never embraced Korea in the first place abandoned it to the Japanese. The bellicose Theodore Roosevelt received the Nobel Peace Prize for brokering peace between Japan and czarist Russia at Portsmouth, Maine, in 1905, but in doing so he relinquished any American interests in Korea to the Japanese for assurances of "noninterference" with more important American interests in Asia.[5] During the war the Japanese had already signed two protocols with the Korean government that provided the Japanese with more financial concessions and stronger advisory powers in Korean affairs. After the war what was emerging as a system of overt control was formalized in a five-point treaty that turned Korea into a Japanese protectorate. The Protectorate Treaty of November 1905 coerced the Korean government to cede control of its foreign affairs to Japan and established Residency-General *(tōkanfu)* with one of the premier statesmen of Meiji Japan, Itō Hirobumi, as its first resident-general.

Itō was part of a faction in the highest levels of the Japanese government that had long argued for indirect control of Korea (Duus, 1995). This group preferred a reformed, stable, and docile Korea run by Koreans but controlled by Japan over direct Japanese rule of the peninsula. In the face of stiff Korean resistance at all levels of society, Itō restructured the Korean government, gradually increasing the power and influence of Japanese "advisors" at all levels. By 1907 the Residency-General abandoned any pretext of indirect control because continuing Korean resistance required sterner measures. After Kojong dispatched envoys to plead for outside intercession in Korea at the World Peace Conference at The Hague, the Japanese forced his abdication in favor of his son, Sunjong (1907–1910, reign title Yunghŭi) in 1907. In the same year they disbanded the remaining Korean army and assumed direct control of police and judicial functions of the government.

As a result the Residency-General's power to sway the Korean government increased dramatically after 1907. It passed numerous laws and regulations to

Resident-General Itō Hirobumi moving through Seoul under armed guard. The Norman Thorpe Collection.

bring the Korean press under stricter controls, and it promulgated stiff regulations for government and private schools that included the introduction of pro-Japanese texts and curriculum in Korean schools. By late 1909 Korea's fate was sealed. During that summer the debate about whether or not to annex Korea was concluded in favor of the hard-liners. Itō resigned as resident-general, and while on another state mission was assassinated by Korean independence fighters in Harbin the same year.[6] Shortly thereafter, the former war minister of Japan, the humorless General Terauchi Masatake, arrived, empowered by the Meiji cabinet to terminate Korea's independence. On August 16, 1910, Terauchi forced Sunjong to affix his seal to a treaty of annexation already signed by the Korean prime minister Yi Wanyong. For his signature Yi has earned a place of permanent vilification as the archetypal collaborator in modern Korean history. After 518 years, the once-proud Chosŏn dynasty was gone.

This summary reflects the inexorable progress of the Japanese seizure of Korea without doing justice to the turmoil and trauma of the process. Korean journalists continued to raise a hue and cry over every Japanese move to consolidate their position. The Protectorate Treaty provoked outright denunciation of the traitorous officials who had collaborated in such a disgraceful document; the editor of the *Hwangsŏng sinmun,* Chang Chiyŏn, wrote a now-canonical piece, "Today We Cry Out in Lamentation," in a special edition that was distributed free in Seoul. Moderates who had believed in the benign intentions of the Japanese reform propaganda expressed their sense of betrayal, and a number of officials in the Chosŏn government committed suicide in protest. The most renowned of these acts of martyrdom was that of Min Yŏnghwan (1861–1905), military attaché to Kojong. He left a testament decrying the treaty and enigmatically declaring that he was "dead but had not died"; news of his testament spread rapidly and provoked in the press a torrent of patriotic letters, poems, and essays that echoed Min's insinuation that the spirit of the nation must live. Rumors that bamboo had sprouted on the spot where he died further enflamed patriotic passion. But however eloquent and impassioned the words, they fell on deaf ears abroad and in the precincts of the Japanese overlords.

And not all Korean resistance was prose and poetry. As early as the mid-1890s, particularly after the assassination of Queen Min, small, armed bands of guerrilla fighters emerged to harass the Japanese and other foreign enemies of the kingdom. Known as the Righteous Armies *(ŭibyŏng)*[7] these groups were often organized by local literati, and their patriotism focused on supporting the monarch and the Chosŏn system (Yong-ha Shin, 1989). The movement grew rapidly after the announcement of the Protectorate Treaty. In 1905 the venerable Ch'oe Ikhyŏn raised a force in North Cholla province, and Na Inyŏng gathered another small army in South Cholla. Their pronouncements were very traditional: their goal was to protect the monarch, resist the Japanese, and restore independence to Chosŏn. The disbanding of the Korean army in 1907 further swelled the ranks of *ŭibyŏng* groups, as demobilized soldiers joined the guerrilla movement. Most bands numbered in the hundreds, but some *ŭibyŏng* were able to put several thousand together against the Japanese army. The largest encounter involved an army of as many as 10,000 that was turned back in heavy fighting eight miles from the heart of Seoul. In the last years of the dynasty the slogans of the *ŭibyŏng* subtly shifted to more contemporary nationalist language, reflecting the training and indoctrination of the disbanded Korean soldiery. The Righteous Army activity reached its peak in 1907 with Japanese estimates of nearly 70,000 irregulars challenging Japanese forces in 1,500 clashes. The guerrilla struggle waned after 1907, but it forced the Japanese to strengthen their military garrison, and sporadic fighting continued for a year after annexation. The meticulous Japanese military ultimately numbered Korean deaths in the conflicts at 17,690.

It took the Japanese several years after 1910 to pacify the peninsula. In doing so they faced all manner of Korean resistance: sabotage, assassination of Japanese officials and their Korean collaborators, armed confrontation, secret political organizing, journalistic broadsides, appeals to foreign powers, and in the end all manner of acts of daily resistance. After 1910 opposition to the Japanese presence and their colonial state became the main unifying force among those disparate forces that had fought to preserve Korean independence. Now anti-Japanese sentiment unified and mobilized most Koreans—conservative Confucians, radical Westernizers, and everyone in between. The fall into colonial status primed the movement to both articulate a modern national identity and organize a struggle to regain political independence. Faced with a sullen populous and lingering armed resistance, the Japanese began the process of ensuring their domination by creating a colonial state of unprecedented reach and power in Korean society.

Chapter Two

COLONIAL STATE AND SOCIETY

어

WHILE THE CHOSŎN STATE is usually described as bureaucratic, centralized, and authoritarian, its powers had been limited in a number of ways, and its reach into local affairs had been always circumscribed. This was not the case with the Government General of Korea (GGK) as the new colonial state came to be known. The GGK penetrated Korean society more thoroughly than had any previous traditional government, and by the end of their rule the Japanese had left their mark everywhere. They used their experience building the Meiji state and twentieth-century technology to advance their strategic, economic, and political goals with breathtaking single-mindedness and rigor. Not content with simple compliance, the colonial state not only dominated Korea following the usual paternalistic logic of colonialists, but they also believed they could actually "assimilate" Koreans culturally. Indeed, the Japanese attempts to efface Korean culture, even its language, exacerbated colonial exploitation, repression, and racism. And the poisonous memory of this experience continues to plague Japanese–Korean relations more than half a century after Liberation.

Japan was the only non-Western nation to assemble its own colonial empire. The geographical proximity of metropole and colony was also unique in the annals of modern colonial history, a feature it shared with only France and its North African colonies. This proximity encouraged settlement of large numbers of metropolitan émigrés and facilitated colonial migration into the metropole. By 1942 over 1.5 million Koreans were living and working in Japan, and the Japanese population of the colony was approaching 800,000, almost 3 percent of the total population (see Table 2.1). But unlike France and its colonies, Japan and Korea shared a racial and cultural affinity and a long, complex historical relationship. The relationship was analogous to that of England and Ireland where England's domination of Ireland produced the bitter and seemingly intractable legacy of distrust apparent to this day. The Japanese colonialists mobilized archeology, ethnography, and historical studies to justify their rule in Korea as a matter of lifting up a wayward sibling culture and returning it to its proper course as part of the destiny of the Yamato race. This was all the more galling because Koreans had historically considered themselves culturally superior to their new colonial masters.

Pacification and the Mechanisms of Power

Terauchi Masatake (1910–1918), protégé of the powerful Meiji elder statesman Yamagata Aritomo, became the first steward of the state-building process as governor general. His tenure exemplified the enormous power and prestige vested in this office. The home government appointed the governors general from amongst the highest ranks of the Japanese leadership. In all cases save one, Saitō Makoto (1919–1927, 1929–1931), who was a retired admiral, they were high-ranking generals in the Japanese army. Other appointments held by governors general included minister of war, commander-in-chief of the Kwantung Army, army chief-of-staff, and even prime minister. The Japanese prime minister appointed the governor general, and oversight of the office was placed variously in the Diet (budgetary issues), the Home Ministry, and the Ministry of Colonial Affairs. But throughout the period the governor general reported to the emperor directly, creating an ambiguity in the lines of authority that gave this office considerable autonomy. All of Japan's other colonies—Taiwan, Karafuto (Sakhalin), the Pacific Islands (Nanyō), and the Kwantung Lease Territories (Kantōshū)—remained firmly under the thumb of the home government. This was no mere satrapy; he governed 25 million subjects, controlled enormous tax revenues, commanded Japanese military forces in Korea as well as the colonial gendarmerie, issued laws, and directed a bureaucracy that by 1945 employed 246,000 people.[1] This was a state of enormous size, particularly compared with other colonial regimes; France, for example, ruled Vietnam with a 2,920 bureaucrats and a small army of 11,000. The British famously ruled India

TABLE 2.1   POPULATION OF KOREA: 1900–1944

Year	Korean	Japanese	Japanese Population as % of Total	Seoul
1900	12,000,000*	15,829	0.1	190,000*
1910	14,766,000	171,543	1.3	197,000
1920	17,764,000	347,900	2.0	251,000
1930	20,438,000	501,900	2.5	677,000
1940	24,326,300	712,583	2.9	935,464
1944	25,133,352	752,830 (1942)	3.0	988,537

Sources: *Estimated; Korean population statistics prior to 1945 are based on Japanese Government General Yearbooks; Japanese residents in Korea taken from Japanese Resident General and Japanese Government General statistics used by Andrew Grajdanzev (1944) and Peter Duus (1995).

with several thousand civil servants, and the ratio of officials to population was much smaller than that of the French in Vietnam (Cumings, *Origins of the Korean War,* 1981). The governor general was not equal in rank to the prime minister, but the position was almost as prestigious and came with considerable autonomy of action.

The first task of the GGK after annexation was to pacify the colony. The colonial military police and Japanese army regulars worked until mid-1912 to subdue the remnants of righteous army resistance. Concurrently, the GGK gave stipends and titles in the Japanese peerage to 84 high Chosŏn officials and *yangban* and pensioned off another 3,645 officials in the old Korean government (Henderson, 1968). The upper *yangban* were stripped of political power, but they were left with their lands intact and considerable residual social prestige. While the Japanese curried favor with the traditional elite, they began sweeping arrests using lists prepared earlier of "malcontent and rebellious Koreans" *(futei senjin).* The police arrested 700 people including the core leadership of the New People's Association (including moderate reformers such as An Ch'angho and Yun Ch'iho) in connection with a blatantly fabricated plot to assassinate the governor general in 1911. Ultimately 105 were prosecuted (only 5 received prison sentences) in the first major political show trial in the colony. Cases of torture and abuse were common among the tens of thousands of arrests between 1910 and 1912, establishing a pattern of brutal policing that continued to the end of the colonial period.

With armed resistance at an end and virtually the entire leadership of Korean society either mollified, in jail, or under surveillance, the Japanese established the institutions of their rigid, highly intrusive administrative colonialism. They counted everything and created a myriad of regulations governing daily life from slaughtering a worn-out draft animal to the placement of a family grave; they established new land and family registers, health regulations, detailed sanitation procedures in the reorganized city administrations, fishery regulations, rules governing water rights and irrigation ditches, standard operating procedures for periodic markets, and licenses and permission forms for just about everything else. The gendarmerie—swords dangling from the men's uniforms as symbols of their authority—was given summary powers to enforce the regulations. This allowed the police to be both judge and jury, deciding punishments on the spot for minor infractions. Nothing could have prepared the Korean population for such an invasion into what had heretofore been matters of local and customary practice. In addition, the Japanese renamed geographic features of the peninsula and its cities and towns. For a generation after Liberation Western maps frequently still used the Japanese names.[2]

The GGK built upon a base of administrative law already promulgated during the Residency General to create what became in effect a dual system of jurisprudence. Unlike native Koreans, Japanese residents in Korea retained their rights as citizens under the Meiji Constitution as well as those granted by special laws in the colony. This meant two sets of laws and punishments, one for Japanese residents, another for the Korean population. Perhaps the most obnoxious feature of this legal apartheid was the use of traditional punishments, such as whipping, for Koreans, while the practice was deemed too barbaric for Japanese citizens. One Japanese official fatuously explained the practice as "culturally sensitive," asserting that Koreans would more readily accept their own "traditions" in this arena (Robinson, *Cultural Nationalism*, 1988, p. 60). To enforce the new legal and regulatory structure, the Japanese created an expanded judicial system, with all judges appointed by the governor general, except for high judges, who were appointed by the emperor. As with most middle and high ranks in the bureaucracy, the majority of judgeships were held by Japanese until the very end of the colonial period, when more Koreans were appointed to the higher courts.

The lion's share of enforcement for all GGK regulations, laws, and special orders lay with the colonial police. The numbers and reach of the colonial police expanded rapidly in the first decade of Japanese rule. At this time the police were still a military police, this meant the entire Japanese army garrison (roughly 40,000 troops in 1911) was available for security work. Gradually, a centralized police system emerged as the GGK created civil police bureaus in all thirteen provinces and then extended the placement of stations, substations, and police boxes downward into the counties, the rural districts and urban wards, and then into urban neighborhoods. Between 1910 and 1920 the police were organized as a military police; after 1920 it became a civilian force, but it was still organized as a colony-wide structure. The police force grew rapidly from 6,222 in 1911, to 20,771 in 1922, and to roughly 60,000 in the 1940s (a ratio of 1 to 400 of the Korean population). If we add to this the small army of informers who worked for the High Police to covertly monitor political behavior, the numbers would be even more impressive. Over half of the police force were Koreans, and these people became the most reviled group of collaborators after Liberation. But for many Korean men without family connections, resources, or land, and with little education, careers in the colonial police became one avenue of mobility during the period.

The GGK extended its regulatory and legal penetration of Korean society by conducting, at enormous expense, a comprehensive cadastral survey of land ownership and use on the peninsula between 1910 and 1918. The survey was designed to establish a broad tax base and to rationalize ownership and title to all agricultural land (paddy and dry field), untilled upland, river floodplains, tidal basins, and forest land. It plotted, assessed, and fixed ownership for every piece of land on the peninsula. The Land Survey Ordinance required all landowners and tillers to register with the government documentary proof of any claims to ownership or other cultivation rights. The new land laws swept away centuries-old local practices, informal cultivation rights, seasonal claims on land of ambiguous provenance, and informal customs that had mitigated landlord-tenant relations in traditional Korea. Hereafter, land was to be governed by a strict and rational system of title in order to fix tax obligations and to rationalize land transfers and sales. Postwar nationalist historians claim that the survey was no more than a vehicle for a massive expropriation of land—that thousands of peasants lost their land because they did not understand the new registration procedures, or because they filed claims improperly. Certainly, many did lose their land, but probably not in the massive numbers claimed. Other studies indicate that there was considerable continuity in landownership before and after 1910 (Gragert, 1994). It was the colonial takeover itself that was the real land grab; the GGK assumed control of all Chosŏn state agricultural, forest, and mountain lands as well as a large portion of the Royal Household's holdings. Large tracts of the agriculturally useful portion of these lands were sold to individual Japanese and Korean investors and private land companies such as the Fuji Land Company or the huge semigovernmental Oriental Development Company. When the land survey was completed in 1918, the government controlled 21.9 million acres or almost 40 percent of all farm and forest land in Korea.

While the survey expropriated land from peasants and placed what had been in effect common land under strict government control, the new rationalized land system was a boon to landowners and landlords of whatever ethnicity. While large Japanese land companies and individual investors did control enormous areas of the best paddy land, large and medium Korean landlords also increased their holdings during the period, and they made up the majority of the landlord class. Rent for paddy land customarily was paid as a percentage of the harvest, with tenants assuming the bulk of cultivation expenses. In bad years or at times of depressed rice prices landlords still received 40 to 50 percent of the harvest, but tenants might not have enough left to cover expenses, let alone enough rice for subsistence. Over time, population increases drove up rents, rice prices were increasingly tied to the volatile world market, and the world depression after 1930 drove rice prices down, further increasing peasant indebtedness. Exposure to the extractive effects of world capitalism and upward pressure on rents caused an alarming rise in landlessness in Korea during the 1930s. By the end of the colonial period, tenancy rates approached 80 percent in the densely populated and most productive rice-growing areas of the Cholla provinces in the southwest. And many peasants chose to leave the land altogether, ending up in the cities in search of jobs.

Land and the rents therefrom remained one of the safest investments in Korea during the colonial period. Over time, Korean landowners, Japanese investors, and the large land companies expanded their holdings, causing increased concentration of landownership in the hands of the few. Absentee landlords living in the growing cities worked through agents in the countryside, and they became a staple of satire and loathing. It is likely that the odious Master Yun, archetypal absentee landlord and protagonist of Ch'ae Mansik's serialized novel *Peace Under Heaven* (1930–1931), seemed to readers like many landlords, Korean or Japanese, when he waxed eloquent in praise of the law and order brought to the countryside by the Japanese police; speaking to his captive servant audience at his palatial compound in Seoul, he notes with great satisfaction how he no longer has to consider the incessant demands of his tenants for relief, rent breaks, or gratuities depending on yearly conditions—he could live under his motto of "let everyone else go to hell" (Ch'ae Mansik, 1993, p. xx). The new land system with its advantages for owners encouraged quiet support for the GGK among the landlord class, but it set in motion the gradual rise in tenancy and rural immiseration that created the explosive class conflict that emerged in the era immediately following Liberation.

The GGK regulated finance and business activity through the Company Law of 1910 and its close control of the Bank of Chōsen and later the Chōsen Industrial Bank. The Bank of Chōsen became the central bank for the colony; it issued currency and provided capital for GGK projects (mostly agricultural development) and infrastructure development (railroad and port construction). Over time the Bank of Chōsen grew to assume great importance in the regional economy of Northeast Asia by providing loans for Japanese investment in Manchuria and north China. The Chōsen Industrial Bank, established in 1917, rivaled its sister bank in size and dominated capital inputs for the industrial development in Korea during the 1930s. The GGK's initial economic policy focused on "underdeveloping" Korea, that is, restricting investment to raw materials extraction and increasing rice production for the Japanese market. The Company Law required all businesses, including those of the Japanese, to be licensed by the GGK. In effect, the GGK stifled business development in Korea in the face of loud complaints from Japanese businessmen, not to mention its almost complete refusal to charter Korean corporations of any kind.

Between 1910 and 1920 the colonial state restricted cultural and political life in Korea. All privately run newspapers were closed down, and the presses of the largest pre-colonial paper, the *Korea Daily News*, were impressed to print an organ paper for the GGK of the same name. The GGK fine-tuned its system of publication permits and prepublication censorship begun during the Residency General with the 1907 Newspaper Law and 1909 Publication Law. All private organizations were abolished, and another permit system was created to regulate public assembly of any kind. Only religious organizations escaped the crackdown, and, as we shall see, Christian, Buddhist, and Ch'ŏndogyo (the modern church of the Tonghak religion) churches provided the only available organizational cover for a major political upheaval in 1919. National histories refer deservedly to the first decade of colonial rule as the "dark period" *(amhŭkki)*, and with particular reference to any overt political expression, the term is apt. A limited number of publications did, however, see the light of day. Small and short-lived academic, literary, and religious publications survived the blackout. Perhaps most notably, Ch'oe Namsŏn's magazine *Youth (Ch'ŏngch'un* 1914–1918) continued his project begun with *Boys* (*Sonyŏn*, 1908–1911) to pioneer new style vernacular prose and poetry as well as politicized "educational" features on national heroes in Western and Asian history.

Finally, this early period inaugurated a sustained building boom as the Japanese invested millions of yen in the bricks and mortar of colonial rule. Cumulatively the government buildings, shrines, railroads, motor roads, power and telephone lines, hydroelectric dams, barrages, and irrigation works transformed Korea's visual geography and became potent symbols of Japan's domination of the modern sector of society. In the 1920s a colonial architectural style emerged, an eclectic and grandiose style that might be described as beaux arts authoritarian, as the GGK raised imposing edifices for the new Seoul (renamed Keijō) City Administration Building, the Bank of Chōsen, and a new capitol. The capitol, completed in 1926, dominated the Seoul skyline and its placement directly in front of the south gate (Kwanghwanmun) of the Kyŏngbok palace was deliberately calculated to efface any symbolic residue of the ancient regime.[3] The GGK built large shrines in Korea's major cities as sites for extending centralized state Shinto into the colony. After 1937 these became sites for obligatory—and for Koreans despised—rituals promoting loyalty and devotion to the Japanese emperor. The shrines, principle among them the enormous Chōsen Jinko on Namsan in the middle of Seoul, represented the most objectionable reminders of Japanese power, and of all the colonial-built structures, they were the first to be destroyed after Liberation.

Even more important to the GGK than buildings was the communications

Overview of Seoul looking north to the new Capitol Building in 1927. Source: The Norman Thorpe Collection.

infrastructure of the colony. Over the thirty-five years, from 1910 to 1945, the Japanese laid thousands of kilometers of railroad track, north-south lines that linked Korea's southern ports to Seoul and Manchuria, and, on the bias, east-west lines that connected the mines and rice-producing areas in the interior to the newly built ports along the coasts. Viewed as a whole, the entire grid quickly conformed to the strategic and extractive logic of Japanese colonial policy. By the time the Korea Railroad Corporation was amalgamated with the huge Southern Manchurian Railway Corporation in the 1930s, Korea was the strategic and economic center of Japanese-dominated Northeast Asia. The railroad also altered the human geography of Korea. Towns and cities sprang up at important railroad junctions or at the new ports, drawing population and economic activity from the hinterland. Small villages such as Iri on the Honam plain, Taejŏn in central Korea, Najin in the extreme northeast, and Ŭiju, now Sinŭiju, on the Yalu River and Chinese border grew topsy-turvy; all have become major centers in contemporary Korea. Telegraph and telephonic systems connected the colonial administrative centers and, ultimately, every police box in Korea to the center. In 1945 Korea possessed an impressive communications infrastructure—unprecedented for a recently liberated colony—an unintended legacy of Japanese strategic, economic, and political control policies.

Cultural Control and the Ideology of Empire

The Japanese relied on coercion and tight control of public life in the first nine years of their rule, and the first decade of Japanese rule has become known as the period of Military Rule *(budan seiji)*. The global repression of Korean society ultimately backfired, for it provoked major upheavals in 1919 that forced the GGK to modify its control policies in a series of reforms under the third governor general, Saitō Makoto, after 1920. These policy changes ushered in the so-called era of Cultural Rule *(bunka seiji)*, with culture here referring to limited Korean cultural autonomy.

From the beginning of their colonial rule, the Japanese had intended that Korea would not be absorbed just politically by the empire but that it would also be culturally assimilated *(dōka)*, to become one with Japan in all respects. At first glance this seems completely preposterous. How could the Japanese contemplate the deracination of twenty million Koreans and the effacement of a culture and historical memory thousands of years in the making? Such questions seemed not to bother leading Japanese statesmen such as Count Okuma Shigenobu, who commented in the preface of Yamamichi Jōichi's *The Korean Peninsula (Chōsen hanto,* 1910):

> From ancient times, our country's race and that of Chōsen have been the same. . . . Furthermore, in the past we have had frequent contact, especially since last year when the peninsula became a part of our empire. In order to

rule, many political, economic, and educational issues must be resolved. Compared to other, Western imperial powers who have encountered innumerable problems in their attempts to rule over very different races, however, in our case, the path to *dōka* (assimilation) will transform the Koreans into loyal and obedient subjects. (Pai, 2000, p. 37)

The logic behind this belief was grounded in the scientific racism of the turn of the century and the emerging discourse on Japan's manifest destiny to lead Asia against the white race. Assimilation of Korea was the political expression in colonial ideology of the theory of the "common ancestral origin of the Korean and Japanese races" *(Nissen dōsoron)*. Japan had already evoked this shared background to legitimate their late-nineteenth-century drive for ascendancy on the peninsula. With the advent of colonial rule an array of research institutes, both private and GGK-sponsored, burgeoned to prove how the two cultures were linked by race, culture, and history, with Japan being the more advanced culture and thus the natural one to absorb the lesser (Korea) into itself. For the first twenty years of Japanese rule assimilation remained a long-term goal, and the Japanese were content to lay the historical and archeological foundations of assimilation theory while doing what was possible to spread Japanese language use and inculcate the proper values of good imperial citizens among their Korean subjects. Only after 1935, and with a vengeance after the outbreak of war in China in 1937, did assimilation become an urgent priority, realized in the Movement to Create Imperial Citizens (Kōminka undō), the general mobilization for war, and the attempts to efface Korean culture of the late colonial period (see Chapter Four).

To Koreans the first decade of colonial rule must have seemed like a massive inventory project because not only was the cadastral survey in full swing, but the GGK had also begun a comprehensive cataloguing of archeological sites, historical relics, tombs, artwork, and temples. In retrospect this was part of a vast cultural control project, to find, name, and integrate the entirety of Korea's physical historical legacy into a Japanese version of Northeast Asian history (Pai, 2000). The state mounted a number of research and publishing projects, extending archaeological, ethnographic, and historical studies already begun by 1900. In copious detail, the studies advanced two fundamental propositions: that Korean and Japanese had evolved fundamentally from the same prehistoric ancestors, and that the Japanese had developed to a higher level to which their less-developed Korean cousins could certainly be assimilated. Between 1932 and 1937 the GGK published a *History of Korea (Chōsenshi)* in thirty-seven volumes that rewrote the entire history of the peninsula into an elaborate justification of colonial rule. Korean intellectuals fought back with their own studies even though they were hampered by lack of resources and Japanese scrutiny. In spite of Japan's massive cultural and historical production, the assimilation program ultimately failed along with Japanese colonialism, but because of the professionalism and sheer volume of studies the Japanese produced, they continue to influence debates on the early history of Northeast Asia. Contemporary historians and archeologists in Korea and Japan still fight over the interpretation of the colonial materials as they try to unscramble this narrative in an academic climate still dominated by nationalist passions (Pai, 2000).

Education was a prime means of social and cultural control, but in the 1910s school expansion was very slow. As with the legal system, the GGK created separate schools for Japanese and Koreans. Japanese residents in Korea could send their children to school in Japan proper or they could use equivalent schools established for Japanese in the colony. For Koreans, the GGK created a separate but not equal system of four-year primary and four-year secondary schools for boys (three years for girls). The Korean schools' avowed purpose was to create "good and loyal subjects of the Emperor" (Robinson, *Cultural Nationalism*, 1988). The Educational Ordinance of 1911 also placed a number of new regulations on and required the use of GGK-approved textbooks at the roughly 1,200 private schools established before the Japanese takeover. These regulations caused the number of these schools to drop to less than 700 by 1920. Japanese language study was compulsory in all accredited schools, and the Korean secondary system stressed vocational and technical education. The only higher liberal arts education available to Koreans was in private religious or secular colleges; in short, opportunities for Koreans in Korea to study law, medicine, engineering, and the humanities remained very limited. Ambitious students with financial backing began to go to Japan for upper-level schooling in increasing numbers during the 1910–1918 period. By 1919 only 84,306 Koreans (3.7 percent of eligible children) attended primary school. The rate of growth for primary and secondary schools was painfully slow and hardly served the tremendous latent demand for education. The competition for slots in the few colleges was very intense. Over time the GGK was constantly under pressure to expand the educational system, and by 1944 about 40 percent of Korean children between the ages of seven and fourteen were attending either a two- or four-year primary school. Yet in spite of the increase in secondary schools (public and private), the 1944 data show only 13 percent of the total school population received secondary education and 7 percent some college (Nahm, *Korean Tradition*, 1988).

Between 1910 and 1920 the new colonial rulers relied heavily on systematic, repressive policing of all aspects of daily life. The administration sucked the life out of the public sphere by banning newspapers and other publications with political content, prohibiting public assembly, and outlawing most private-interest organizations. But its treatment of the landed elite and its land policies encouraged tacit support by a large proportion of the upper class. More insidiously, the Japanese dominated all aspects of early modernization in the colony. Almost all prestigious, modern, white-collar jobs were in Japanese-dominated enterprises: banks, large companies, trading houses, land corporations, public schools, the railway corporation, and the huge bureaucracy of the GGK itself. To work in the modern sector meant getting at least a secondary school degree, if not a college education. The route to the best jobs lay in upper education in Japan. Therefore, from the beginning, attaining Japanese cultural and linguistic skills became de rigueur for the ambitious sons of the elite and Korea's tiny middle class if they were to have any chance at even the middle- and low-level, white-collar jobs in the cities.

The draconian repression of the first decade had limited opportunities for educated Koreans to cultural production or journalism, and by 1919 the tremendous political tension in the colony exploded in a political upheaval that ultimately compelled the Japanese to rethink their policies of rule in Korea. After that, however, the selective inclusion of educated Koreans in the modern sphere tended to remove potential political leaders from the nationalist independence movement. Even worse their modern schooling, which emphasized how to survive in a Japanese-dominated world, alienated this educated class from the masses of uneducated, ordinary Koreans toiling in the fields, menial service jobs, or factories. Over time this came to have significant political implications.

By 1919 the Japanese appeared to have successfully pacified their Korean colony and created a draconian state that put them in total control. But their policies had sealed a lid over political and cultural expression while turning up the heat under the pot; ultimately the Korean pressure cooker exploded. After ten years of Japanese rule, the increased physical mobility provided by the railroads, the intensifying economic contacts stimulated by the increasing influence of the international rice market, and a steady internal migration to the new administrative centers and cities brought Koreans from all walks of life and all regions together on a scale never before possible. This, combined with the relative increase in education, literacy, and use of the vernacular, helped mobilize Koreans and create awareness of politics on a nationwide basis, what Benedict Anderson refers to as the imagined community of the nation (Anderson, 1991). The severe military rule, the blatant legal and educational discrimination, and the arrests of political and intellectual leaders ensured that resentment and loathing of Japanese colonialism were shared by all members of this imagined community. Even at the level of the peasantry, ten years of colonial rule had galvanized anti-Japanese consciousness. The new power disrupted life in villages and urban neighborhoods that had previously been governed by local custom. Moreover, the arbitrary exercise of summary powers, not to mention the use of flogging by the hated gendarmerie, further heightened Korean consciousness of collective discrimination. As the Japanese public in the metropole followed news of the Versailles Peace Conference ending World War I and wondered what spoils might accrue to Japan for their late entry into the war on the Allied side, Japanese colonial policy and Korean resentment of colonial rule at all levels of society were on a collision course.

A Brief Shining Moment: The March First Uprising

The March First Uprising of 1919 was a defining moment in modern Korean history. And the memory of this uprising plays a significant role in the narrative of modern Korea and the evolution of Korean nationalism. The Japanese today have little reason to note this event, since they have spent the better part of the last fifty years trying to forget that they colonized Korea. But for Koreans the March First Uprising marks a shining moment of national unity during the long dark night of Japanese rule. Moreover, the movement was connected in important ways to global flows of information and the movement of people; it placed the plight of the Korean people briefly on the world stage, precipitated a major shift in Japanese control policies, and was a public relations disaster for the Japanese.

In January of 1918 the stage had been set by the publication of Woodrow Wilson's famous Fourteen Points, which outlined the American agenda for the Versailles Peace Conference. To the consternation of his allies, all colonial powers, Wilson declared that that the principle of humanism, respect for the self-determination of peoples, and international cooperation must become the basis of a new era of peace. Although Wilson's comments were made in the context of the postwar disposition of the Austro-Hungarian Empire and the remaking of political boundaries in Eastern Europe, Asians struggling under colonial rule felt they had found a world power willing to guarantee political self-determination for all people. Thus the American propaganda machine indirectly encouraged a number of petitions to the conference from Asian nationalist groups demanding self-determination for their nations. Korean nationalists exiled in Shanghai, the Russian Far East, and the United States all tried to send delegations to Versailles. Simultaneously Korean students in Tokyo drafted an independence declaration and sent it to the Japanese Diet. By February of 1919, Korean students returning from Tokyo had joined with students in Korea to plan a nationwide demonstration to appeal to the powers at Versailles.

Student activists gained the cooperation and financial support of Ch'ŏndogyo leaders, and further work brought Christian and Buddhist activists on board. Recruiting an older generation of moderate religious leaders was important because the planners needed the churches' nationwide networks to successfully stage their demonstrations and spread their message. Important leaders of various women's groups in the 1920s, both moderate and radical, such as Kim Maria (1891–1944), Hwang Hedŏk (Esther Hwang 1892–1971), and Na Hyesŏk (1896–1948), were central in the effort to mobilize girl students for the demonstrations. The leaders of the various church organizations, however, insisted on a nonviolent demonstration. The movement's declaration, authored by Ch'oe Namsŏn, asserted Korea's "natural" right to nationhood by evoking Korea's long history of political and cultural autonomy. In mildly Confucian fashion the declaration declared the start of an "age of restoration and reconstruction" that would fulfill Korea's promise as a nation in the world community; it closed by enjoining Koreans to eschew violence and to carry out the demonstration in an "orderly and solemn" manner, with an "honorable and upright" attitude.

In contrast to the idealistic, radical motivations of the movement's student organizers, the March First Declaration expressed the more moderate ideas of the senior religious leadership who became the public leaders of the movement—men such as Son Pyŏnghŭi, Yi Sŭnghun, Pak Hŭido, and Han Yong'un. But the tactical logistics depended on the energy of younger students, many of whom were still teenagers. The planners had originally chosen March third for their demonstration, the day of former king Kojong's funeral, when large crowds would be gathered in Seoul to pay their respects. To avoid police detection, however, the date was moved back to March first. Copies of the March First Declaration were printed and secretly distributed. On March first the thirty-three signatories to the declaration, all well-known intellectual, religious, and social leaders, gathered at a downtown Seoul restaurant for a formal reading of the document; simultaneously throughout Korea crowds gathered in parks, markets, city squares, and school grounds for public readings, followed by parades of celebration, with people chanting, "Long live Korea."

The size and number of the demonstrations caught the Japanese police by complete surprise. Perhaps as many as a million people from all walks of life took part in the marches or were swept into spontaneous demonstrations that continued into the early summer of 1919. The Japanese response bordered on hysteria; they used brutal force to contain the demonstrations and Koreans fought back in kind. By mid-April rioting was widespread, and police violence led to a number of well-documented atrocities: the burning of villages, shooting on crowds, mass searches, arrests, and the disappearance of demonstrators. The police also seized printing presses, closed schools, and declared a colony-wide curfew. Still the rioting continued sporadically into the summer of 1919 and was controlled only after additional troops arrived from Japan. Korean historians claim that over 7,500 people died, 15,000 were injured, and over 45,000 arrested; even the GGK admitted to 553 deaths, 1,409 injured, and 12,522 arrests, a serious conflagration by any estimate. Notably, the statistics list 471 arrests of women and girls participating in the movement. This is strong evidence of the increased participation in nationalist activities of a new generation of women who attended or had graduated from the new schools for women that mushroomed in the 1910s.

The movement failed in the sense that it neither dislodged the Japanese nor gained the attention of the Western powers. But it did demonstrate to Korean nationalists of all political stripes that it was possible to organize a mass following around appeals to nation and anti-Japanese sentiment. Within months a number of disparate and, seemingly, politically incompatible exile organizations had come together in Shanghai to form a government in exile, the Shanghai Provisional Government, with high hopes of unifying their efforts to regain Korean independence. The Japanese lost face internationally as word leaked out of atrocities and the martyrdom of young students, both boys and girls. Missionaries published eyewitness accounts in the American press, and funds were collected to help Koreans injured in the riots. In Japan by mid-summer of 1919, the first party cabinet headed by the newly elected liberal Prime Minister Hara Kei met to assess the situation in Korea. A new governor general was appointed and charged to reform colonial policy under the softer label of *nisen yūhwa* (harmony between Japan and Korea). Indeed, while the March First Movement did not unseat the Japanese, it did succeed in forcing the Japanese to ameliorate their most obnoxious policies in Korea. But it was a Pyrrhic victory. With their will to hold Korea unchanged, the Japanese replaced naked coercion with a softer but even more effective policy of manipulation and co-optation.

Course Correction: The Cultural Policy

Punctuating the tense situation still prevailing in December 1919, the new governor general, Saitō Makoto (1858–1936), and his administrative team were greeted at Seoul Station by radical nationalists' failed attempt to detonate a bomb. Saitō was an urbane, well-traveled diplomat with strong ties to the new party government as well as the Japanese military establishment. He brought with him former Home Minister Mazuno Rentarō and another technocrat, Maruyama Tsurukichi, whose job it would be to reorganize the colonial police system. The Cultural Policy *(bunka seiji)*, as the Saitō reforms came to be known, reformed the overtly abusive practices used by General Terauchi and his successor, Hasegawa Yoshimichi. The overall objectives in Korea remained unchanged, but the colonial administration replaced naked repression with a softer—in retrospect, more effective—policy of manipulation. The GGK reorganized its administrative structure and increased the size and number of local and provincial advisory boards staffed by prominent Koreans in order to create more "participation" in government affairs. In legal matters, the Japanese concentrated on areas where Korean cultural sensibilities could be mollified without diluting colonial authority.

Responding to Korean outrage at obviously discriminatory laws, Saitō abolished whipping as a punishment for minor offenses. He modified unpopular laws regulating traditional burial practices as well as police interference with rural markets. A new pay scale for civil servants responded to Korean demands to reduce the difference between Korean and Japanese employees of equal rank.

The Cultural Policy also featured several fundamental changes in economic policy. There had been massive protests in Japan over the sharp increase in rice prices at the close of World War I. The Rice Riots of August 1918 had already stimulated increased interest in raising Korean rice production. Saitō inaugurated a new program for investment in irrigation works and agricultural extension activities in order to increase rice yields and make more rice available for export. During the 1920s rice production rose by 40 percent, with most of the increase finding its way into the export market. The millions of yen invested in agricultural production stimulated the rural economy of Korea, and the 1920s turned out to be a period of relative prosperity for farmers and landlords. This helped to reduce tension in the countryside. On the other hand, rapid expansion of rice-growing raised water rates for peasants, and while the extra rice helped lower rice prices in Japan, the per capita rice consumption in Korea continued to fall as peasants substituted cheaper grains in their diet in order to market the more valuable rice.

A second major economic change was the rescinding of the 1910 Company Law. Thereafter companies, whether Korean- or Japanese-owned, had only to register their existence; they did not need government permission to come into being. While this encouraged native entrepreneurs, the main intent was to open Korea to private investment from Japan. Flush from the economic boom of World War I, Japanese companies greedily eyed the cheap, abundant labor in Korea. Concurrently, tariff barriers between Japan and Korea were largely eliminated, anticipating the regional autarkic economy that developed in the 1930s. However, Japanese firms already in Korea complained that fledgling colonial companies needed subsidies to protect them from larger, well-financed competitors from the homeland. The issue of subsidies was explosive, because if Korean-based Japanese companies were granted subsidies, then Korean capitalists, although few in number, would point to the new slogan of *nisen yūhwa* and demand equal treatment.

Saitō went so far as to promote policies that would promote a "bridge between Japanese and Korean capitalists." In 1921 he invited important Korean businessmen to participate in the Chōsen Industrial Commission. Ultimately, selected Korean companies received subsidies; one well-documented example was Kim Sŏngsu's Kyŏngsŏng Spinning and Weaving Company, a firm that would later become one of the largest pre-1945 Korean-owned companies (Eckert, *Offspring of Empire*, 1991). The subsidies came at a time when Korean nationalists were promoting a Korean Production Movement, a campaign to spur the development of native manufactures. It is clear the subsidies were intended to dilute Korean entrepreneurs' enthusiasm for this program, even those devoted to the development of national (Korean) capital (see Chapter Three).

Other important reforms completed Saitō's program of Cultural Rule, but that of the police system was perhaps the most significant. The semiautonomous military gendarmerie was abolished. In its place Saitō established a purely civilian police authority; civilian uniforms without swords replaced military dress both for policemen and colonial officials. Simultaneously, Saitō announced measures to expand the education system with the ambitious goal of one primary school in every district *(myŏn),* more secondary schools, and the creation of an imperial university. The press blackout was broken, as the GGK relaxed its censorship standards and offered permits for vernacular newspapers and journals with political content. Throughout the reform process, Saitō held meetings with foreign residents and a broad spectrum of Korea's social, political, and economic elite. He expanded the Central Advisory Council (Chusuin) to assist the GGK in policy formation on all cultural matters, and the elected provincial, prefectural, and village councils were expanded in order to give the appearance of reinvigorated Korean self-governance. Prospective publishers negotiated with the police to establish the guidelines and mechanics of the new press system. Thus the Cultural Policy created an aura of change and moderation by showing the GGK as open and sensitive to the needs and opinions of important residents in the colony; they also publicized the changes abroad with a new propaganda offensive to redress their flagging public relations in world opinion.

The Cultural Policy strategy was to mollify public opinion through administrative reshuffle, selected legal reforms, cosmic changes in police practices, and the currying of favor with Korean elites. Behind the face of conciliation, however, they reinforced their entire control apparatus. The police got new uniforms, but suddenly their numbers were also greatly increased. Promises for new schools turned out to be bait and switch. While Saitō discussed expansion of the school system, the GGK had, by the end of 1920, increased the number of police stations from 151 to 251 and quadrupled the number of substations to 2,495 to cover every subdistrict and neighborhood in Korea. Moreover, the administration added a new police bureau, the High Police (Kōtō Keisatsu), that was in charge of covert surveillance, censorship, thought control, and counterterrorism. In short, the new cultural policy was about tone and appearances; it gave up nothing in the important area of control.

Nonetheless, the reforms were significant concessions. In particular, the new freedom to publish and organize immediately expanded the public sphere, and for the next few years an atmosphere of excitement and experiment prevailed as Koreans tested the new boundaries and as administrators contemplated the limits of their tolerance. And if the Cultural Policy led to a dramatic increase in nationalist activity in the colony, it also stimulated the national independence movement abroad.

Scholars who see conspiracies everywhere will dismiss the new policies as calculated and Machiavellian, and in hindsight they do appear to have been a brilliant political maneuver. The reforms were not, however, as calculated as it might appear in retrospect. Saitō did meet with a broad spectrum of Korean opinion-makers, most of them moderate to conservative intellectuals, publishers, and religious leaders. He worked tirelessly to gain the trust of moderate, middle-of-the-road nationalists, those who most directly benefited from the new climate of tolerance in the crucial areas of speech and assembly. Saitō's diary is mostly silent on the substance of these negotiations, but clearly he was granting favors even if we will never know the exact quid pro quo. Although the growing leftist element within the intelligentsia was not invited to the table, they did take advantage of the new rules to organize students, youth groups, and peasant associations. Particularly between 1920 and 1925, it appears that the GGK was groping to find the middle ground between complete repression that had characterized the Military Rule period and tolerance for relatively benign activities. In short, the new freedoms were calculated to blunt overt dissent and encourage a cooperative attitude in Korea. This was a considerable gamble, given the ferocity of the disturbances that had precipitated the reforms in the first place. Colonial rule thus evolved into a flexible rule of divide and conquer. In hindsight, the policy worked very well—by providing outlets for mild forms of dissent and by making the governance and economy slightly more inclusive of Koreans, the Japanese strengthened their hegemony. But in 1920 it was unclear whether it would work at all.

Exiled Nationalist and Students Abroad

The harsh repression that accompanied the advent of Japanese rule drove many political activists into exile after 1910. Although overt political resistance had been stymied inside Korea, a growing number of organizations emerged abroad, many of them supported by large Korean communities in Manchuria and the Russian Far East, and by a smaller number of émigrés in the United States. The movement in exile continued throughout the period of Japanese rule, and although it was fragmented by political differences and personal ambitions, it kept the flame of resistance alive and provided some international awareness of Korea's plight as a colony. When these activists returned to Korea in 1945, they brought with them the legacy of this divided and contentious movement. The complexity of post-Liberation politics was in no small part driven by the competing, and often grandiose, claims of the exile leaders.

Worsening economic conditions and continued political instability between 1905 and 1910 had led to increased Korean emigration, especially into southeast Manchuria. In 1910 there were already 109,000 settlers in the Kando (Jiandao) region, and by 1913 they were joined by an additional 60,000 refugees. Moreover, tens of thousands of Koreans had crossed the Tumen River into the Russian Maritime Province. The Korean community in the United States grew from the roughly 7,000 Koreans recruited for labor in Hawaiian sugar plantations between 1902 and 1910; subsequently many of the original contract laborers moved to the west coast of the United States, where they settled around Los Angeles and San Francisco. These communities provided funds and manpower for a number of exile nationalist groups that burgeoned between 1910 and 1920.

The political and tactical orientation of all these exiles varied widely. In Manchuria Yi Siyŏng (1882–1919) organized a military school to train future independence fighters. In the Russian Far East Yi Tonghwi (?–1928) established another military unit called the Government of Korea Restoration Army. Manchuria and Russia provided cover for numerous small groups who were able to cross back and forth over the Korean northern frontier to communicate with the underground resistance or commit small-scale acts of sabotage. This region proved to be the most fertile region for Korean nationalist activity; by the late 1920s it had become home to early Korean socialist groups allied with either the new Soviet government to the north or the nascent Chinese Communist Party (CCP) to the south. In the mid- to late 1930s socialist Korean-led guerrillas, among them and most famously a group led by the later leader of North Korea, Kim Il Sung (Kim Ilsŏng, 1912–1994), fought the most enduring armed struggle against the Japanese until they were either subdued by Japanese encirclement campaigns or escaped into Soviet territory as did Kim Il Sung and his band in 1941. During World War II Koreans fought with units of the Chinese Communist Party against the Japanese. Some even stayed on in China after 1945 and contributed to their victory in the civil war.

More moderate groups that were focused on diplomatic maneuvers or long-term training of future leaders emerged in China proper and the United States. Sin Kyusik's (1880–1922) Mutual Assistance Society forged the first ties with the early Chinese nationalist movement led by Sun Yat Sen. Thereafter, various Korean nationalist groups worked on and off with the Chinese Nationalist Party (KMT) for the next twenty years. During World War II, moderate and conservative Korean nationalists found succor with the KMT and organized a small liberation army in common cause against Japan. The man who would become the first president of South Korea, Syngman Rhee (Yi Sŭngman, 1875–1965), had been living outside of Korea since his release from prison in 1904. He had been arrested in conjunction with the disbanding of the Independence Club in 1897. In 1909 he organized the Korean National Association in San Francisco before returning to his original Hawaiian base in 1913; he was picked as president of the Shanghai Provisional Government in 1920 and continued working for the independence movement until the end of the Pacific War. An Ch'angho (1878–1938), a founding member of the New People's Association, left Korea and eventually arrived in southern California in 1902. After the March First Movement he was drafted into the Shanghai Provisional Government and became a leader of a nonviolent, gradualist faction within this conglomeration of exile groups. His most enduring contribution to the national cause was his founding of Hŭngsadan, an organization devoted to the cultivation and training of future leaders that continues to thrive today.

Of greatest import to the continuing struggle against Japanese rule within Korea was the steady stream of returning students from Japan. In 1909 there were already 790 students studying in middle schools, high schools, and universities in Japan. By 1912 this number had swelled to 3,171; the limited educational opportunities in Korea fostered this exodus of students who were mostly privately financed, although there were also a number of scholarship programs offered by the Ch'ŏndogyo, youth associations, other churches, and the GGK itself. One of the most important intellectual leaders in the 1920s, Yi Kwangsu (1892–1950?), received his university training at Waseda University on a Ch'ŏndogyo scholarship

without which he would never have been able to study abroad. The new generation of Korean professionals, intellectuals, and political activists overwhelmingly
received their advanced education in the metropole. A tiny minority left to study
in Europe or the United States, but Japan remained the destination of choice for
most students going abroad. Japanese language knowledge was key to good jobs
upon return as well as for gaining access to the huge literature on Asia and the
world produced during the Meiji period. Only after Liberation did the United
States become the new Mecca, and English the new power language, for ambitious
students with means to study abroad.

Around the time of the March First Movement, many of these students being
educated in Japan began to fall under the influence of radical ideologies popular-
ized by the simultaneous disenchantment with the West (caused in part by the
bloodbath of World War I) and the enthusiasm for the Russian Revolution. Korean
nationalist groups in Russia were the first to be influenced by Bolshevik ideology.
This was manifest in the founding of Yi Tonghwi's Korean Socialist Party (Hanin
sahoedang) and Nam Manch'un's "Korean Section" of the Communist Party in
Irkutsk, both in 1918. Korean and other Asian students in Japan—the largest group
was from China—studied subversive literature together and bonded in their common experience of ethnic discrimination as outsiders. They made common cause
as well with young Japanese radicals who were disenchanted with the politics of
their older generation. Moreover, the students were in Japan during the postwar
recession, when labor and tenant strife had become widespread. Ironically, the
more open intellectual climate and less rigorous censorship in Japan fostered political organizations of all types. One group with the awkward name of The Korean
Self-Supporting Students' Fraternal Association (Chosŏn kohaksaeng tong'uhoe)
even published its own magazine *Comrade (Tongmu),* an early source of Korean
leftist thought and one that would have never passed the censor in Korea.

In the 1910s, as Japan clamped down on Korean organizational and political
life, the movement of students became the most important conduit of information and transnational knowledge in Korea. By the time of the March First explosion, students were the couriers between the underground nationalist movement
in Korea and the widely dispersed exile groups. For example, one contingent of
students who were deeply involved in the March First planning moved to Shanghai in 1920 to participate in the planning of a united government in exile. Among
them was Yi Kwangsu, author of the 1918 Student Declaration, who returned to
Korea two years later to begin his influential career. Indeed, it was this generation
of students who fostered the cosmopolitan colonial culture of the 1920s and 1930s
in Korea. With the unfolding of the Cultural Policy at home, students returned to
a broader array of opportunities in Korea: in journalism, publishing, education,
even business.

Upon returning to Korea, however, students faced difficult choices. They
returned to the high expectations of families who had invested heavily in their

schooling and had, no doubt, already made plans for their futures. On the one hand, an education abroad provided entrée into elite society in colonial Korea. It meant access to jobs in the growing modern sphere, which in turn usually meant working in Japanese institutions. On the other hand, to engage in nationalist projects of whatever political orientation meant insecurity and potential danger, while working for a bank, company, or even the colonial bureaucracy meant relatively good wages and potential mobility.

The tension between youthful idealism and mature practicality would work itself out in thousands of ways for this generation of Korea's best and brightest. Whatever choice each made, they all experienced the culture shock common with students moving back from the developed economy of the metropolitan power to their poorer, subjugated homelands. Students returning on the Shimonoseki ferry from long sojourns in Japan were greeted by the dismal sight of bare hills along the Korean coast, a stark contrast to the verdant Japanese mountains. Disembarking amidst the coolies and porters swarming over the quay to offload cargo, they must have also thought of the contrast provided by the more mechanized ports of Japan.[4] They returned to a Korea in the throes of change. And they added their youthful enthusiasm to what was to become an intellectual renaissance under the Cultural Policy in 1920s Korea.

Chapter Three

CLASS AND NATION IN COLONIAL KOREA
The 1920s

삼

A T LEAST FOR KOREA'S middle-class intellectuals, the early 1920s marked a time of hope and renewed cultural and political activity. The Cultural Policy permitted new avenues of expression for writers and ideologues of all stripes in the form of vernacular newspapers and journals. The reforms also inaugurated an era of frenetic organizational activity as a new generation of Korean leaders emerged to create local, provincial, and national associations formed around interest groups of all kinds. Readers of the inaugural editorials in the new press or the charters of the new organizations have to be struck by the optimism and expansiveness of the rhetoric. It was as if an entirely new era had begun for Korean society, an era of cultural construction, education, and social reform. Notwithstanding the fact that Korea was still a colony and that the new press had emerged under a strict censorship regime, within its first year one of the new vernacular papers, the *East Asia Daily (Tonga ilbo)*, was bold enough to have proclaimed itself the "voice of the nation" on its masthead.[1]

We must remember that this intellectual ferment and organizational innovation remained on the surface of Korean society. For the most part it expressed the views of the urban, literate minority in Korea only. This minority could say they spoke for the masses, but their papers and journals were still not accessible to the vast majority of Korea's preliterate population. The experience of Korea's agrarian masses in the 1920s differed profoundly from that of the intelligentsia. Given the differences in class and social status that separated elites from those working on the land, this was not unusual. Moreover, during the 1920s the remnants of the old "moral economy" in the countryside disappeared. Rationalized land laws, the explosion of the export market for rice, and the commercialization of agriculture brought most peasants under the dominance of capitalist market relations. But in the short term, the decade was a relatively good time for agriculture and peasants because the new Cultural Policy had increased GGK investment in rice production for the Japanese market. During the 1920s rice prices quadrupled, and agricultural productivity increased.[2] Conflicts between tenants and landlords, therefore, were forward-looking, that is, peasants were more interested in bettering their situation within the improving agricultural economy. This was in contrast to the defensive and more desperate conflicts that characterized the post-1930 depression years, when peasants struggled to keep what little they had in the face of increasing tenancy rates and rising rents (Gi-Wook Shin, 1996).

The divide widened between the experience and concerns of peasants, whether small owners, partial owners, tenants, or agricultural laborers, and absentee landlords, the scions of Korea's elites, and the small urban middle class. To read the glowing accounts of national unity surrounding the March First Movement, we might assume that Korean nationalism had become that bridge. Common loathing of Japanese rule, however, was a negative bond, and it was some time before such sentiments reached the unified intensity characteristic of contemporary Korea's fierce nationalism. After all, while there had been significant changes in Korean society since 1900, the lives of most Koreans were still more informed by the class relations, values, and habits of traditional Korea. Indeed, the 1920s may be viewed as a pivotal decade in which the hold of the old society gave way to startling new ways of thought and action as well as new forms of economic behavior as changes in the class structure of society became manifest. To the extent this was true, at least in the realm of politics and ideas, was due mostly to the post-1920 cultural and nationalist renaissance and the effort of Korean ideologues to provide shape and form to a national unity. But the rising political consciousness was complicated by an emergent class politics that would challenge the nationalist vision. The discourse that emerged in the 1920s became a struggle over who would claim leadership of the nation and what class of Koreans defined the nation. In terms of political debates, the 1920s were the beginning of a fundamental ideological schism between left and right that continues to plague a divided peninsula eighty years later.

The Nationalist Renaissance
and Reopening of the Public Sphere

Renaissance is an apt description of the outpouring of essays, commentary, literature, and political analyses that fueled the reemergence of a Korean press after 1920. It was a renaissance because the cultural production of the 1920s revived the nascent journalistic and literary movement of the period between 1896 and 1910 as well as the discourse on national identity and social reform. Moreover, the Cultural Policy's relaxation of publication controls permitted Korean journalism to exploit a market of readers that had expanded during the first ten years of Japanese rule. Even though there had been no Korean-owned newspapers between 1910 and 1920, educational opportunity had continued to expand during that time in the private and colonial schools. Furthermore, Korean linguists had continued to experiment with and standardize the vernacular, and their work had been adapted in the small number of Korean-owned publications published between 1910 and

1919. The period had been "dark," but not completely devoid of progress in this arena.

The magnitude of the 1920s publishing boom was enormous in relative terms. The Japanese had issued permits for only forty magazines and journals during the entire 1910–1920 period, but in 1920 alone, they granted permits to 409 different magazines and journals, not to mention the coveted "current events" *(sisa)* permits to two daily newspapers, the *East Asia Daily* and the *Korea Daily (Chosŏn ilbo)*, and almost half a dozen politically oriented journals.[3] In 1910 the combined circulation of Korean daily papers and important journals probably did not exceed 15,000; by 1929 the circulation of the two Korean newspapers alone had increased tenfold to 103,027. The *sisa* permit allowed discussion not only of current events, but also of political and social commentary. Moreover, no cumbersome change in the legal system that governed publishing had been necessary. Suddenly permits that for the most part had been denied Koreans for a decade were forthcoming. There was no lag between policy and practice, and given the youth and energy of the new publishers—the founder of the *East Asia Daily*, Kim Sŏngsu, was only thirty and his reporters were in their twenties—new publications hit the streets weekly in the early years of the 1920s.

In the early 1920s the new publications were poorly financed; there was plenty of patriotic enthusiasm but little business sense. With journals it did not matter; the goal was to get ideas and plans into the open for discussion. Many of the political journals were supported by donations, and they almost always lost money. The newspapers did not make money for several years, but they were sustained by investors' patriotic fervor. By the mid-1920s, however, increasing advertising revenues (ironically from Japanese commercial sources) brought them into the black, and by the early 1930s each was publishing successful entertainment monthlies aimed at segmented audiences such as youth, women, sports fans, and children. Publishing was becoming a profitable business that competed with other enterprises for a share of the expanding market for entertainment. This called forth lamentations from political activists, who decried the commercialization of the press and the corresponding enervation of its political commitment.

The new journals' disinterest in profits in the early 1920s insulated them from the threat of the censor in interesting ways. Seizure of an issue only increased readers' interest in obtaining the banned goods. The daily press also took many more chances during their early years for political reasons, such as building a reputation for resisting Japanese pressures to conform. At the same time, however, the Cultural Policy expanded the police organs charged with oversight of publishing and organizational activity. Originally, the GGK Publication Department (Toshoka) had administered the prepublication censorship system that vetted all publishing in Korea.[4] After 1920, the new High Police Bureau inherited the responsibility for overseeing the vastly expanded amount of material seeking approval. Once a publication permit was granted, each publication (a book, each issue of a journal, each issue of the daily newspaper) required screening before it was actually distributed. Books and periodicals were controlled more easily with such a system, but practical problems made this cumbersome for the daily press. Ultimately, a system emerged in which the newspaper publisher provided the censors with a galley while simultaneously beginning its print run for the day. The memoirs of early journalists tell wonderful stories of tricks that evolved to avoid or subvert the system. When the editors knew a certain article would draw attention or be prohibited, they would plan for an early press run and hire more delivery people to get as many copies out before an order banning an issue could be issued. Once the papers were distributed, they were virtually impossible to recover.

It is important to note here that colonial censorship was a work-in-progress in the first years of the Cultural Policy. By 1925 the system was easily handling the volume of publications, for by then it had created a general framework for interpreting the law. Application of the standard was quite subjective and varied over time; had the censors followed the letter of the law, practically everything published could have been questioned. But in the early years, particularly between 1920 and 1922, there was considerable negotiation between publishers and the High Police. The most serious issues for the police were statements critical of or demeaning to the emperor, outright advocacy of class warfare, the revealing of military information, or anything that impugned the legitimacy of the GGK itself. If this was not enough, there was always the catch-all last article in the law: ". . . and anything deleterious to the general welfare and moral health of society" (Robinson, "Colonial Publication Policy," 1984). The High Police reserved their most potent weapons—seizure, suspension, abolition, and prosecution—for the most serious thought crimes such as advocacy of class warfare or disparaging the emperor. Most frequently, they simply used erasure; working from an ever-changing list of offensive words, the censors would simply delete portions of text and replace it with dashes or broken lines. The result would be pages that resembled a brick wall, hence the contemporary slang *pyŏkdol sinmun* (brick-wall newspapers) used during the period. Mechanically effective and easy, this technique was ludicrously simple to subvert by any reasonably educated reader, who had only to try a few substitutions to understand such violated passages. The erasures, moreover, alerted readers to the proscribed and illicit.

Associations, Clubs, Unions, Leagues, and Parties

Perhaps even more startling than the outpouring of publishing after the Cultural Policy thaw was the mushrooming of organizations of all types. In 1920 there were 985 organizations of all types registered with Colonial Police. These were local youth groups, religious organizations, educational and academic societies, and social clubs. Two years later this number had swelled to almost 6,000. These included occupational groups, tenant and labor associations, savings and purchasing cooperatives, temperance unions, health and recreational clubs, and groups clustered by Japanese statisticians into a vague category called "self-improvement." The Cultural Policy clearly set loose an enormous pent-up demand for associational life in the colony. And while most groups restricted their activities to politically innocuous social, enlightenment, or self-help projects, even a cursory glance at their charters reveals that many linked their goals to national self-strengthening. There were, however, many groups who forsook nationalism altogether in order to promote social reform among Koreans themselves, most notably, early feminist groups and the movement to eliminate discrimination against the traditionally low-status *paekchŏng*.[5] In the short term the Japanese chose to ignore the potential for nationalist mischief that these organizations represented, but they were very keen to monitor and selectively suppress what they saw as class-based—and therefore more dangerous—tenant and labor organizations.

In addition to the rapidity of organizational growth, there was a significant structural change in the interrelations between groups. With increased operational freedom similar groups began to coalesce into nationwide federations and leagues. This trend was most obvious within the Korean youth movement. In June 1920, 600 groups joined together to form the Korean Youth League (Chosŏn ch'ŏngyŏn yŏnhaphoe); by the mid-1920s there were similar tenant and labor federations. Such organizations became the instruments through which major nationalist projects were mounted during the decade. The organizational boom of the 1920s fulfilled the promise of the earlier growth of nationalist associations before annexation. A decade of colonial rule, expanded education, urban growth, and development of communications had only increased the Koreans' capacity for collective action.

Another important feature of the organizational boom was the increasing participation of women in public life. Women's clubs and educational associations had appeared on the heels of the Independence Club's activities in the late 1890s. Thereafter aristocratic and middle-class women took the lead to establish schools for women and to reform oppressive customs such as child-marriages and the prohibition of widow remarriage (some of these customs had been outlawed already by the Kabo social legislation of 1894–1895). Before annexation, women in the Christian churches had formed groups around a number of social reform issues. Soon the number of patriotic women's associations *(aeguk puinhoe)* burgeoned, and they played an important role in the largest private campaign mounted in Korea before annexation—the National Debt Repayment Movement. After March First the term "new woman" *(sinyŏsŏng)* became standard usage in the press to describe modern, educated women who had become a very visible part of public life. By the 1920s more radical demands for a true liberation of women emerged in Korea's first avowedly feminist journals, Kim Wŏnju's *New Woman (Sin yŏsŏng)* and Na Hyesŏk's *Women's World (Yŏjagye)*. In these publications women's issues were not justified by merging them with the agenda of national self-strengthening. Instead, for the first time, Na and Kim directly confronted the inequity and oppression of Korean patriarchy. Radical feminism, however, was ultimately marginalized, while the less confrontational agenda of Christian-dominated, reformist women's groups found favor within the male-led nationalist movement (Wells, "Price of Legitimacy," 1999).

Cultural Nationalism: Working within the System

As the 1920s wore on, political activists of differing ideological and strategic orientation struggled to gain control of the larger federations in order to use them as a mass base for opposing Japanese rule. And this struggle exposed major rifts within the Korean nationalist movement. A number of educational, social reform, and national cultural movements emerged in the 1920s that were unified around the idea of transforming Korean society from within in order to prepare for full nationhood. The leaders of these projects believed it was possible to work within the political limits of the colonial system in order to establish the strength for future independence. While more radical activists mocked the idea that anything could be accomplished under the oppressive weight of the colonial system as hypocritical and accommodationist, nevertheless these moderate projects came to dominate the domestic nationalist movement during the 1920s.

The contemporary press used "cultural movement" *(munhwa undong)* to describe these moderate nationalist projects, and "culturalism" *(munhwajuŭi)* became the code for the movement's generally shared ideology. Another code word for this nationalist self-strengthening ideology was reconstructionism *(kaejojuŭi)*, a term derived, probably, from the title of a well-known tract, "The Treatise on National Reconstruction" ("Minjok kaejoron") by Yi Kwangsu that first explicated these ideas.[6] Yi elaborated a conservative approach to nation-building through long-term social and economic reforms as a prerequisite to Korean independence. Moreover, in a move criticized by many, he asserted that for now Koreans had no alternative but to work within the confines of colonial society. This pragmatic stance outraged radicals who wanted to directly challenge Japanese colonialism with peasant and worker mobilization. While this agenda earned the unwavering contempt of the radicals, it provided a loose ideological frame that at least the Japanese police viewed as harmless. Most probably the GGK hoped that these moderate programs would ultimately self-destruct.

Clearly the basic program and tactics of the cultural nationalists were offshoots of the earlier turn-of-the-century enlightenment ideology. The culturalists' efforts to spread education and literacy, raise national consciousness, and cultivate a cadre of future leaders resonated strongly with the ideology of the Independence

Club in the 1890s and other organizations such as the New People's Association and the Self-Strengthening Association that followed in the 1900–1910 period. The later fall of Chosŏn had confirmed in the leaders' minds that enlightenment, social change, and economic strengthening were the only solution for Korea's future. Added to this was an emphasis on gradualism and nonconfrontation that unified what otherwise was a diverse set of projects and movements within the moderate camp.

Yi Kwangsu's "Treatise on National Reconstruction" was perhaps the most coherent elaboration of the cultural movement's agenda. Interestingly, it appeared immediately after Yi's return from Shanghai, where he had been working with a moderate faction in the self-proclaimed Korean government in exile, the Shanghai Provisional Government. Yi's essay faithfully reflects many of the early ideas of his mentor, An Ch'angho, not to mention the fact that at times it seems cribbed verbatim from the prominent Chinese liberal ideologue Hu Shih. And Hu Shih's moderate and gradualist agenda had also been savaged by more youthful and radical elements of China's May Fourth era. Nevertheless, it provided a common vocabulary for several major projects mounted by moderates in the early to mid-1920s.

The first, the National University Movement led by the Society for the Establishment of a National University, was the natural outcome of the intelligentsia's interest in educational issues. Korean intellectuals were outraged from the beginning by the colonial school's stress on the acquisition of Japanese language, cultural values, and a Japanized version of Korean history. Even more galling was the fact that opportunities for higher education were limited to a small number of technical and vocational high schools that offered agronomy, sericulture, or commerce. College-bound Koreans had few choices. They could fight for a spot in one of the small Christian or private colleges or go abroad (the primary destination being Japan) at considerable expense to complete their educations. Thus it was thought that creating a Korean university would respond to a number of current problems. It would provide more space for bright students to study a broad array of subjects without leaving the country; it would serve as a base for the best Korean scholars as teachers; and it would counter implicitly the undesirable effects of Japanese education.

In November 1922 the venerable enlightenment reformer Yi Sangje was chosen to front the new Society for the Establishment of a National University. Led by Song Chinu, then editor-in-chief of the *East Asia Daily*, the organization built an impressive national network of offices that mobilized support by working through existing networks established by youth and other local organizations. The goal was to raise ten million yen to build the university by relying on large numbers of small contributions. The society also sent representatives to Manchuria and the United States to solicit funds. Within six months, however, the project began to falter. Mismanagement of donations, infighting between chapters, and withdrawal of support from the important All-Korean Youth League, slowed the early momentum. Moreover Japanese authorities further diluted interest in the project when they announced with great fanfare plans to open an imperial university in Seoul (Keijō Imperial University) by 1926. This seemed to co-opt any residual public interest in the fund-raising campaign, and before long the movement had become moribund.

A second important movement coalesced around the issue of national economic development. A combination of the worsening economic conditions, economic reforms that augured more Japanese investment, and renewed discussion of Korea's economic dependence engendered in 1923 what would become the largest nationalist project of the early 1920s in terms of numbers of participants and the breadth of its organizational networks. The Encouragement of Korean Production Movement (Chosŏn mulsan changnyŏ undong; hereafter, Korean Production Movement). Korean businessmen were already fighting for subsidies and freedom to participate on an equal footing with Japanese enterprises, but the moderate nationalists approached the problem on a different tack. Their plan was to mobilize national sentiment in support of Korean industry and handicrafts, and thus encourage self-sufficiency and the development of national capital in competition with Japanese capital. Korean businessmen quickly grasped how this movement benefited their own interests and enthusiastically supported the new organization.

Linking patriotism to economic development was not a new idea. Nationalists had been quick to see the link between economic power and political autonomy; the Repay the National Debt Movement (1907–1910) during the Protectorate period had raised money using just such appeals. The first Korean joint stock company, the Masan Porcelain Company (1908) in P'yongyang was a project of An Ch'angho's New People's Association. In fact, the company's founder, Yi Sŭnghun, became one of the leaders of the Korean Production Movement. The situation in the early 1920s was peculiarly suited to the launching of a large, sustained economic movement. Korean enterprises were reeling under competition from large Japanese companies. Korean goods could not compete with the cheaper, higher-quality imports from Japan and the West. Moreover, the discrimination inherent in the 1910 Company Law had seriously inhibited the growth of Korean corporations between 1910 and 1919. With the upsurge of nationalistic fervor after 1919, the time seemed ripe for a movement that would combine patriotism with the promise of Korean-generated economic growth.

The idea of self-sufficient national economic development had already fostered a number of consumer cooperatives. In P'yongyang, Cho Mansik, often called Korea's Gandhi, had created the Society for the Promotion of Korean Production in July 1920. Cho had absorbed Gandhian ideas of nonviolence and self-sufficiency while attending college in Japan. In addition, there had been a spate of articles in the press describing Gandhi's Swaraj movement in 1922 and 1923. Clearly Gandhi's ideas inspired the leaders of the Korean Production Movement; his emphasis on nonviolence, self-sufficiency, and national unity across class lines supported their culturalist agenda. Cho Mansik brought together others who had already begun to organize cooperatives and small Buy Korean groups, and in December of 1922 formed the nationwide Korean Production Movement.

The addition of businessmen to the usual coalition of intellectuals, students, and journalists was unique. Kim Sŏngsu, president of the *East Asia Daily* and the Kyŏngsŏng Spinning and Weaving Company, and Kim Tongwŏn, president of the Kyŏnggi Spinning Company, both played important roles in the genesis of the project. The leaders recognized that women, as primary consumers, had to be involved as well. Ultimately women created an auxiliary association, the Women's Local Products Promotion Association (T'osan aeyong puinhoe), in order to mobilize at the grassroots level. The appeal was simple: all must patronize Korean stores and use Korean-produced clothing, textiles, foodstuffs, and other daily necessities whenever possible. There was a strong emphasis on the spiritual benefits of consuming native products, and the leaders were also aware that by focusing on an affirmation ("buy Korean"), they avoided the confrontation a boycott of Japanese goods might provoke. The movement organized provincial chapters and published a journal, *Industrial World (San'ŏpgye)*, as a clearinghouse for ideas and to advertise various campaigns.

At its height in the summer of 1923, the movement became the most successful mass mobilization of Koreans since the March First demonstrations. Consumption of Korean-produced goods increased to the extent that certain items became unobtainable. Understandably, prices of Korean-made goods rose, demanding, ironically, further financial sacrifice for the patriotically inclined. Clearly the movement heightened mass awareness of economic issues, and it altered, at least temporarily, Korean consumption habits. However, economic and political realities blocked its sustained growth, and by 1924 the movement was in steady decline.

The movement threatened the Japanese in a curious way. It was not illegal or tactically confrontational. But at its core it was still deleterious to the long-range goals of the colonizers. The police decided to control it indirectly by censoring publicity and prohibiting rallies in the capital. Perhaps more effectively, they continued to implement tariff restructuring, negotiate subsidies for select Korean companies, and discuss economic concessions with key business leaders in a behind-the-scenes campaign to undermine the resolve of the movement's leadership. The first such subsidy, to Kim Sŏngsu's Kyŏngsŏng Spinning Company, helped it at a crucial time; Kyŏngsŏng Spinning went on to become one of the largest Korean-owned companies during the period (Eckert, *Offspring of Empire*, 1991). Subsidies were important because they allowed Korean businesses to compete on a level field with Japanese corporations. Of course, subsidies were also more attractive than the uncertain market, even with a Buy Korean campaign in progress. In this way, by alternating intimidation and conciliation, the Japanese successfully drove a wedge between large businessmen and the nationalist leaders of the movement.

There were other problems as well. Korean merchant cooperation was vital to the movement's success, but many merchants felt threatened by consumer cooperatives, fearing competition for customers. Importers worried that the movement would drive them out of business. And, finally, a number of highly publicized scandals challenged the integrity of the entire enterprise. In March 1924 it was discovered that several textile merchants had been importing cheap Japanese broadcloth from Osaka and representing it as "Korean-made" in order to profit from the higher price. Such gouging and other exploitative practices were demoralizing to people who were making sacrifices to patronize Korean stores exclusively.

These problems opened the movement to growing criticism from within the ranks of the nationalist movement. Leftists charged that such an economic movement could never succeed in a colonial situation and that only Korean capitalists would profit in the struggle with Japanese monopoly capitalism. Even more to the point, critics declared that the very leadership that exhorted the masses to use native goods were, themselves, the most Westernized group in Korea, in dress, style, and education. Why should the masses sacrifice to enrich a small group of Korean capitalists at the behest of foreign-educated intellectuals? The arguments attacked not only the project itself but also the underlying idea of working within the colonial system. In 1924 and 1925 the Korean Production Movement became the focus of a bitter ideological struggle between moderate and more radical nationalists that anticipated the deepening rift in the movement. The polemical warfare ended in a stalemate, but the damage had already been done to the morale of leaders at the grassroots. The Korean Production Movement declined steadily in its second year. By the end of 1924 it was having problems meeting the rent for its central offices in Seoul. Although the movement continued to organize New Year's parades and enjoyed a brief revival during the depression years, its mass appeal and significance waned after its first year. The organization did maintain, however, an official presence and continued publishing *San'ŏpgye* until the abolition of all nationalist organizations following Japan's invasion of China in 1937.

The Flowering of Korean Language and Literature

The Korean University and the Buy Korean movements were large nationwide projects coordinated by centralized organizations. Both failed to sustain the broad consensus among Koreans of all classes that might have led to a more successful outcome. Nevertheless this was also a time when the cultural production of small academic associations, scholars, artists, and writers increased dramatically. With more and more students returning from abroad to a generally restricted job market for intellectuals, this underemployed group turned to literary and academic pursuits. They often self-consciously thought of or organized their work as a defense against the torrent of Japanese cultural influences that was pouring into Korea. The large mass projects of the moderates tended to invite the attention of the Japanese police, but this was less of a problem for individuals and groups engaged in more purely academic subjects. Although they were still subject to censorship, novels, poems, and histories that were not explicitly political found their way through the system to a modest but growing audience.

On the part of the Japanese colonial administration, what was evolving during the 1920s was a policy that only became explicit during the later period of forced cultural assimilation. Assimilation policy intended to inculcate Koreans with the core values needed to be a good subject of the Japanese emperor, but it recognized that Korean ethnic identity could not be quickly effaced. Japanese bureaucrats discussed this ethnic identity in ways similar to how Americans might think of ethnicity within the broader identity of citizenship. At the height of the later forced assimilation campaigns, Japanese officials were discussing how to speed up assimilation by emphasizing the values and habits that they believed were most important, while accepting as inevitable the annoying background noise of their subjects' residual "peninsular consciousness" *(hantō ishiki)*.

The language movement was, more than any other cultural project in the 1920s, tied directly to the effort to maintain and foster a strong national identity. The Independence Club in the late nineteenth century had placed a premium on the spread and use of the vernacular as a means of defeating the traditional divide between elite Sino-centric cultural norms and the culture of the common man. For nationalists the language itself was the means to unify a Korean identity and to give voice to its unique sensibilities. In contrast to more highly politicized movements in the era before annexation, the Vernacular Language Movement survived the early repression of 1910–1919, reorganized itself in the 1920s, and even continued to work during the height of the Japanese policy to discourage Korean language use of the early 1940s. By the first decades of the twentieth century, the Korean vernacular movement pioneered by Chu Sigyŏng in 1897 had grown into a national network of scholars and writers. Chu's students came of age in the early 1920s and created the Korean Language Research Society (Chosŏnŏ yŏn'guhoe, 1921) in the aftermath of the Cultural Policy reforms. This organization, the precursor to the present Korean Language Society (Han'gŭl hakhoe), continued the work of systematizing rules for grammar, orthography (1933), and the transliteration of foreign loanwords (1940). It published a dictionary of standard vocabulary in 1936 and began the compilation of the first comprehensive Korean language dictionary *(K'ŭn sajŏn)*.

On the surface these activities seemed to be the exclusive provenance of linguists and intellectuals, with little connection to the political drama of colonial life, but they made one of the most important, and perhaps the most permanent, contributions to the future of Korean national and cultural life. In addition to their scholarly work, the society worked closely with Korean publishers and newspapers to implement unified usage. Another primary activity was the society's effort to urge Japanese education officials to accept changes in Korean-language texts and to upgrade Korean language instruction in private and colonial schools. Although frustrated by Japanese official resistance to their suggestions for editing textbooks already in use in the colonial schools, the society staged a series of training institutes for Korean language instructors to improve their teaching techniques. The society also created texts on the language for the growing student population and for distribution at circuit lectures in the provinces.

The language movement survived and prospered throughout the 1920s and 1930s because it connected itself to the projects of both moderate and radical nationalists. As specialists and intellectuals, leaders of the language movement worked easily with publishers, journalists, and educators, and the goals of the society fit comfortably into the moderate and gradualist cultural nationalist philosophy. Yet the Language Society also worked with radicals. In spite of their opposition to the general cultural nationalist program, radicals supported the language movement because they were interested in the link between mass literacy and the creation of a truly mass culture in Korea. With the help of the two Korean newspapers, the society created special materials for and helped to organize a very successful, multiyear literacy campaign in rural areas. Students went to the countryside during their summer vacations to teach basic reading skills. The movement, known as the *punarodu,* a transliteration of the Russian *"v narod"* (to the people), found support in the Korean socialist camp as a means for direct action and connection with the Korean masses. Interestingly, these summer campaigns anticipated similar programs to merge with and learn from the peasant masses that were organized by college students in the 1980s. In the 1980s, however, it was the students who were trying to absorb from the peasantry the essence of national consciousness that they believed had been lost in the rush to economic modernization (see Chapter Six).

By the end of the colonial period, work in the language movement became a progressively more dangerous act of political defiance. As part of the intensified cultural assimilation program after the outbreak of war with China in 1937, the GGK gradually restricted the use of Korean in public: first in government offices (1937), then schools (1938), and finally by eliminating private vernacular publications (1939). The society continued its work on the comprehensive Korean dictionary in spite of the increased pressure. But in 1942 the police purged the society by arresting fourteen members for violating of the national security law with their work as lexicographers. The police seized the incomplete manuscript of the dictionary, the product of twenty years of research, as evidence for the later trial. In the confusion at the end of the colonial period the manuscript was lost for several years until rediscovered in a warehouse at Seoul Station. The list of charges against the language society read at the subsequent trial provided a suitable tribute to their efforts. The scholars in the dock were undoubtedly proud to hear their crime described as "working to ensure the future independence of Korea by reviving the national spirit and fostering national strength through a cultural movement" (Hiseung Lee, 1973, p. 41).

Literary output exploded in tandem with the language movement. Modern Korean literature traces its origins to the 1910s and the experiments in new-style vernacular poetry, short stories, and essays that filled the pages of magazines such as *Boys (Sonyŏn)* and *Ch'ŏngch'un (Youth)*. With the publication of Yi Injik's (1854–1915) *Tears of Blood (Hyŏl ŭi nyu)* in 1915, followed shortly thereafter by Yi Kwangsu's *Heartlessness (Mujŏng)* in 1917, the modern Korean novel was born. By the mid-1920s poetry and serialized novels could be found in the daily press and virtually all monthly journals and magazines. Young authors like Ch'oe Namsŏn and Yi Kwangsu not only pioneered the production of new literary forms, they were influential stylists as well. They were joined by other talented writers whose work in the rapidly evolving vernacular expanded its expressive possibilities and gave voice to a diverse set of experiences and ideologies. Indeed, the new literature movement quickly split into a number of different artistic and political groupings. In 1922 one group of authors began publishing the journals *White Tide (Paekcho)* and *Ruins (P'yehŏ)* as vehicles for "pure" literature—a literature divorced from political and social reform ideology. Two of the leading writers in this group, Yŏm Sangsŏp (1897–1963) and Kim Tong'in (1900–1951), experimented with naturalist and romantic forms in reaction to the heavily didactic tone of earlier so-called "enlightenment" novels.

Shortly thereafter, there was a reaction to the "art for art's sake" movement by leftist writers, who believed that literature should serve the cause of class liberation. By 1925 this group had consolidated to form the Korean Artists Proletarian Federation (KAPF). The KAPF attracted writers, painters, actors, and musicians who experimented with "socialist realism" as a device to promote class-consciousness among the intelligentsia as well as expose the abysmal condition of the proletarian masses *(minjung)*.[7] Among the well-known works that emanated from within this school were Cho Myŏnghŭi's *The Naktong River (Naktonggang)* and *Fire Field (Hwajŏn)* by Yi Kiyŏng. Many of the young intellectuals associated with KAPF were also organizers with the Korean Language Society of the summer literacy campaigns in the Korean countryside as well as teachers in night schools in Seoul and provincial cities. KAPF writers also translated the major works of Marx and other socialist classics. The KAPF suffered constant Japanese police harassment—its members under surveillance and liable for arrest, its publications heavily censored. KAPF managed to continue as an organizing focus for leftist intellectuals into the 1930s but collapsed after the mass arrests of its membership in 1935.

Radical Nationalism and Social Revolutionary Thought

The KAPF writers were part of a large movement of leftist intellectuals and radical activists who in the 1920s were attracted to social revolutionary thought. Throughout Asia the cataclysm of World War I had begun a process of disenchantment with the West in general and liberal thought and governmental models in particular. Nor was this disenchantment assuaged by the calls for global cooperation, internationalism, and pan-humanism as the fundamental bases of a new world order that emanated from the Versailles Peace Conference of 1919. Such abstractions rang particularly hollow in the ears of colonial intellectuals and political activists in Asia, who felt betrayed by the failure of the imperialist powers to apply any of their high-minded ideas in their overseas colonies. Indeed, the great powers at Versailles had already ignored the March First leaders' moderate appeals for Korean self-determination. They had also refused to recognize the fledgling Shanghai Provisional Government. Socialism and the dream of an international alliance of anticapitalist forces liberating people in the colonial world offered a potent alternative ideology. The Bolshevik victory in the Russian Revolution, the later formation of the Communist International (Comintern), and the evolving Leninist doctrine of an Anti-Imperialist United Front fostered an entirely fresh set of ideas and tactics that could be applied to the problems of the colony. By the early 1920s, these ideas were solidly entrenched among Korean exile nationalist groups as well as among the younger intelligentsia in the colony.

The Russian Far East and Tokyo provided a breeding ground for Korean socialists. Yi Tonghwi formed the first Korean Socialist Party (1918) in Khabarovsk, and a rival organizer, Nam Manch'un, created a communist party in Irkutsk in 1919. They drew their supporters from among Korean partisans who had made common cause with the Bolsheviks against the remnants of the czarist forces and their Western and Japanese allies fighting in the Russian Far East. These groups and others that followed ultimately established themselves in Soviet territory and Manchuria, and they became a constant irritant to the Japanese and an important source of support for their colleagues inside Korea well into the 1930s. The Japanese metropole, however, was by far the most important source of socialist and radical ideology for Korean intellectuals during the 1920s.

By the early 1910s the trickle of Koreans traveling to Japan for schooling had become a river; by the mid-1920s it was a flood. Middle- and upper-class families saw that their mobility and status maintenance was directly linked to their children attaining advanced degrees from Japan. Even poorer students were supported by GGK scholarships or fellowships offered by Korean social and religious organizations.[8] In Japan, Korean students encountered a society that was beginning to feel the effects of a generation of rapid economic and social change. The post-World War I recession brought significant hardship to both industrial laborers and farmers, and labor and tenant strife increased; 1920–1925 was a period of prolific leftist organizing, the origins of the Japanese labor and tenant movements, and increased urban unrest. It was also an era of "isms." Popular journals such as *Reconstruction (Kaizō)* and *Liberation (Kaihō)* were samplers of diverse ideologies. The doctrines of democracy, Bolshevism, social democracy, syndicalism, guild socialism, anarchism, Fabianism, and National Socialism whirled about in an atmosphere of experimentation. Korean students became caught up within these organizations and ultimately brought home the ideas and organizational techniques learned firsthand in Japan. For example, Kim Chunyŏn, whose career included work for both of the major Korean nationalist newspapers and who was later first secretary of the Third Korean Communist Party (1926), was introduced to socialism as a member of the left-leaning New Man Society (Shinjinkai) at Tokyo University.

Thus many of the early Korean socialist organizations can be traced to student organizations in Japan. These overseas Korean student groups began as self-help organizations that provided a community for isolated students far from home. The obvious futility of the March First Movement, as well as the impotence of the putative Korean government in exile, encouraged a leftward shift of student activism. One group in particular, the Korean Self-Supporting Students' Fraternal Association (Chosŏn kohaksaeng tong'uhoe), became the first openly socialist organization among the students. By 1922 the group was publishing its own periodical, *Comrade (Tongmu)*, and shifting its attention away from student and worker relief to foment class struggle directly. Returning students became leaders in the youth movement that had appeared after the Cultural Policy reforms, and toward the end of the decade they provided much of the energy for creating a United Front Movement that would bridge the gap between nationalist and leftist radicals.

While the vast majority of radicals within the colony dabbled in socialist ideology and informally carried its message to youth, tenant, and other organizations established for workers and peasants, a more organized Korean communist movement had emerged within the exile movement. Yi Tonghwi joined forces with the recently formed Korean government in exile in Shanghai. His group, soon to be known as the "Shanghai faction," quickly came into conflict with other Korean communists who traced their origins to the Irkutsk group organized by Kim Manch'un. By 1922 these two groups were competing for the patronage of the newly established Communist International (Comintern) in Moscow, setting the stage for the endless factional struggles that would plague the Korean communist movement throughout the 1920s.

At the urging of Comintern, the exiled Korean communist movement tried to organize a base in the colony between 1920 and 1925, but factional disputes and Japanese police vigilance made this difficult. It was not until April 1925 that the first official Korean Communist Party in Korea was formed. Unfortunately this coincided with an increase in Japanese police pressure on radical organizations of all types. The police crushed the first Communist Party and four successive attempts to create a formal party apparatus met the same fate in the following years. In spite of the organizational ineptness of the Korean Communists, they had already in the early 1920s competed successfully for the hearts and minds of Korean youth. They gained positions in the important All-Korean Youth League, led by conservative nationalists O Sanggŭn and Chang Tŏksu. And Communists were an important part of a radical youth movement that coalesced under the banner of the Seoul Youth Association (1921). Ultimately they dominated an important conference of youth leagues in 1923, writing into its position statement a pledge that committed the league to leading and helping the Korean masses.

In 1924 the rising socialist movement in Korea also gave birth to the Korean Women's Socialist League (Chosŏn yŏsŏng tonguhoe). Women's liberation was seen as a logical corollary to socialism, so the issue of women's liberation was directly linked to class liberation. The problem for socialist women resembled that of the mainstream women's movement and its relationship to the nationalist movement. Women's issues were subordinated to national liberation on the one hand or class liberation on the other. Since men dominated the press, women's liberation was most often viewed through the lens of nationalist or socialist politics. Indeed, Korean men, already subjugated under the Japanese, were sensitive to loss of any prerogatives in their own homes (Wells, 1999).

The growing split between moderate and conservative nationalists and Korean Communists and leftist sympathizers was very bitter. Leftists criticized the moderate wing for playing into the hands of the Japanese by avoiding confrontation. Even more vehemently, leftist journalists such as Kim Myŏngsik and Sin Ilyong lambasted moderates like Yi Kwangsu for daring to suggest that Koreans must work within the colonial system to prepare the groundwork for future independence. Others attacked the University Movement as a project that would only benefit the sons of landlords and middle-class elements, while it ignored the ignorance and poverty of the masses. The Korean Production Movement came under attack as a transparent device that used patriotism to enrich Korean capitalists. Leftists mocked as completely specious the Production Movement ideologues' argument that national capital was in competition with foreign capital. To them, capital was capital and ethnicity was not relevant, and they attacked the patriotism of Korean businessmen by asserting that the movement simply served the class interests of rich Koreans at the expense of the poor.

The United Front

The growing split within the nationalist movement coincided with a renewed crackdown by the Japanese police. The Peace Preservation Law of May 1925 provided police with broadened powers to control political life in the colony. In November of the same year they arrested a number of Korean Communists and leftist leaders. In June 1926 the funeral of the last Chosŏn emperor, Sunjong, was the focal point of widespread anti-Japanese riots that precipitated additional police reprisals against nationalist organizations. Concurrently, the High Police began to eliminate radical publications as well as increase censorship actions against the nationalist newspapers. Because both the right and left had failed repeatedly to sustain any broad movement, each side realized that the nature of the liberation movement had to change from one driven by elites to one powered by a mass base. Finally, early in 1927, the decisive move for a united front came from the forces of the left.

The New Korea Society (Sin'ganhoe), active between 1927 and 1931, was the culmination of the search for a united front organization. Founded in 1927, with top posts going to prominent moderate nationalists, the Sin'ganhoe provided a common base for moderates, radicals, and Korean Communists. The Japanese tolerated the organization because of its moderate leadership, and they undoubtedly took advantage of its formation as a means to further penetrate the nationalist movement. Once formed, however, the leadership, especially at the branch level, fell to radicals and Communists. By 1930, according to nationalist sources, the Sin'ganhoe claimed 386 branches and 76,939 members. It coordinated the activities of youth, labor and peasant groups, and intellectual societies, and it had become a vehicle for coordinated nationalist activity that served the ends of both the right and left.

The rise of the Sin'ganhoe stimulated a similar joining of moderate and more radical women's groups in the establishment of the Friends of the Rose of Sharon (Kŭnuhoe), a "sister" body to the Sin'ganhoe. The Kŭnuhoe brought together mainstream reformists with women socialists in an attempt to bring women's issues to the fore of united-front politics. This was an uphill battle; like the struggles within the Sin'ganhoe proper, there was a constant battle for control within the divided leadership of the women's movement. The Kŭnuhoe continued the social work and reformist agenda of the mainstream movement, returning to "safer" projects after the Japanese crackdown following the 1929 demonstrations initiated by the Kwangju Student Movement. In 1929 the Kŭnuhoe had 2,970 members, evidence of the increasing participation of women in public affairs. Ultimately the Kŭnuhoe suffered the same fate as the Sin'ganhoe because its socialist leadership campaigned for and succeeded in dissolving the organization in 1931 (Wells, "The Price of Legitimacy," 1999).

The Japanese police carefully watched the Sin'ganhoe from the beginning. They prohibited it from holding national conventions, and their periodic roundups of leftists within the leadership exacerbated factionalism within its ranks. Factional struggle had arisen in its first year when leftists had proposed a number of radical amendments to the society's original charter. They had called for the waiving of student fees for the poor, the withdrawal from Korea of Japanese companies such as the notorious Oriental Development Company—it was the largest landlord on the peninsula, and the abolition of all laws inhibiting free speech and assembly. The Sin'ganhoe's support of student demonstrations in the southwest provincial capital of Kwangju in 1929, and its role in levering them into a nationwide disturbance, was the beginning of the end of the United Front. In the wake of the demonstrations, a number of Communists were arrested, bringing a shift to the right in the Sin'ganhoe leadership. The generally Communist-led local branch leadership, already directed by Moscow's Comintern (December Thesis) to resist domination by reformist elements, began to consider dissolving the organization.[9] In May 1931, the first national conference of the Sin'ganhoe to be allowed by the police was convened. The moderate leadership fought to save the organization, but they were defeated by radicals who voted for dissolution. Ironically, the Japanese police watched the process with relief, for their interests coincided with those of the Communists.

Beyond Nationalist Politics

As with all political histories, this discussion highlighting activities in the intellectual and political world of the colony has emphasized the activities and ideas of only a small percentage of the population. Standard historical narratives give disproportionate attention to political movements, highly publicized campaigns, and dramatic personal struggles and martyrdom. While the debates between nationalists, whether of conservative or radical bent, were important and established new ideas of collective action and new ideologies of national belonging, most of the Korean population continued their daily lives and coped with the continuous and accelerating pace of social and economic change. It is not certain to what degree the poorly educated and overwhelmingly rural population understood or even cared about the high-minded calls for cultural and social reform in the name of nation-building. And it was also unlikely that the abstruse doctrine of class warfare advocated by socialists made much sense initially to conservative peasants mired in the daily struggle to survive another growing season. Certainly, almost all felt the reality of colonial rule, but we cannot assume that simple resentment over foreign rule automatically turned all Koreans into nationalist patriots.

Foreign rule, as opposed to centuries of independence and autonomy, was certainly an unnatural situation for Koreans after 1910. But probably it was more unnatural for those who had traditionally ruled. The Japanese simply completed a process that disenfranchised the traditional elites that had begun in 1895. Yet however resentful they may have become, the upper *yangban* could fall back on their landed wealth. What of other groups in Korean society long blocked by the barriers to social mobility policed by the upper aristocracy? The secondary status groups—the lower (middle class if you will) aristocracy—had seized opportunities that came with the reforms of the Chosŏn administration after 1895, and many continued their upward rise as the colonial bureaucracy expanded. These groups no doubt looked on Japanese colonialism with ambivalent feelings (Hwang, 2004).

But what about the vast majority of Koreans who composed the peasantry? Certainly the rule of foreigners was distasteful, and the colonial state was much more intrusive than the old Chosŏn government. Nevertheless, the peasantry had long suffered under the domination of the Korean upper class, tilled its fields, paid rents, and put up with labor service and other indignities. Was not the colonial government just a new and more efficient version of traditional oppression? The answer is certainly yes, it was. In a negative sense, the very presence of the Japanese as foreign oppressors was the major source of national consciousness formation. But I would submit that by the late 1920s, this negative sense of being Koreans, bound together by outside oppressors, had not yet been fully transformed into a positive sense of belonging to the Korean nation.

In fact, more was going on in the countryside than this discussion of Korean nationalists and Japanese occupiers may suggest. During the late 1910s and first half of the 1920s an economic boom occurred based on rising rice prices and increased production for the Japanese export market. Landlords, small owners, and even partial tenants were doing better, but tenants and landless peasants were also spurred to fight for an increasing share of the expanding rural economy. The Cultural Policy reforms made it easier to organize, and the 1920s witnessed an increase in landlord tenant disputes. Given the fact that most landlords were still Koreans, this meant that for many peasants the most important drama was with their own people, not with the larger political struggle between Korean nationalism and Japanese occupation. These disputes in the agricultural sector were reformist and practical, not revolutionary or ideological. The economic downturn and later depression of the 1930s brought increased class polarization; disputes at this point became more defensive, indeed, a matter of survival (Gi-Wook Shin, 1996, p.74).

The fact was that Japanese colonialism brought new oppressions and new opportunities in Korean life. The opportunities arose out of the new economic, social, and cultural patterns that had emerged since Korea's inclusion in the nation-state system and its global capitalist economy, and they brought new opportunities and political realities to all Koreans. By the late 1920s all Koreans were enmeshed in a system of economic and social relations embedded in a new, highly uneven modernity. The new modernity provided opportunities heretofore absent in Korea. To take advantage of education, service in the colonial bureaucracy, employment in Japanese companies, investment in the Japanese dominated colonial economy, or profiteering in the new international export markets meant stepping into the Japanese-dominated sphere of modernity. To do so required deemphasizing one's identification with Korean nationalism and its fierce anti-Japanese logic in favor of cultivating the colonial system to one's advantage. In the end, Japanese colonial rule succeeded insofar as many Koreans chose to passively include themselves within the colonial system.

By the 1930s, to which we turn next, the vast majority of the population still lived in a similar fashion to that of the pre-colonial era. The growth and complexity of the state and its interventions in society, the domination of capitalist market rule, urbanization, and the cultural expressions of modernity existed, but were unevenly distributed in the colony. The most obvious examples could be found in the new administrative centers and the growing cities of the colony.

Chapter Four

COLONIAL MODERNITY, ASSIMILATION, AND WAR
1930–1945

사

THE YEARS BETWEEN the collapse of the United Front in the fall of 1931 and the outbreak of the war with China in 1937 brought colonial Korea's ironies and contradictions into sharp focus. While the fall of the United Front meant the collapse of overt nationalist resistance, what emerged in its place was a more violent anti-Japanese movement represented by the guerrilla movement in Manchuria and the Red Peasant Unions in the far northeast of the peninsula. Japan's seizure of Manchuria in 1931 altered Korea's position in the empire, for Korea then became a middleman in the empire's development of northeast China's vast untapped resources. The subsequent, seemingly anomalous industrialization of North Korea provided new jobs for peasants, but at the price of dislocating them from the densely populated south and moving them to the north; furthermore, Korea's industrial labor force expanded simultaneously with the deepening immiseration of the Korean countryside. Finally this period witnessed the flowering of a capitalist mass culture in Korea's cities, a popular culture providing the façade of a modernity that had evolved unevenly in the colony. The alluring consumer culture and glittering nightlife in the cities contrasted with abject poverty in the countryside, symbolizing each end of the economic spectrum of a dual economy—dual in the sense that parts of Seoul were as modern as anything in Tokyo, yet in rural backwaters profound poverty and wretched material conditions remained unchanged from the nineteenth century.

The addition of Manchuria caused large-scale shifts within the Japanese Empire. Increasingly isolated in world affairs and threatened by economic isolation as trading nations erected tariff barriers to protect their own economies, Japan began to create an autarkic economy formed around its colonies. The main axis of this system ran from Japan proper through Korea and Manchuria, with Taiwan playing an important, but less crucial role. Because Korea was more firmly integrated politically, had a more developed infrastructure, and was labor rich—not to mention its being geographically central—Japan began to industrialize Korea in order to exploit the raw materials of Manchuria. The state-led industrialization of Korea in the 1930s was an anomaly in colonial history. No colony had ever before been industrialized to the level of Japan's Korea colony, a process that shifted labor from the densely populated south to the sites of huge new factories in northern Korea and Manchuria and spurred urban growth as well.

The increasing economic importance of Korea within the empire motivated Japan to intensify its efforts to spread Japanese values, language, and institutions within the colony. By the mid-1930s Japanese authorities were demanding active Korean participation in Shinto ceremonies, stepping up the pressure within the education system to spread Japanese language use, and trying to eliminate the last differences in legal and administrative practices that distinguished the Japanese *naichi* (inner lands) from the colonial *gaichi* (outer lands). The goal in the minds of colonial officials was a seamless cultural, legal, and administrative assimilation of Korea, and where this could not be accomplished in reality, cosmetic fiction would do. This was especially true in the dark years of the Pacific War (1941–1945), when the Japanese assimilation policies became increasingly hysterical and unrealistic.

By the end of the colonial period in 1945, Korean society was suffering under a cripplingly harsh mobilization for total war. It was no consolation that the Japanese Diet had recommended the complete elimination of the distinction between *naichi* and *gaichi,* or true Japanese from their imperial subjects on the periphery. Becoming assimilated meant that Koreans would be allowed the same privileges to sacrifice for the emperor granted the citizenry of the main islands—namely, to be conscripted for the military and labor forces, to render their rice and precious metals to the imperial treasury, and to be forcefully moved wherever manpower was needed. Of course while distinctions disappeared in theory, Koreans and other colonials still carried identity cards designating their ethnicity.

Colonial Modernity

The material, structural, and intellectual underpinnings of what is normally thought of as modernity was inextricably bound up with imperialism in the non-Western world. Since the expansion of the global capitalist market system often required the use of force, the colonial system had emerged as the political super-structure of market expansion. East Asians fought against inclusion in the new global political-economic system of capitalism, but ultimately their societies were joined to the international system whether willingly or not. Market opening began the process of technology transfer, creation of trade circuits, as well as the importation of Western ideas and values. Ultimately political control (indirect control in the case of China) cemented the connections between these "less-developed" economies and the West. In Korea's case, its opening and later domination at the hands of the Japanese began their drama of social and economic transformation similar to that of other colonies around the globe.

After 1910 the direct and massive Japanese colonial intervention in Korea speeded the process of change in unique ways and created a form of modernization in which the process may be usefully termed "colonial modernization" and the state of being "colonial modernity." These terms help us distinguish the modernity of the Korean colony from that of the West, or of Japan for that matter. The usual elements of the modern are manifest, but in a highly skewed form. Most importantly, colonial modernity is one in which the modern sector is dominated by the political control of the colonizers. The presence of colonial domination adds ethnic power relations to the usual formation of class difference and competition. Finally, the association of the modern sector of colonial society with the dominant culture of the colonizers creates an added element of complexity. To be part of modernity will therefore mean adopting the culture of the ethnically distinct and advantaged colonizer community. This engenders cultural hybridity because it forces the colonized to adopt the colonizers' language and values if they want to participate in the new modernity.

Japan used the most advanced technology of the times in fashioning their colonial state. They also had the advantage of followership, that is, they were able to learn from the mistakes and successes of older colonial regimes like the English and French (Pyle, 1974). As a consequence, Japan not only forced Korea into contact with the global market and the attendant influences that began the transformation of traditional Korea, but its colonial state also took an active role in shaping and accelerating this transformation. It began by penetrating the countryside with railroads, telegraph, and telephone lines. Later motor roads began to creep out from the new administrative centers to link smaller periodic markets to the larger county and provincial centers. The new communications infrastructure tied together the military and police control apparatus. Within a few years of annexation, police substations with phone lines radiating out from its modern façade and a new motorcar parked in front put the trappings of modern culture directly in the view of a peasantry who lived in an entirely different material universe. The brutal reality of Japanese rule, the tumult of changing laws and regulations, new administrative procedures, health inspections, market regulators, and all the appurtenances of modern colonial administration brought with them the additional shock of the modern.

Colonial modernity describes the striking contradictions inherent in a juxtaposition of the modern and the backward, the developed and the undeveloped. Indeed, this binary in the minds of the colonialists justified their controlling presence. It appeared to them as a temporary contradiction that placed the latest technology and consumer objects next to what might be considered the traditional and primitive. Certainly one feature of this modernity was the sense of time warp encountered when moving from the modernizing cities to the still unchanged rural countryside. Even in the post-colonial 1960s, travelers could still feel a backward movement in time the further they traveled into Korean's rural hinterland, leaving behind the comforts and conveniences of modern life and encountering a material world of another century. Such a feeling, of course, assumes that what is left behind in the city is a present progressively moving toward the future, and what is encountered in the hinterland is a past as yet unchanged.

The shock of the modern must have been even more acute in the 1930s. The Japanese used this play on time and their domination of the modern to legitimate their rule. Wielding still and movie cameras, Japanese anthropologists had fanned out into the countryside from the early moments of colonial rule; to know and record the past as represented in Korea's present backward (and "natural") state was an important part of justifying Japanese rule—just as it was in the entire colonial world. By the 1930s legions of Japanese and foreign tourists consumed this backwardness, moving back and forth in time from modern hotels to the sites of the "traditional past." They could buy in any hotel postcards that documented the quaint rural customs and costumes of their colonial subjects, or they could choose to send images of Seoul's Honmachi, the main Japanese shopping district, and one that was virtually identical to any modern Tokyo street.

Colonial modernity was also defined by an ethnic bifurcation between the modern (Japanese) and the backward (Korean), a bifurcation enforced by Japanese economic and political ascendancy. And the large population of Japanese who lived and worked in Korea enhanced this split. By 1940 over 800,000 Japanese residents clustered in the urban centers. The lifestyle of this large expatriated enclave defined modern living. They were colonial bureaucrats, intellectuals, teachers, and businessmen whose residences and the service economy that supported them represented islands of Japanese modernity surrounded by a developing Korea.

Honmachi, center of the Japanese quarter in Seoul, 1930s. Source: The Norman Thorpe Collection.

To enter Japanese enclaves was to enter a different cultural zone, making explicit the colonial modernity's hybrid predicament. For the socially and economically ambitious Koreans, working for or playing within the modern sectors of Korea's new cities meant participating in a blend of Korean and Japanese cultures. Colonial modernity privileged Japanese cultural and material influence in Korea and skewed its reception by Koreans because of the power realities that it only lightly masked. In the end, the attraction of the modern explains in part how the Japanese successfully established a stable hegemony in Korea after 1920 (Gi-Wook Shin, "Colonial Corporatism," 1999). By including (and implicating) Korea's ambitious middle class in the burgeoning modernity of the colony, the Japanese served their long-term interests of gaining this key social class's compliance, or at least passive acceptance, of the colonial order.

Modernity in Korea also contained elements of potential liberation within its cultural and intellectual matrix. Development created different occupations and introduced new avenues of mobility. Liberation from traditional ways of being did not mean life would necessarily be easier, but movement to the cities, working in industrial settings, and even leaving the country to seek employment in Manchuria or the metropole itself changed peoples' consciousness of life's possibilities. The expansion of the educational system, however its message was twisted to justify imperial rule, brought literacy, new skills, and a widened consciousness to the hundreds of thousands of Koreans who heretofore had no access to even a rudimentary education. Educating women was particularly revolutionary. The old taboo against educating women had been broken at the turn of the century, and by the 1920s entire journals were devoted to discourse on the modern women (sinyŏsŏng). Educated young women challenged traditional roles by appearing in public wearing Western clothes and engaging in activities previously the monopoly of men. At least among the middle-class women of the cities, the evolution of colonial modernity had opened a space for them, by creating new roles and styles and asserting rights for women. Finally, within the visual and aural representations of cinema and popular song, an entirely new dreamworld emerged that created a whole new set of longings and desires in everyone from the poorest rural peasants to the urban scions of the wealthy new commercial class.

Economic Growth and Developmental Colonialism

After 1920 the economic policy in Korea continued to encourage increases in agricultural production through selective investment in irrigation, introduction of chemical fertilizers, and the spread of modern farming technology. Because of demand for Korean rice from the metropolitan markets and increasing rice prices, Korean agriculture faired well during the decade. Landowners increased their holdings and large landlords in particular received a windfall in rents. While twenty years earlier the only obvious investment of profits from rents was in more land, by the 1920s landlords began to funnel their profits into modern enterprises. The Japanese stimulated this move by removing formal restrictions against incorporation by Koreans with its new Company Law of 1920. More Koreans began to participate as entrepreneurs or stockholders in commercial enterprises, and a select group of very successful capitalists emerged.

Indeed, by 1920 there was a pent-up demand among wealthy Koreans to profit from the growing colonial economy. The governor general recognized this demand and knew that to continue to restrict Korean investment would work against Japanese long-term interests for control and pacification of the colony. Just as the Cultural Policy provisions within the cultural sphere had worked to provide an outlet for repressed intellectual energy and deflect it away from resistance to Japanese rule, so too changing the economic policy, they believed, would allow them to use to their advantage their perception that political instability also worried Korean economic elites. These elites would be included in the colonial economy under the new banner of Japanese-Korean harmony *(nissen yūwa)*.

In 1921 the colonial government convened an industrial commission of businessmen and Japanese officials to discuss the shape of economic policy in the post-World War I era. At the commission both Japanese and Korean businessmen beseeched the GGK to moderate restrictions to investment in the colony. Japanese investors had chafed under earlier obstacles to investment from Japan, but they were now worried that the GGK was getting ready to provide advantages to Korean entrepreneurs at their expense. In the end, the colonial economy was opened to more Japanese businessmen, and subsidies were given to a select group of Korean businessmen (Eckert, *Offspring of Empire*, 1991).

The Korean economy remained dependent on Japanese capitalism, but a space for Korean participation had been opened. And while colonial economic policy continued under the slogan of agriculture first in the 1920s, commercial and manufacturing sectors in Korea began to develop more quickly. Although this anticipated future industrial growth, the unique government-led economic development would only come in the 1930s. Still, the distribution of economic activity had changed significantly by 1930. Korean businessmen were important players in the new service and manufacturing sectors. Most notably, Kyŏngsŏng Spinning and Weaving Corporation, directed by Kim Sŏngsu and his brother Yŏnsu, established itself as the largest Korean-owned company in the colony. By the 1930s the Kims' company was poised to take advantage of opportunities in Manchuria and China, and during the war Japanese procurement swelled its profits (Eckert, *Offspring of Empire*, 1991). In trading and retail, several Koreans also established large business empires. Pak Hŭngsik built a retailing empire from a modest trading company. His ultra-modern, six-story Hwasin department store on Chongno in downtown Seoul anchored a unique chain of stores that successfully competed with Japanese retail giants such as Mitsukoshi and Chōjiya.

In spite of increased Korean participation, however, the economy remained dominated by Japanese. After 1935 and the promulgation of the Export Association Law, some investment flowed into the colony from the large Japanese business combines known as *zaibatsu*.[1] Mitsui, Sumitomo, Yasuda, and Mitsubishi all had stakes in the colony by the late 1920s, and even more notably there were the so-called new *zaibatsu*, large combines that had emerged after World War I, which specialized in joint ventures with the GGK that were financed by bank loans and special subsidies from the Bank of Chōsen. Such was the case of the businessman Noguchi Jun, who in the early 1930s began a series of large projects in Korea that ultimately included the world's largest nitrogen-fertilizer plant. In the mid-1920s Noguchi had met with Governor General Saitō to help with planning the expansion of Korea's hydroelectric sources, and a decade later their planning bore fruit in the completion of enormous dams on the Yalu River that provided abundant, inexpensive power for the industrial boom of the war years. The pattern of close ties between private entrepreneurs and capital, state-run banks, and the economic and strategic planning of the GGK came into focus by the late 1920s. Thus the contours of a unique developmental colonialism, a product of Japan's strategic and economic interests in Northeast Asia, were already apparent in the years just before the Great Depression (Cumings, "Northeast Asian Political Economy," 1984).

The Great Depression: Rising Tenancy and Rural Misery

The global depression after 1929 hit the Korean countryside very hard. It signaled an end to the relatively good times of the 1920s and steady or increasing rice prices. The program to increase rice production had been moderately effective, but the increased production had generally found its way into the export market, enriching landlords and rice merchants but not the ordinary peasants themselves. Perversely, as rice production increased, Korean peasants consumed less rice in favor of cheaper grains such as barley and millet so they could market the more valuable rice for cash, thus further degrading their caloric intake. The fall in rice prices caused by the Great Depression, as well as by protectionist pressure from Japanese rice growers, exacerbated negative trends within the land-tenure system that were already apparent in the 1920s, namely, rising rents, increased concentration of landownership, and higher percentages of tenancy. During the Depression, the situation in rural Korea worsened. A rapid increase in the Korean population after 1920 compounded market forces that were increasing the rate of tenancy. Between 1910 and 1940 tenancy steadily increased with a tremendous spike during the Great Depression and war years. Because of the intense pressure on available land resources, landowners raised rents almost at will, further exacerbating peasant distress. Large numbers of peasants were forced off the land in search of jobs as casual laborers or as workers in the service sector or in small urban factories.

Another indicator of rural distress was the rising number of landless peasants who were resorting to upland slash-and-burn agriculture, the so-called fire-field people *(hwajŏn)*. In 1936 over 300,000 families were engaged in such marginal farming, a 300 percent increase over the number in 1916. Increases in landowner-tenant disputes also marked the deterioration of life in rural Korea. Disputes recorded by the GGK increased from 667 in 1931 to 7,544 in 1934; a year later they had tripled to 25,834. By 1933 the situation was so grave that the GGK revised its tenancy and arbitration laws in order to provide some relief for peasants caught in the spiral of rising rents (Shin, *Peasant Protest,* 1996). In 1934 Governor General Ugaki formally ended the rice production program under pressure from Japanese agricultural interests who were demanding relief from the downward pressure on prices caused by the continuing flow of cheap Korean rice into Japan. Ostensibly to meet the food problems in the colony, Ugaki now instituted a self-regenera-tion campaign to encourage rural self-sufficiency and frugality, a campaign that anticipated a similar move in the 1970s—Pak Chung Hee's New Village Move-ment—which was also intended to help spur economic growth.

In spite of GGK efforts to ameliorate the worsening conditions in the coun-tryside, landownership concentration continued to increase and became one of liberated Korea's major problems in 1945. As the number of absentee landlords increased, more tenants came under the supervision of agents, who often worked under an incentive system that tied their income to the amount of rents collected. In addition, the system further depersonalized owner-tenant relations already strained by the impersonal market. An increase in Japanese investment in Korean

A Korean village in the 1930s, from a postcard series entitled "Korean Customs." Source: The Nor-man Thorpe Collection.

land in the 1930s had the same deleterious effect; although relatively few in number, Japanese made up a good proportion of the largest landowners in the colony. Still, the majority of landlords were Korean, and the real tragedy of the colonial land-system was that it served landowners' interests so well. Throughout the colonial period, the landowning strata continued, in general, to profit from secure investments in land. By 1945 the overall tenancy rate (including partial tenants) in Korea was 69.1 percent, but in some areas of the southwest Cholla provinces the rate approached 80 percent.

The Seizure of Manchuria and Colonial Industrialization

On September 18, 1931, the Kwantung Army created a pretext that led to the invasion and seizure of Manchuria, and the puppet state of Manchukuo was established a year later. This act was the logical outcome of Japan's long-term strategic effort to control Manchuria, the rise of radical military influences within domestic Japanese politics, and what heretofore had been the implicit emergence of a yen-bloc economy embracing Japan's colonies. The seizure of Manchuria solidified linkages with Korea's growing economy that the GGK had been promoting for years. Now the Japanese could refer explicitly to Korea as a supply base for their Kwantung Army stationed in China; after 1931 Manchuria was quickly integrated into Japan's economic and strategic policy to create a self-sustaining regional economy that would counter the effects of increasing diplomatic and economic isolation in the world. The GGK coordinated Japanese private and public investment in Manchuria, with the Bank of Chōsen and the Chōsen Industrial Bank playing a primary role in capitalizing Manchurian industrial projects. Korean entrepreneurs also moved into Manchuria. The governors general of Korea, all military men, had long understood the strategic importance of Manchuria to the defense and welfare of Japan. In the mid-1930s Governor General Minami described Japan as the "torso" *(dōtai),* Korea the "arm" *(ude),* and Manchuria as the fist *(kobushi)* when he characterized the integration of Northeast Asia under Japanese control (Eckert, *Offspring of Empire,* 1991, p. 115). Such thinking anticipated the subsequent invasion of China, but at least a decade before the colonial government in Korea had started developing the economic links between Korea and Manchuria in the service of the empire's greater good.

The inclusion of Manchuria into the empire accelerated the industrialization of Korea in the 1930s. This industrialization was accomplished by a state-private sector cooperation that anticipated similar arrangements characteristic of what is now referred to as the developmentalist state. Already begun in the 1920s, Korea's hydroelectric capacity was increased to provide power for the new factories. Cheap power, in particular, was a prime motivation for Noguchi Jun to develop his chemical manufacturing empire in Hamhŭng. Japan Steel Corporation established plants to exploit high-grade iron-ore deposits in Manchuria and newly discovered ones in north Korea. This formed the core of an expanding metals industry. By 1940 Korea, still an impoverished colony in most respects, boasted a disproportionately developed manufacturing sector (chemical, tools, metals, and textile industries) that accounted for 40 percent of Korea's entire economic output, a figure up from a 17.7 percent in 1931. The increased economic output was tightly bound to Japan, where 95 percent of all Korean exports went. For its part, Korea was, by 1939, absorbing fully 34 percent of all Japanese exports. A further dimension of this development was the participation of Korea-based Japanese companies, Korean entrepreneurs, and Korean labor in Manchuria. With Japanese political control and the infrastructure they had already developed, capital and labor flowed freely over the Korean-Manchuria border. By the outbreak of the war in China, the close economic linkage between Japan, Korea, and Manchuria envisioned a decade earlier by GGK bureaucrats and businessmen had become an accomplished fact.

The economic development of Korea during the 1930s, featuring its characteristic combination of overdevelopment and underdevelopment, had a profound effect on the Korean population. As industry expanded, hundreds of thousands of peasants found themselves in factory jobs. The factory work force in Korea doubled in the 1930s and increased further after the outbreak of the Pacific War, from 384,951 in 1932 to 1,321,713 in 1943, a 343 percent increase (Cumings, *Origins of the Korean War,* 1981). If the mining industry and transportation sectors are added, the increase is even more dramatic. Moreover, this does not count the tens of thousands of Koreans working in plants in Manchuria by 1945. The expansion of the manufacturing economy not only pulled peasants off the land and into the alien factory labor, it also displaced large numbers of Koreans from their home regions. Recruitment generally moved labor from the populous south to north. Before 1937, private industry had to recruit its own labor, but their task was simplified by the increasingly desperate situation in the Korean countryside. Recruitment by the market alone, however, was insufficient after the outbreak of the war in China. After 1937, government labor conscription moved even larger numbers of Koreans throughout the empire to fill the various needs of war production (see Table 4.1).

Just as Korean entrepreneurs were handicapped in competition with Japanese capitalists in the area of large-scale industry; similarly, Koreans found themselves largely relegated to secondary jobs in an ethnically demarcated workplace. Koreans occupied the bottom of the labor hierarchy, and before the war only a small percentage rose into leadership or technical positions. The foremen of most factories were Japanese, and the skilled trades were dominated by Japanese labor. The few Koreans who rose into management were restricted to middle levels of authority or to clerical positions. With the coming of the war and the draining away of Japanese personnel through army conscription, Koreans were able to advance to higher positions on the factory floor and in offices, yet the numbers were still

Table 4.1 GROWTH OF THE WORKING CLASS: 1933–1943

Type of Worker	1933 N of Workers	1943 N of Workers	% 1943 Workforce
Factory workers	99,400	390,000	22.3
Mine workers	70,700	280,000	16.0
Transportation workers	n/a	170,000	9.7
Construction workers	43,600	380,000	21.7
Miscellaneous workers	n/a	530,000	30.3

Source: 1933 Shokusan Bank Monthly Survey Report; 1943 Imperial Diet Summary Report; in Soon-Won Park (1999, p. 29).

meager and the phenomenon of too short a duration to have a meaningful effect in labor training by the end of the war (Park, 1999).

Anti-Japanese Resistance in the 1930s

While the overt nationalist movement within the colony faded after the fall of the Sin'ganhoe in 1931, Japan's seizure of Manchuria helped to revive the exile movement. The increased presence of the Japanese in Manchuria galvanized Korean exiles in China proper to create a common cause with the Nationalist Chinese government (KMT) in Nanking. A new group led by Kim Ku, the Korean Independence Party, inherited the legacy of the now defunct Korean Provisional Government. This party staged a series of successful terrorist attacks, bombings and assassinations, on Japanese targets in China. Another more powerful group coalesced around the leftist Korean National Revolutionary Party headed by Kim Wŏnbong. Although these two groups tried to create a unified front, personal and doctrinal differences and fickle KMT support prevented any successful union. Only in 1944 did the two groups merge to revive the Korean Provisional Government and receive Chiang Kai-shek's imprimatur as the de facto Korean government in exile. The group ultimately received support for the formation of a Korean Restoration Army. Numbering 3,600 in 1943, the army languished in rear areas, but they did participate in limited propaganda, intelligence, and guerrilla operations.

In the period before 1937, most Korean Communists who had been working within the various nationalist parties in China proper moved their operations to Yenan and Manchuria. In Manchuria, they waged a protracted guerrilla war harassing the Japanese. Between 1931 and 1935 an estimated 200,000 guerrillas composed of bands of all sizes and levels of discipline and organization were fighting in Manchuria. Koreans represented the largest percentage of guerrillas in proportion to population of any other ethnic group (Cumings, *Korea's Place*, 1997; 160). A protracted and bloody anti-insurgency campaign reduced the levels of opposition, but guerrilla bands, some numbering in the thousands, were still operating in 1935.

The most successful guerrilla groups were part of the Chinese Communist military units that operated in loose coordination under the banner of the Northeast Anti-Japanese United Army. Korean detachments within this army carried out a desperate and ultimately losing battle against the Japanese pacification campaigns. Most effective among them was a group led by Kim Il Sung, the future "great leader" of North Korea. Kim's detachment made a number of raids in Manchuria as well as Korea in the 1935–1940 period. The Japanese at one point created a special counterinsurgency unit that enlisted Korean Communist defectors from other groups to hunt him down. His group was small, numbering between 50 and 300, and it maintained itself on forced contributions from wealthy farmers. Eventually, Japanese pressure forced Kim, with his last followers, to cross into the Kabarovsk area of the Soviet Union to wait out the war in Soviet training camps with other retreating Korean partisans.

After Liberation, Kim Il Sung and his loyal partisans dominated the leadership of what became North Korea. Over time, the significance of his guerrilla activities became grotesquely distorted within the fantastic claims of the personality cult woven around the person of the Great Leader. Indeed, the portrayal of Kim's single-handed defeat of the Japanese remains central to North Korea's legitimacy claims as the true leader of the Korean people. Official South Korean histories have tried to write Kim completely out of the record. The fact remains that Kim was one of the last resistance fighters standing in Manchuria in the 1930s; while his accomplishments were considerably more modest than is claimed in North Korean lore, he was, according to Japanese sources, a formidable enemy who had gained the support of the Korean peasantry in Manchuria. (Suh Dae-Sook, *Kim Il Sung*, 1988) And Kim as well as his guerrilla loyalists ended up leading postwar North Korea until the mid-1990s.

Origins and Maturation of a New Mass Culture

For decades after Liberation, Korean nationalist historians ignored important cultural developments that had taken place during the colonial period. This was an understandable backlash against Japanese cultural repression during the forced assimilation campaigns of the late 1930s and war years. Nevertheless, in recent years there has been a considerable effort to exhume the full picture of Korea's early modern mass culture in order to understand the antecedents of contemporary Korean modernity. As noted earlier, modernity began to evolve on the peninsula in the late nineteenth century and matured in Korea's urban space under Japanese rule. It was necessarily linked to the modern mass culture of the metropole, a hybrid phenomenon shaped by the transnational forces of global capitalism, technology transfer, and blended forms of cultural expression. Most important, new mediums of cultural expression and new styles of cultural consumption that were brought into Korea not only introduced foreign culture, they also began transforming traditional Korean culture within these new styles and new media.

Mechanical reproduction of musical and visual culture changed how people consumed entertainment. Modern mass culture is characterized by the passive consumption of culture rather than its active production. Traditionally people were responsible for their own entertainment. In a traditional village setting in Korea for example, villagers performed for each other as entertainment. While some might specialize or form special groups within the village, dance, song, drama depended on villagers for its production. Within the leisure world of the upper class, performance by professionals mixed with the elites' own production of arts and culture. It has been noted that certain forms of Korean cultural expression had already begun the process of professionalization in the mid-nineteenth century. Itinerant performers of song, *p'ansori* for example, earned their living collecting fees on the market circuit where the elite and an emerging class of merchants had the means to buy such entertainments (Pihl, 1994). The expansion of market forces accelerated this trend, and by 1900 there were many more opportunities to consume the services of hired entertainers. Thus the transition from local performance on the village common *(madang)* to performance on a stage requiring admission fees had already appeared in the late nineteenth century. By the turn of the century, Western-style theaters opened in Seoul, speeding the movement of entertainment from *madang* to stage to the silver screen and, ultimately, into the ether via radio waves in the next several decades.

What became the content of mass popular culture in colonial Korea was necessarily a mixing of traditional Korean culture with Chinese, Japanese, and Western cultural forms; given the increasing interconnectedness of the world even in the early twentieth century, it is hard, if not impossible, to find any "pure" national culture. That Japanese influences were prominent in this mix is not surprising, given the power realities of colonialism. We cannot, however, dismiss this cultural production as somehow not truly Korean culture because of its colonial origins. On the contrary, it is just as easy to see the adaptation of Korean folk culture into the new media as something that preserved kernels of the tradition within the corrosive assault, at least as perceived by colonial intellectuals, of modernity during this period of modern transformation.

Print capitalism was an important part of this transformation. Even before Korea's opening in 1876, reading patterns had already begun to change. In the late eighteenth century publishers expurgated old-style, didactic novels written in classical Chinese to create the popular, plot-driven "new novels" *(sinsosŏl)* for wider distribution among the lower classes. Ironically, by the early twentieth century Japanese publishers were taking advantage of the demand for these new novels, while Korean publishers ignored this market in favor or publishing more modern Western-style newspapers and intellectual journals. The revolution in vernacular language use after 1890 had spurred the production of newspapers, journals, and books, and after 1920 the print market expanded rapidly with the revival of Korean daily newspapers. By the 1930s publishing was truly a creature of the market; niche magazines, the equivalent of dime novels, newspapers, pamphlets, consumer guides, sheet music, genealogies, and broadsheets all competed for a share. Nationalist intellectuals worried that commercialization of the press reduced its political commitment and debased its cultural value, but nevertheless it encouraged standardization and expanded the use of the Korean vernacular, whatever message it might convey (Robinson, *Cultural Nationalism,* 1988). Print capitalism also inaugurated and spread the use of line art, photographs, and their combination in advertisement. By the 1930s this, together with film, another powerful visual medium, became an important stimulant of material desires and style.

Korean traditional music was forever transformed by the importation of Western music and instruments in the 1880s and by devices for the mechanical reproduction of music in the early 1900s. Song and dance had already begun to move onto the stage in the nineteenth century, and by 1900 variety shows in theaters created for audiences a new spectacle that would become a staple of popular culture throughout the twentieth century. Western music did not replace Korean music so much as it augmented the musicality of an already rich tradition. While interest in traditional court music had sunk to an all-time low, Western-style songs and new hybrid song forms captured the imagination of Koreans of all classes. With the arrival of phonographs Western classical music, traditional folk songs, "new" folk songs *(sinminyo),* and the Western/Japanese/Korean hybrid popular song genre *(yŭhaengga)* all became staples of a rapidly expanding consumer music market. By the 1930s and the advent of radio broadcasting in Korea, the recording industry produced an amazing array of music for a relatively mass audience. Even peasants in the countryside who never dreamed of owning a radio or phonograph could recite lists of the top recordings and tell stories of the fabulous and scandalous lifestyles of major recording artists.

In the 1930s mass culture had progressed to the point where all the new trends in entertainment had combined in the now-familiar tightly woven nexus of capitalist production, marketing, and consumption. Newspapers were full of ads for variety performances that featured the latest star performers; record releases were timed to coordinate with these performances; and radio programming was similarly timed to produce the maximum play for new material. A hit record would sell 50,000 copies in the colony alone, and Korean hits also sold well in Japan. In fact, Korean singers were in demand for tours in Japan and forged an important link to the more cosmopolitan popular culture of the empire itself. Postwar critics in Korea are quite ambivalent about the musical legacy of the colonial period. Some insist that popular songs were a major covert source of anti-Japanese resistance while others dismiss them as simply a debased form imported directly from Japan. Ironically, post-colonial nationalists have celebrated a similar, but more intense, outpouring of popular cultural exports—the so-called Korean Wave or Hallyu— to Japan and the rest of East Asia since the late 1990s as proof of Korea's creativity and cultural dynamism (see Epilogue). Whatever their political meaning or lack thereof, popular songs were an important part of the new modernity and played a role in reshaping Korean imaginations and sensibilities at the time.

Colonial Mass Culture and National Identity

The emerging mass culture was a double threat to those who had placed themselves in the position of protecting or reviving traditional Korean cultural forms. The new media and mediums of cultural construction, dominated as they were by Japanese and Western modalities, appeared as a juggernaut of cultural destruction as it crushed any feeble attempt to protect or revive traditional ways and hurtled into the modern world of consumption and leisure. Both the foreignness of the modern mass culture and its "baseness" plagued the self-appointed cultural standards police of the nationalist movement.

For example, in the mid-1930s programmers for JDOK, the Korean-language radio station, struggled to preserve and maintain traditional Korean art forms while simultaneously providing entertainment to a mass audience.[2] Korean intellectuals considered radio a didactic medium for elevating public culture, and they took a keen interest in the content of programming. They encouraged high-toned fare such as Western classical music, traditional Korean instrumental music featuring the *kayagŭm* (twelve-string zither), or formal court music. Programmers, however, were caught between their own cultural pretensions and public demand for more popular music. Nationalist intellectuals disparaged the popular song genre *(yŭhaengga)* as vulgar and saw no redeeming cultural value in its focus on the trials of love or the melodrama of emotion in general. Ironically, postwar nationalists have resuscitated this genre, reading them as allegories of national resistance. A compromise was eventually struck by increasing playtime for popular songs, but at the same time introducing more Korean folk songs and the so-called "new folk songs" *(sinminyo)*, arrangements of old folk songs that used new instrumentation and experimental combinations of Western and Korean tonalities.

Radio, while tightly controlled, became a medium of both experimentation and preservation for Korean traditional culture and by doing so undercut GGK cultural assimilation programs. In their search for broadcast content, Korean programmers worked with artists to recast traditional forms of music and drama into forms suitable for radio. By any measure this was preservation of cultural identity; that it was implicitly supported by a GGK subsidy of broadcasting put in place for completely different reasons was another irony of colonial modernity. The Japanese had to allow significant airtime for entertainment programming in order to spread the use of radio among the population, but in doing so they inadvertently provided a cultural space that challenged their own assimilation policies. Radio broadcast was a major stimulus to the continued evolution of the Seoul dialect as the standard pronunciation for the language generally. Linguistics lectures and Korean language lessons (featured in the popular children's hour entitled "Radio hakkyo") continued on air into the late 1930s concurrent with the increased prohibition of Korean language use in public institutions and schools.

Modern Women

Modernity in Korea meant changes for the position of women in colonial society. Within the general reforms sought by nationalists beginning in the 1890s was an emphasis on elevating the position of women. The Christian church brought men and women together for public worship; it established schools for women; and it encouraged the organization of emergence of women's groups devoted to practical reform issues. Women had participated in the early nationalist movement, and their patriotic associations had been instrumental in the movement to repay the national debt and other nationalist projects at the end of the Chosŏn period. Indeed, early women's activities were quickly absorbed into the larger national struggle, setting a precedent that continued to link women's liberation with national liberation. Educating women was a particularly important goal and by all measures it was succeeding; and long before the 1930s, uniformed girls commuting to schools in Korean cities had become a common sight.

By the 1930s the women's movement split between a smaller and more radical feminist movement and the majority reformists who urged a moderate reform program that focused on education and enlightenment of Korea's women. One reason more radical feminism failed to take hold was that the general goals of the more conservative women's groups coincided with formal colonial programs to educate a new generation of wives and mothers in scientific methods of child rearing, hygiene, nutrition and food preparation, and other women's arts. Such education changed only the content and not the social role of women in Korean society. For the colonial authorities, such reforms were for the benefit of raising a new generation of strong and healthy subjects. For the less radical mainstream women's movement, it was to become better mothers for their children. This also jibed with the role of modern women—at least urban middle-class women—as the most important consumers in the expanding commodity markets. How to manage the household budget and make the right consumption decisions was a frequent subject of articles in women's journals and newspaper features.

But while a more radical idea of female liberation may have been subordinated to a reformist agenda within the mainstream women's movement, or, in the case of the socialist women's movement, taken a back seat to the primacy of class liberation, women leaders in general pushed anti-traditional life choices with their own behaviors. Many leaders in the women's movement chose to remain single, cut their hair short, refused to follow restrictive clothing traditions, and became public figures. In the 1920s and 1930s these were still radical choices and drew social disapprobation, even ostracism. Such was the case with Na Hyesŏk, feminist, writer, and painter, who was much in the public eye in the 1920s. Na wrote one of Korea's significant feminist short stories, "Kyŏnghui," won awards for her painting, spent time in jail for political activism in the March First Movement and in association with the anarchist group, the Ŭiryŏldan, and she published an early women's journal. But as a very public figure Na's unconventional lifestyle and outspoken commitment to female autonomy made her a target of the conventional press and an object of scorn and gossip. After an affair in Europe that became public, she was divorced by her husband in 1929 and thereafter effectively ostracized. She died destitute in 1948.

Finally, the rise of women entertainers in the public spotlight of the new mass culture decisively changed perceptions about women's roles in society and broadened the spectrum of possible action and identity. It was during the 1920s and 1930s that the modern girl appeared. Wearing Western fashion in public and confidently cruising the byways of the modern city, the modern girl became a symbol of change and an inspiration to young girls. Much of this was a construction of the popular press, which used the characteristics attributed to the modern girl for sensational and prurient content in order to sell publications. And, indeed, the number of women who could afford such display was still small. To see and be seen in the new department stores, tearooms, or at the public cinema or theater challenged hundreds of years of custom that restricted women to the home precincts. The voices of women announcers on the Korean radio network, the songs of female entertainers (kisaeng) heretofore unheard in public, the images of Korean actresses in the cinema, and the pictures, records, and news stories of the first generation of Korean popular song stars all created a different world of images, roles, and imagined possibilities for Korean women.[3]

The End of Colonial Rule:
Forced Assimilation and War Mobilization

The gradual, but ultimately complete cultural assimilation of Korea by Japan had been a guiding principle of colonial policy from annexation onward. This principle flowed from a colonialist construction of racial, cultural, and historical kinship between the Korean and Japanese people. The Japanese treated Koreans as distant, poor kinsman. Their theory asserted that Japan had followed a different, more beneficial path of evolution and had now turned to help lift up its backward cousins. The GGK devoted tremendous resources to the study of Korean history, archeology, and folk culture. In part this stemmed from the seemingly universal curatorial impulse of all colonialists—the impulse that produced much of our knowledge about the non-Western world up to that time. This knowledge was always filtered through the lens of the colonialists' perceived superior culture. But there was a twist to the Japanese obsession with Korean culture; the Japanese were bent on producing knowledge that proved a link between Japan and Korea in order to legitimate Japan's benevolent task of ruling Korea. Concurrently, however, much of the ethnography of Korea produced at this time emphasized Korea's pre-modernity and difference from Japan. Thus the assimilation discourse was laden with contradictions: it was an anthropological salvage operation, a source for demonstrating how Korea and Japan were one body (Naisen ittai), nostalgia for the pure/primitive culture of the past rapidly disappearing in Japan, and simultaneously a denial of mature equality.

Between 1910 and 1930 assimilation remained largely an unrealized theory whose practical implementation lay far behind the year-to-year exigencies of ruling Korea. The addition of Manchuria to the empire in 1931 and the new emphasis on Korea's increased economic and strategic importance led to an acceleration of assimilation programs in the mid-1930s. The intention was to create subjects who would actively support imperial goals, not merely comply passively. Forced assimilation can be dated from the policy debates over education and the new reg-

"Modern girls" and "modern boys" at Ŭlmildae in P'yŏngyang in the 1930s. Source: The Norman Thorpe Collection.

ulations regarding charters for schools in December 1934. Only a month later, in January 1935, Governor General Ugaki Kazashige promulgated a policy of obligatory worship at Shinto shrines, which required Korean attendance at shrines on all occasions of national importance. This meant all school students and members of Japanese organizations (official and private) were required to attend formal ceremonies organized by group leaders. Such "forced worship" was deeply offensive to all Koreans, but they precipitated a particular crisis within the large Christian community (Clark, 2003). Each church had to decide whether to obey or defy the order as a religious matter; some refused, others found ways to comply. The GGK only applied real pressure for compliance after the outbreak of war. Between 1935 and 1940 the Japanese closed 200 churches, revoked the charters of all Presbyterian schools, and arrested 2,000 Christians who continued to resist on religious grounds.

Formal assimilation programs began in earnest in October 1937 when the new Governor General Minami Jirō (1936–1942) ordered recitation of the "Oath as Subjects of the Imperial Nation" at all public gatherings and by students at the beginning of every school day. Minami was a former commander of the Kwantung Army, a major power within the Japanese high command, and a leading member of the "control faction" within the Japanese military that by 1939 dominated the home government. He brought to his post a reputation as a hard-liner and alliance with expansionists and ultranationalist elements at the highest rungs of power

High school matriculation ceremony at the Chōsen Shrine in Seoul, 1943. Source: The Norman Thorpe Collection.

in Tokyo. What came to be known as the Movement to Create Imperial Citizens (Kōminka undō) emerged under his hand, and the gloves were off. Only a year later Japan was at war with China, and Minami intensified the campaigns; by 1937 Saitō's and Ugaki's relatively "soft" approach to assimilation was a memory, and preparations for total war waited in the wings.

Another pillar of assimilation was language use. Japanese had become the "national language" *(kokugo)* of the colony in 1910. Surprisingly, the dissemination of Japanese skills in Korea remained tied to the public education system and its use was voluntary until the 1930s. The GGK appears to have tacitly framed language policy as a program of attraction rather than coercion. In the 1930s, Korean language classes continued in the schools, and the language movement successfully mounted programs in the countryside and established night schools in the cities to spread Korean literacy. It was clear, however, to any ambitious Korean that success in the modern sector of the colony required Japanese fluency, and a high percentage of colonial intellectuals were bilingual. In 1938, however, Japanese became the language of instruction for all subjects in the colonial schools, and Korean language study was formally removed from the curriculum in 1942. In the same year the GGK arrested the entire leadership of the Korean Language Movement and seized the manuscript of the comprehensive Korean dictionary, then nearing completion. Unlike Japan's language policies in Taiwan, formal Japanese outreach programs in Korea were only begun in 1938, and the movement to establish a registry of "National Language Families" that had been very successful in Taiwan failed in Korea. In 1944, even by the overly optimistic GGK estimates, barely 12 percent of the Korean population had functional Japanese. The corollary to forced use of Japanese was censorship of the printed word. Censorship of all Korean publications increased with the coming of the war; by 1940 the Japanese had closed the independent Korean-run daily newspapers and many of the monthly journals.

In retrospect the language programs within the assimilation project failed. It was clear by 1945 that the Japanese had not even begun to stamp out Korean language use. The symbolic abomination of required Japanese use affected mostly middle- and upper-class Koreans—or those Koreans enmeshed in Japanese organizations, companies, bureaucracies, and schools. But Koreans in these institutions were already using Japanese by necessity. The language policies were a classic example of the GGK trying to do by instant fiat what their own experts had already told them would take a century or more. Even as the GGK made preparations for repressing the Korean Language Society, the totally Japanese-controlled broadcasting system was still airing Korean classes, and pronunciation purification programs on the Korean language station were silenced only in 1944.

Perhaps the most galling program was the notorious decision to change Korean names that Minami announced on February 11, 1940. The formal term for the process was *sōshi kaimei* (to change family names). The ostensible reason was reform of the Household Registration Law, for the new regulations would bring colonial practice in line with Japanese norms with regard to head of household, registration of births and deaths, and family law in general. Noting that Korean names were based on lineage *(sei)*, not family *(shi)*, as in Japan, the GGK announced that the emperor had graciously allowed his Korean subjects to bring their names into accord with the system in Japan. Within the six-month deadline established by the February order, over 3.17 million households or 75 percent of the population had registered new names.

This policy struck at the most personal and perhaps the most cherished source of Korean identity. The heartrending spectacle of family heads abandoning ancient names became a daily event at the local registry offices, and the memory has been recorded in novels, short stories, and memoirs. Richard Kim's well-known novella *Lost Names* offers a vivid account of the psychological trauma and cruelty of the campaign; more of the insensitivity and hypocrisy inherent in this preposterous policy is eloquently traced from the point of view of a Japanese protagonist in Kajiyama Toshiyuki's short story, "The Clan Records" (Richard Kim, 1998; Kajiyama, 1995). And in spite of their changed names, Koreans continued to carry identity cards that signified their ethnicity (Chōsenjin), lest the established colonial ethnic hierarchy be challenged.

Assimilation also had implications for Korean participation in the Japanese military. Military training had become a part of the curriculum in all colonial schools in 1934, and select Korean youth had been accepted at the Japanese Military Academy before 1937. With the opening of the Manchurian Military Academy in 1937, more opportunities were available to Koreans for participation in the military. In February 1938, the "Laws Concerning Army Special Volunteers" created a system to recruit more Koreans into the military. While the Japanese boasted that there was a "flood" of applicants, actual acceptance was circumscribed by high educational and physical requirements. After 1941 and the widening of the war, standards fell as the need for manpower rose. By 1943 general conscription was a fact. Most conscripted Koreans ended up in noncombatant roles, over 200,000 in the army and 20,000 in the imperial navy.

Between 1940 and 1945 the increasing cultural pressure to assimilate—to participate, not just to acquiesce—transformed into a full-scale mobilization of the entire population in the total war effort. In 1940 the Japanese organized the entire colony into 350,000 Neighborhood Patriotic Associations, each consisting of ten households. These were the basic units for a variety of government programs for extracting labor, forced contributions in cash or materials (precious metals, etc.), rice "donations," internal security, and rationing. The GGK organized all professions into "All Chōsen Leagues" of artists, writers, journalists, filmmakers, actors, musicians; in short, all identifiable occupational or interest groups were centrally organized. Cultural organizations sponsored patriotic contests of all sorts: song writing, short stories, art fairs, and poster art, and so forth. Famous Korean writers, intellectuals, businessmen, and the socially prominent were cajoled or forced to give patriotic speeches urging Koreans to "give the ultimate sacrifice" in prosecution of the war.

In short, the last five years of colonial rule plunged Korea into a morass of contradictions. With its cultural memory assaulted from above, its population uprooted, and the war industry booming, life for Koreans became a whirl of mobilization. They were mobilized in the name of an imperium in which they remained, at best, second-class citizens, at worst, draft labor, cannon fodder, or sexual slaves. To object or resist meant prison and disgrace for their families. Compliance among the prominent meant later denunciation as collaborators or, worse yet, assassination.

Labor Mobilization, Comfort Women: Korea's Population Hemorrhage

One of the most appalling incidences among the many Japanese cruelties during the Pacific War was the recruitment of Korean women to work in Japanese military brothels. While the exact number will probably never be known, between 100,000 and 200,000 women, mostly Korean (Chinese, Filipina, and some Western women also served in these units) were recruited either by deception or force into units euphemistically termed the "comfort corps" *(wianfu)*. These unfortunate women found themselves attached to garrisons in the far-flung Japanese military from northern China to as far away as Southeast Asia and Indonesia, where they endured servicing the sexual needs of Japanese soldiers and officers. Under such horrible conditions many of the women died. Some were disfigured and rendered infertile, and most were abandoned in their camps abroad after the war. Those who managed to return came home to lives forever altered by the experience. Because of the moral and social stigma attached to prostitution, many were unable to marry. They had to endure the unwarranted shame for having been prostitutes no matter under what circumstances, one of the uglier aspects of Korean patriarchal attitudes. Only in the late 1980s did the first few courageous survivors step forward and tell their shocking stories publicly (Choi Chungmoo 1992; Howard, 1995). These survivor stories galvanized others to come forward and eventually led to a movement that united women in Korea, Japan, China, and Southeast Asia to demand an accounting, reparations, and a formal apology from the Japanese government.[4]

The comfort women made up only a tiny fraction of the Koreans who were uprooted during the Pacific War. Hundreds of thousands of Korean men found themselves serving all over Asia in the Japanese military, but by far the greater Korean contribution to the war effort was made by ordinary Koreans mobilized to work in factories and mines in Manchuria, northern Korea, and Japan. The number of laborers who were uprooted was staggering. In what has been called a "population hemorrhage," perhaps as many as 4 million people, an astonishing 11.6 percent of the population, were living and working outside of Korea by 1944 (Cumings, 1981, p. 53). And this does not include those moved from the southern provinces to work in the industrializing north. The drainage of manpower into the Japanese army had created desperate labor shortages in Japan. To fill the gap, Koreans, particularly from the southeast Kyŏngsang provinces, were recruited to go to Japan to work in menial positions. Some of the most arduous labor duty was in the mines, where tens of thousands of Koreans labored under the most brutal conditions throughout the war. And at the end of the war, somewhere between 20,000 and 30,000 such Korean laborers in Hiroshima and Nagasaki perished in the atomic bombings.[5]

The internal and external migration of Korean labor during the war years left a bitter legacy. The urban population of Korea increased from 3 to 10 percent between 1930 and 1945. The mass movement raised the political and social consciousness of the population. When the formerly rural population of Korea was shaken up, dispersed, and then brought back together in the space of a decade, it had a politicizing effect, particularly for rural Koreans who returned to missing families, lost land, unemployment, and crowded conditions in the cities. Expectations for life chances and the perception of class differences were irrevocably altered. And beneath the accumulated psychological trauma lurked a deepening resentment of the Japanese and their Korean collaborators. Such resentments fueled major riots and instability in South Korea in the period after Liberation. Indeed, as Bruce Cumings has pointed out, the most unstable areas in South Korea after Liberation were precisely those that had the most population turnover (*Origins of the Korean War*, 1981).

In addition, the war effort had developed Korean industry in curious ways. The chemical industry in the north had become a prime source of munitions and ordnance for the Japanese army. Textile companies profited from the inexhaustible demand to fill the needs of the Japanese army. From a meager beginning, a sophisticated tool and machinery industry emerged to manufacture a host of war-related parts. Korea and Manchuria were spared Allied bombing during the war, and so the Japanese shifted the production of many industrial and manufacturing needs to these safe havens. Understandably, the war also brought opportunities to some Korean industrialists. Indeed, Korean entrepreneurs had ready networks for labor recruitment, and the wartime economy provided them additional access to the capital resources needed to expand production facilities. Those in a position to take advantage of Japanese procurement policies thus profited enormously, to the disgust of their countrymen after the war.

In summary, the last years of Japanese rule were certainly the worst of times for Korea. Society reeled under the weight of the war mobilization and political repression. With almost any act defined as a crime against the state, from linguistic scholarship to sabotage, the prisons of the colony overflowed with political prisoners. By even modest estimates millions of Koreans had been uprooted from their homes and sent to work abroad or in the northern provinces. Households buried their rice to prevent its seizure, and families sent their sons into hiding in the countryside to avoid conscription. War-related shortages made life unbearable; the state rationed dwindling food supplies, melted down personal effects for war production, and apparently even destroyed every film print it could gather—the entire creative product of the early Korean film industry—for its silver, Korean-language publications all but disappeared. As the Korean people waited impatiently for the end of the war, the increasingly bizarre demands of their Japanese overlords doubtless was a signal to some of the growing desperation of the imperial cause.

Chapter *Five*

LIBERATION, CIVIL WAR, AND DIVISION

오

IT WAS CLEAR by the spring of 1945 that the Japanese war effort was hopeless. Information came into the colony in bits and pieces from businessmen
and students returning from Japan. The Korean nationalist government in exile in
Nanking was beaming shortwave broadcasts to Korea on Allied radio from both
China and the Soviet Union; a group of radio technicians working for JDOK, the
colonial broadcasting network, were arrested for monitoring such broadcasts in
April 1945. Intelligent consumers of war news had already figured out and the
increasingly hysterical Japanese propaganda made it obvious that the end might
be near. Nobody, however, expected the sudden surrender of the Japanese on
August 15; indeed, Governor General Abe was informed by Tokyo on the plan
to surrender only on August 11. It is not certain how many Koreans—in schools,
government offices, Japanese businesses and manufacturing plants—heard the
historic broadcast of Japan's concession of defeat by Emperor Hirohito on the
morning of August 15, but by noon the streets were full of celebrating Koreans.
At long last Liberation had arrived. The once-formidable colonial state withered
away in the next few weeks as it scrambled to find some group to assume control of
the country, protect the expatriated Japanese population, liquidate its assets, and
prepare for the evacuation of Japanese citizens and government personnel from
the peninsula.

The colonial prisons emptied themselves of both common criminals and the
more numerous political resisters on August 16, and exiled nationalist groups
frantically searched for ways to return to the homeland where they would swell
the ranks of pretenders to political leadership in the power vacuum that followed
the Japanese defeat. The end of the war also meant the repatriation of millions
of Koreans from Japan, Manchuria, northern Korea, China, and even from the
custody of Allied forces in the South Pacific and Southeast Asia. This prodigious
mass of humanity—everyone from elite exiled political leaders to common laborers and former peasants—returned to a land reeling from the effects of forty years
of Japanese rule (Cumings, *Origins of the Korean War*, 1981). And in the restless
uncertainty following Liberation was a three-week interregnum in the capital
Seoul that found a nervous Governor General Abe waiting to surrender to some
representative of the victorious Allied army, whose first elements did not arrive
until September 8.

In hindsight it is easy to paint a foreboding picture of what was to come. For ordinary Koreans, however, Liberation brought joy and celebration in the streets. People could scarcely have imaged how events would unfold in the coming years. We now know that during five years following Liberation, forces were set in motion that even now continue to adversely affect the lives of all Koreans. The joint American-Russian occupation and the almost simultaneous onset of the Cold War between them anticipated the ultimate division of the peninsula. Once again, foreign power intruded onto the peninsula would complicate or prevent Korean self-determination. In combination with fractious Korean nationalist politics, US-Soviet hostility would abet the emergence of contending Korean nation-states. Ultimately a catastrophic civil war between the North and South, compounded by Cold War politics, solidified the geographic division, producing important consequences for the politics, economic development, and social life of all Koreans to the present day.

The Colonial Legacy

The Japanese colonial rule of Korea left a bitter legacy in the decades following their departure. Mobilization for total war had churned up the Korean population by sending millions away from their homes in all manner of service to the war effort: actual military service in the army and navy, factory labor in every sector of war production often concentrated in the most difficult and brutish jobs, labor service for the Japanese military, and, most heinously, service in prostitution camps for the far-flung Japanese military. It is hard to imagine the chaos as these millions made their way back to Korea. At least half of these mobilized workers were returning from extraordinary experiences abroad. Those who had not been sent out of the country began their journeys home from the factories and mines in the north to their villages and families in the densely populated south. Many returned to find the land untilled, or occupied by different tenants. Enormous numbers collected in the cities to seek casual employment or just handouts at the soup kitchens organized to feed the homeless. This huge movement of people added to the political instability of the first years after Liberation, particularly in the south.

The cumulative effect of colonial rule, particularly in its last ten years, was to heighten class conflict in Korea. In spite of the GGK's attempt to relieve rural distress, tenancy rates approached 80 percent in some counties in the Cholla provinces of the southwest. Pushed off the land by spiraling indebtedness or unable to afford rising rents, peasants had already begun migrating to cities in search of work by 1937. The mobilization of labor during the war, particularly after 1941, accelerated this movement, but it also masked the potential for class conflict as it emptied the countryside of its landless, unemployed peasants. Repatriated laborers returned to the countryside after 1945 with raised expectations that a new

Korean government might solve the land problem. Indeed, in the immediate aftermath of Liberation there was a question as to what would become of the major Japanese landholdings, both public and private. Would these lands simply fall into the hands of the large Korean landowners? After all a majority of the landlord class was Korean. Or would they be distributed more broadly? Rumors of the possibility of a land reform circulated and added tension to the already strained relations between landlords and the peasants, who considered the large landlords profiteers and collaborators in the colonial regime.

The cities were overcrowded with unemployed, rural migrants and returnees after 1945. They made up a *lumpenproletariat* available to all manner of demagogues. The prisons had disgorged political prisoners who were predominately leftists associated with illegal organizing, thought crimes, and other political agitation. Within weeks of Liberation, elements of the exiled nationalist movement in China, the Soviet Union, and the United States began to arrive; all were in search of supporters, and many began organizing their own paramilitary groups. Given contemporary South Korea's staunch anti-Communism, it is hard to imagine socialism's popularity in the 1940s Korea. But in the period after Liberation, the

Repatriated Koreans disembark Japanese transport vessel, Pusan, Korea, October 1945. Source: US Army Signal Corps.

socialists drew tremendous support from the landless, intellectuals, and factory workers. After all, it was the left that had more experience with organizing workers and tenants, and they put it to use immediately.

Japanese colonial rule also left a legacy of political factionalism. Having successfully split the nationalist movement with a divide-and-conquer strategy that had evolved with the Cultural Policy, no broad coalition of nationalists existed to assume leadership of the Korean people. The way was open for diverse factions of the nationalist movement representing the entire political spectrum. Elements of the old conservative nationalist government in exile returned from China. During the war they had reorganized a Korean Independence Party, and, with the support of the Chinese Nationalists, formed the small Korean Restoration Army. Kim Ku, a charismatic nationalist leader and a staunch anti-Communist, returned to trade on a reputation gained in terrorist attacks on Japanese officials and institutions in the 1930s. Syngman Rhee returned from the United States after a forty-year exile; unfamiliar with conditions on the ground, he nevertheless had name recognition and impeccable nationalist credentials. At the other end of the spectrum, arriving with the Soviet army in the north, was Kim Il Sung and his Manchurian guerrillas. Among Communists in Korea, Kim Il Sung was less known than the most prominent Communist, Pak Hŏnyŏng, one of the original founders of the Korean Communist Party. After Liberation he became the head of a southern branch of the party. Moderate nationalist leaders also emerged. In P'yŏngyang, Cho Mansik was working with grassroots committees that sprung up during the vacuum of power after August 15. Another important figure, Yŏ Unhyŏng (1885–1947), had already emerged as organizer of the Committee for the Preparation for Korean Independence (CPKI), a group formed in response to Governor General Abe's request for help with peace and order after surrender. Yŏ had been active in the independence movement abroad, spent time in jail in the late 1920s, and had continued his activism in Korea. He was considered a moderate leftist, having worked with groups on both sides of the ideological divide.

The history of Korean nationalism is replete with patriots, martyrs, astounding acts of selflessness, endurance of severe repression, and, in spite of Japanese repression, an enormous national cultural production. But no one leader or organization could claim credit for defeating the Japanese; Liberation had come as the incidental result of the Allied defeat of Japan. A desperate fight ensued, therefore, immediately after Liberation, among all who hoped to emerge at the head of the Korean nation. The next several years witnessed a violent struggle among the various factions and individual political leaders in Korea; it was a period of recrimination and assassination. Yŏ Unhyŏng and Kim Ku both lost their lives to assassins' bullets, and numerous leftist leaders disappeared in the brutal consolidation of Communist factions in the north.

Compounding the problem of leadership was the wholesale delegitimation of Korea's social and intellectual elite. Many writers, artists, educators, businessmen, and intellectuals—men who might have risen to positions of leadership in a post-colonial Korea—had been compromised by their cooperation with the Japanese during the war. The Japanese had cajoled, threatened, or otherwise compelled many to support the war effort by writing patriotic tracts or speaking at schools and factories where they enjoined their countrymen to make all efforts, including the ultimate sacrifice of their lives, for the imperial cause. Even those whose collaboration was less public, businessmen who profited from the war—large land-owners, and middle-class elements who had worked for the GGK or in Japanese companies—were seen to have profited from or taken advantage of their ties to the Japanese. The specter of collaboration loomed over Korea for decades after the war. Besides the publicity of the anti-National trials after 1945, charges of collaboration were cultivated, by word of mouth, rumor, innuendo, and sheer malice between political or social enemies. Whether such charges were true or not, collaboration remained a card to be played in the often vicious political and social struggles that beset Korea from the years of the joint occupation well into the era of division after 1948.[1]

The Reoccupation of Korea

The question of how to dispose of the Japanese empire had begun at the Cairo Conference in 1943. The conference established a principle of trusteeship for Japan's colonial possessions, the ultimate independence of which would be granted in the now-famous diplomatic phrase "in due course." The concept of trusteeship was reaffirmed at subsequent meetings of the Allied leaders at Yalta and Potsdam in the winter and spring of 1945. The idea of Allied trusteeship projected American power into the Pacific in a leadership role and forced a complete reevaluation of what had been America's low profile in Northeast Asia since the Japanese had first annexed Korea back in 1910. Manchuria and Korea, however, were of considerable strategic importance to the Soviet Union; it bordered Manchuria and Korea, the latter being perilously close to its only major Pacific ports. The USSR had also been more directly involved in the anti-Japanese struggles in Northeast Asia, further highlighting this asymmetry of interests.

The brutality and high casualty rate of the Pacific Island campaigns left the United States dreadfully concerned about the potential cost of life that the ultimate invasion of the Japanese home islands would incur. American war planners were, therefore, anxious to involve the Soviet Union in a joint operation in which the United States was to invade the main islands and the USSR would handle the Japanese army on the Asian mainland. To that end the United States had invited the Russians into the postwar trusteeship by conceding their occupation of Manchuria and Korea at the Yalta conference. American worries were further confirmed by the terrible loss of life in the battle of Okinawa between March and June 1945, the final, decisive battle of the Pacific War before the atom bombing of Hiroshima and Nagasaki in early August. After the Japanese signaled their intention to surrender on August 10, the American planners tried to limit Russian involvement in Korea to a joint occupation. They hastily proposed a North-South division of Korea along the 38th parallel of latitude, a line that put the Korean capital of Seoul and the bulk of the population under US control in the South. To the Americans' surprise, the Soviets accepted this arrangement even though there was nothing to stop their complete occupation of the peninsula. Soviet troops had moved into Manchuria and arrived in northeastern Korea in early August. Using the still-intact railroads they could move freely around the peninsula.

With the Russians already in Korea and appearing to acknowledge the 38th parallel as the line of division, the American command scrambled to find a unit that could be sent to Korea on short notice. The closest troops were elements of the American Tenth Army still in Okinawa recovering from the recent battle. The Tenth Army's 24th Corps, mobilized under the leadership of Gen. John Hodge, left Okinawa on September 5 and finally arrived off Inch'ŏn on September 8. Three weeks had passed since the surrender; Governor General Abe was relieved to surrender authority to US forces, but the Americans had to struggle to assert their control over the rapidly unfolding events in Seoul. Unlike the elaborate preparations that preceded the occupation of Japan, Hodge arrived in Korea with no translators, no area specialists, no background studies—fundamentally, no plan whatsoever. He assumed command over half of Korea, its largest cities, perhaps two-thirds of its population, the largest Japanese expatriate communities, and, as a consequence, the bulk of its political and economic problems. Hodge and his command had scrambled to get to Korea, spurred on by the State Department's urging that the situation there might deteriorate at any moment. They were also painfully aware that Soviet elements had moved as far south as the capital of Seoul before voluntarily withdrawing. How long the Soviets would cooperate was anyone's guess.

General Hodge was greeted by a group of relieved Japanese officials. As for his early contacts with Koreans, he faced the full spectrum of potential leaders, conservatives and radicals alike; more important, he had to decide immediately what to do about a grassroots Korean People's Republic that had emerged in the weeks before his arrival.

In the days before surrender Abe began looking for a Korean leader who might be able to organize a group to guarantee the safety of Japanese citizens after the surrender. Ultimately a moderate leftist, Yŏ Unhyŏng, agreed to accept the Japanese charge. He formed a broad coalition group, the Committee for the Preparation of Korean Independence (Chosŏn kŏnguk chunbi wiwŏnhoe) (CPKI), to begin planning for the maintenance of peace and order and for a future government. It began immediately to spread its organization throughout the country and soon branches of the CPKI sprang up and assumed control of local governments. On September 6, a representative group drawn from these branch committees met in Seoul and announced the formation of a Korean People's Republic (KPR). Thereafter, the

CPKI organs became "people's committees" *(inmin wiwŏnhoe)* that emerged at most local levels of government.[2]

Scholars still debate the true nature of the KPR, but at least in its beginning the leadership represented a rather broad spectrum of political views. Moderates like Yŏ played important roles, but right-leaning nationalists were also represented. Syngman Rhee, a staunch anti-Communist, was chosen as its chairman. The KPR issued a broad twenty-seven-point program of political and social reform. Most important among its articles were a call for land reform, a redistribution of land owned by the Japanese and traitorous collaborators, nationalization of large industries, and a new labor laws that established regulations on child labor, maximum labor hours, and a minimum wage. It also sought a universal franchise for men and women and a denial of such rights to collaborators. The KPR platform reflected long-standing demands of tenants and laborers from throughout the colonial period. Had it been instituted, it would have been quite revolutionary, given the conditions that faced Korea in 1945.

The Russian Occupation of Northern Korea

Sources for studying the Russian occupation strategies and policies are lost or still undisclosed in North Korea today, but enough is known to sketch the rough contours. The Russians, already in Korea at the surrender, decided to recognize the peoples' committees formed under the CPKI. This gave them the advantage of staying in the background at the local level while directing events at the center. The initial leadership of the committees fell to resistance leaders emerging from jails after Liberation; the Russians did not have to worry about the people's committees' politics because the committees had already begun the decolonization process in the North. They removed Japanese and their Korean collaborators from office, froze Japanese assets, and created the beginnings of a police force to keep public order. These early moves were popular, and the relatively broad political composition of the committees masked any show of direct Russian or Korean Communist leadership in the early weeks of the occupation.

With Russians in control at the center, a broad program emerged in the peoples' committees to deal with pressing economic and social demands of the people; as it turned out, however, the committees in the North followed a plan that differed dramatically from what was happening in the South. Most important, in the North a thorough land reform was carried out in February 1946. The new authorities confiscated all Japanese-held land and that of 5,000 large Korean landlords and redistributed it to the tenants. Those landlords who were not considered direct collaborators were allowed to keep a small portion of land only if they promised to farm the land themselves. This was a revolution in Korean society because it attacked the very foundation of the inequitable distribution of wealth that had supported the ruling class in Korea for centuries. In some districts peasants took direct reprisals, sometimes violently, against their landlords, but in the main, the land reform was accomplished quickly and peacefully. It certainly helped that a number of the largest landlords lived in the South and that many of the northern owners had already fled into the southern sector by the time of the reform.

A program of general economic and social reform followed. The major industries in the North were nationalized, but small firms and factories continued to operate privately. New labor laws dictated an eight-hour workday, set a minimum wage, prohibited child labor, and regulated working conditions. Laws to promote gender equality and the rights of women were also an important feature of the program. These regulations prohibited concubinage, female infanticide, and prostitution. Clearly the presence of the Soviet army encouraged the initiatives established by the committees, and the influence of the Korean Communists was also important. But it must be noted that the ultimate shape and direction of the reforms followed remarkably close to the spirit of those advocated by the Korean People's Republic, now defunct in the South. While rightist elements may have chafed under the leftward swing of the decolonization process and the reforms may have exceeded moderates' wishes, the public greeted them favorably. The reforms in general and the land reform in particular solidified mass support for the peoples' committees that by mid-1946 had come more and more under Korean Communist direction.

The United States Military Government in Korea

The policies of the Americans in the South evolved in a very different direction, given the political and social proclivities of the conservative US military authority. Fatefully, one of General Hodge's first decisions was to not recognize the authority of the peoples' committees in the South. Even before arriving, Hodge had been warned by the frightened Japanese to expect Communist subversion within the local provisional authority. By failing to recognize the people's committee, Hodge was foregoing the legitimating influence of the local Korean effort to build a basis for a future Korean government. In place of the committees Hodge established the United States Army Military Government in Korea (USAMGIK) and staffed it by returning to their government posts Japanese and Korean officials who had already been dismissed by the people's committees. USAMGIK had to abandon the use of Japanese officials almost immediately because of the public uproar that followed. Many Koreans, members of the people's committees in particular, were outraged at what amounted to a rollback of the decolonization process. After all, establishing a military authority denied Koreans the very political independence they assumed was now theirs to organize.

The process of ousting the people's committees in the Korean countryside in the South was long and painful. It took a full year to eliminate them, and it was not without major violence. Hodge turned to conservative Koreans for support and found it in the form of the Korean Democratic Party (KDP). The KDP, hastily organized the week after the American arrival, consisted of socially prominent landlords and businessmen who considered with alarm the emergence of a political organization with the socialist-sounding name of people's committees. Emboldened by the American presence in the South, the KDP intended to provide an alternative to the KPR and to protect their interests in the reorganization of governance that would follow. The two highest-ranking police officials appointed by USAMGIK, Cho P'yŏng'ok (1894–1960) (National Police) and Chang T'aeksang (Seoul Police)—among the most unpopular appointees made by the United States—were drawn from the conservative KDP; fully 80 percent of the forces they directed were composed of former members of the colonial police.

In its first year USAMGIK issued a series of social and economic reforms that fell short of Korean expectations and stood in sharp contrast to the reforms already underway in the North. Moreover, many of the new policies were slow to be realized. In spite of the decisive land reform in the North, USAMGIK delayed land reform until 1948, and then it was only a redistribution of Japanese-held land, leaving the holdings of large Korean landowners intact. The failure of land reform in the South was a major problem for USAMGIK, and it was a singular mistake for an occupying authority that was desperately in need of public support. USAMGIK issued new labor laws that limited the work week to sixty hours and provided for time-and-a-half pay for any hours over forty. A new child labor law banned employment of children under the age of fourteen. But the Americans were not enthusiastic to create laws that encouraged labor unions, groups they distrusted as hotbeds of Communist activity. In general the social and economic reform programs in the South failed to legitimize the American occupation government. Indeed, by September of 1946 ill will toward USAMGIK and dissatisfaction with the slow pace of reform boiled over into a general strike sparked by a demonstration of railroad workers in the southern port city of Pusan. The strike provoked massive demonstrations in other southern cities, and American occupation troops and Korean police spent the remainder of the fall fighting what amounted to a major insurrection.

The Formation of Separate States

Looking back over fifty years, it is possible to see the sprouts of separate states, North and South, in the first months of the joint occupation. The Soviet recognition of the people's committees and then the Korean Communist usurpation of them, the land reform, and the early progressive reform program laid the ground work for the emergence of the Korean Communist Party in the North. General Hodge's decision to abolish the people's committees and establish a separate US military government supported by landed interests and businessmen presaged the creation of something very different in the South. Like two strong magnetic forces, these original groups, each sponsored by antagonistic occupation forces, attracted to them like-minded politicians and activists. There were "push" forces operating as well. Land reform and nationalization of the economy in the North motivated the wealthy to migrate South; increasing repression of labor unions, tenant groups, and the southern Korean Communist Party in the South created a similar movement to the North.

In the first year of the occupation, however, both occupying powers labored under the theory that the occupation was temporary—bound as they were by the principle of granting full independence to Korea "in due course" that had been decided at the Allied meetings in Potsdam and Yalta in 1945. To that end the Soviets and Americans established a Joint Commission in December of 1945 to begin negotiations on how to establish a unified provisional Korean government. The trusteeship principle, however, would have had to survive the growing animosity between the United States and the USSR that transformed after 1947 into the Cold War. Moreover, Korean domestic politics divided along a hard line between the Korean Communist Party and their allies in the North and Syngman Rhee and his supporters in the South. Other potential leaders such as Cho Mansik in the North and Kim Ku and Yŏ Unhyŏng in the South were outmaneuvered. In such a climate, compromise within the Joint Commission seemed hopeless. The moderate middle, therefore, buffeted by the cynical maneuvering on the far right and left was left to hopelessly appeal to this already lame-duck commission to salvage a whole Korea. These issues were revisited at the December 1945 Moscow Conference, but the meetings barely created an agenda. The conference simply set meetings for the summer of 1946 that failed again, and by the spring of 1948 the Joint Commission was moribund. Events in the North and South, as well as the opening rift between the Soviets and Americans in global affairs, pushed the issue of a unified Korea permanently into the background.

Again in hindsight it is clear that neither the Soviets nor Americans were willing to compromise. This animosity heightened as the Soviet's tightened their grip on Eastern Europe and as Truman moved toward a new policy of global containment of Communism that would become formal US policy by mid-1947. Although this oversimplifies the position of the United States in Korea, where the State Department continued to honor the formal commitment to trusteeship into the fall of 1947, Hodge had never been committed to allowing an open coalition of Korean political groups to decide the future form of Korean governance. He continually subverted State Department orders to form a broad coalition committee to prepare for independence (Cumings, *Origins of the Korean War,* 1981). Although he personally considered Syngman Rhee to be an obdurate, narrow-minded leader, he could find no alternative who he believed could stand up to the left while unifying popular support .

In the spring of 1947 all the ingredients for a separate southern Korean government were in place. Rhee became the head of the Representative Democratic

Council, which gradually purged itself of moderate elements and became a true creature of the right. A national police force and the beginnings of what would become the Republic of Korea's military were also in place. The National Police had already been busy for a year repressing insurrections, aiding in the suppression of labor disputes, and working in tandem with paramilitary youth corps formed by rightist parties.[3] In January of 1947 USAMGIK moved closer to the creation of a separate government by establishing an Interim Korean Representative Assembly. With the Joint Commission at an impasse in the spring of 1947, the Americans asked the United Nations to form a commission, the United Nations Temporary Commission on Korea (UNTCOK), to supervise general elections that would legitimate an independent Korean government. The Russians refused entry of UNTCOK to the northern zone, but elections proceeded in the South in May 1948. The newly elected National Assembly passed a constitution, and the Republic of Korea (ROK) was formally inaugurated on August 15, 1948. On September 3, the Communists in control in the North responded in kind by declaring their own formal Korean state, the Democratic People's Republic of Korea (DPRK).

Portrait of Syngman Rhee, circa 1957. Source: ROK Ministry of Communications.

The Road to Civil War

Perhaps the Korean War began in the fall of 1948, with the formation of separate states in North and South Korea. As Bruce Cumings aptly puts it: ". . . civil wars do not start: they come. They originate in multiple causes, with blame enough to go around for everyone" (*Korea's Place*, 1997, p. 238). Factors to blame would include the enervation and factionalism of the Korean nationalist movement, the Soviets and Americans for dividing the country after Liberation, Kim Il Sung and Syngman Rhee for sweeping away the moderate elements of Korean politics with the connivance of their superpower partners, the general instability of the country after forty years of Japanese control, and the demoralizing experience of the war mobilization. War could have started at any moment after the fall of 1948. The fact that it did not was simply that neither state felt prepared to gamble its future in its first two years.

The Republic of Korea, led by its new president, Syngman Rhee, faced a number of problems in its early years. Political instability had been chronic in the South since Liberation, but it evolved into open rebellion in the guise of guerrilla insurrections by the summer of 1948. Rhee faced little opposition within his own government, and the ROK constitution granted few powers to the newly elected National Assembly with which it might curb the power of the ROK presidency. Rhee could also use a National Security Law as the legal basis for deploying his growing military and National Police against his political enemies, both large and small. For example he intimidated the National Assembly at one point by arresting thirteen members, using a vague clause in the National Security Law that prohibited "disturbing the tranquility of the nation." More dangerous for the new government was a series of rebellions and a guerrilla movement that tested the mettle of his new security forces.

The insurrection on the southern island of Cheju, South Korea's smallest province, began with demonstrations against the separate elections announced in South Korea in summer 1948. The demonstrations were suppressed, but insurgents fighting from mountain caves in the interior began a guerrilla war against the police. The ROK National Police and army suppressed the insurrection with great difficulty and brutality. The National Police organized a village-by-village encirclement campaign to root out the estimated three to four thousand insurgents, who were known as the *inmin'gun* (people's army). A year later the island was pacified but at a terrible price. Estimates of casualties differ, but over 27,000 islanders died in the fighting, fully one-seventh of the entire population, and half of the island's villages were destroyed. Years later an anthropologist studying shaman rituals and stories noted how the large numbers of deaths during the rebellion had produced an army of wandering ghosts that continued to plague the memory and mental health of the residents of this otherwise beautiful volcanic island (Kim Seung-nae, "Lamentations,"1989).

The Cheju Rebellion was the indirect cause of another uprising that began in the southern port city of Yŏsu and spread in the adjacent Cholla provinces in the fall of 1948. The immediate source of the rebellion was the mutiny of several units within a contingent of troops awaiting transport to participate in the suppression campaigns on Cheju island. They simply refused to participate and began their own rebellion, which captured and controlled large areas in the southwest before the rebellion was suppressed. Their initial success was a direct result of the sympathy and material support of local residents. Although the rebellion was suppressed, it further estranged the poor in this region from the conservative ROK and the hated National Police. Later, during the first phase of the Korean War, many in the southwest rose again to greet the North Korean People's Army as liberators.

Politics at the center of the ROK assumed patterns that would characterize South Korean political culture for the next forty years. The constitution vested enormous power in the presidency, and neither the courts or the legislative branch, the National Assembly, had the power to check presidential prerogatives. During the run-up to elections and the creation of the ROK, Rhee had, out of necessity, maintained an uneasy alliance with the KDP, the party of landed and business interests. His alliance with southern elites provided him a political base that he lacked upon his return to Korea. And for their part, Rhee's wealthy supporters in the KDP needed Rhee's influence and protection because of their collaborationist backgrounds. In the 1948 elections—elections marred by violence and the disruptive tactics of the left—no party could claim a majority. While Rhee was elected as president by a large majority in the National Assembly, his abuses of presidential power soon placed him in contention with the constitutionally weaker legislative body.

The party system in Korea became a simple affair; there was the ruling party and several opposition parties too weak, even in coalition, to affect policy. Ultimately the KDP, part of Rhee's initial base of support, coalesced with other smaller opposition parties to form the Democratic Nationalist Party (DNP), and it subsequently became a permanent opposition party. Not until the election of Kim Dae Jung in 1997 did a member of an opposition party ever accede to the presidency.[4] To the extent that Rhee tolerated debate within the National Assembly, there was at least a semblance of open dissent, but a sustained democratic discourse would have to wait until the 1980s. By 1950 Rhee had established a pattern of authoritarian rule based on his alliance with conservative social and economic elites, his large and intrusive National Police apparatus, and finally, the support of the growing ROK military. Of course, the United States supported Rhee by providing military training and advice, economic assistance, and most importantly a legitimating context for Rhee's militant anti-Communism.

In its first years the DPRK in the North began its social revolution in earnest without the civil unrest that drained the energy of the ROK in the South. Indeed, many features that would characterize North Korea's economy and society had already emerged, such as the early land reform (a prelude to the later formation of cooperatives following the Korean War) and the nationalization of industry. But in the first years the DPRK focused on consolidating control of the Korean Workers Party, building an army, and constructing a police and internal security apparatus. The result was a thorough purge of "bourgeois" elements within the party and government and the beginnings of a mass indoctrination and reeducation of the population.

Before 1948 the first northern government, the People's Interim Committee, under the leadership of Kim Il Sung, already had purged itself of its moderate membership. In particular Kim eased out the leader of the moderate Christian faction, Cho Mansik, while concurrently establishing what would become the mass party of the North, the Korean Workers Party. The northwest and P'yongyang in particular had been a Christian stronghold since the arrival of missionaries in the late nineteenth century. And Christians had been active in all aspects of social and economic life in this area, but as a group particularly hostile to the socialists, they became a target for elimination along with the petty bourgeois, landlords, and other "bad elements." The small parties that provided window dressing for a coalition government in the North between 1945 and 1948 disappeared soon after the creation of the DPRK as the ranks of the Korean Workers Party swelled to become the state's mass base.

The Korean Workers Party maintained its base in the northern peasantry. Its original recruitment policy had simply been to open its doors to all ranks of society. Peasants and the poor found succor in the party and joined in mass numbers in its early years. Even the leadership had a large percentage of people from "poor peasant" backgrounds. The party, however, found ways to include educated groups within its ranks as it anticipated its need for leadership and expertise. The party was the central organizer, along with the police, of a massive effort to reeducate the public politically. Schools, factories, businesses, government offices, and villages all served as venues for reeducation. In the early years this education took the form of socializing peasants, workers, and bureaucrats into the protocols of the meetings themselves, difficult as it was to train people to simply show up.

The DPRK created a formidable internal security apparatus in order to gather intelligence on its own population and provide the muscle for the enforcement of state directives. To that end it comprehensively organized, studied, and classified the population of the North to an extent perhaps unprecedented in modern history. It developed the means to store information on all its citizens: names, addresses, class backgrounds, party affiliation, pre-Liberation activities, political attitudes, work records, and general ratings of political reliability. In order to indoctrinate people to the correct line from above, it strove to understand every minute nuance of thought within the population—all the better to shape political education toward changing these opinions. The police placed all people with suspect political opinions under surveillance; this included remaining Christian leaders, capitalists, former landlords, officials of the old colonial government, and people with relatives in the South.

The training and expansion of an army was a priority. Kim Il Sung himself had emerged from guerrilla origins, and many among the select group that dominated the government were military men. The greatest advantage the North had in creating its army, however, was the significant participation of Koreans in the then-raging Chinese Civil War. Return of experienced troops from that conflict gave the North a tremendous advantage in building its military compared with the South. Korean units, including Kim Il Sung's guerrillas, had worked with the Chinese Communists in north China and Manchuria all during World War II. And some Korean Communists were closely associated with the highest levels of the Chinese Communist Party (CCP). Perhaps as many as 100,000 Koreans, both Manchurian Korean residents and North Koreans, fought with the Chinese People's Liberation Army (PLA) in the civil war. In 1947 Kim Il Sung sent large units to Manchuria at a critical point in the war, thus earning Chinese gratitude that would be repaid a thousand times over during the Korean War. After 1948 Korean units began trickling back to the North and with the Chinese Communist victory over the Chinese Nationalists in 1949, larger units returned as a whole. By the spring of 1950, not only did North Korea have an army, but its army was also battle-trained and tested. With the addition of modern equipment and heavy armor, it would become a formidable force.

The Korean War

For much of the post-World War II period, if people in the West knew anything at all about Korea, it was in relation to the Korean War. But any understanding of the origins of the war remained obscure, not to mention any knowledge about the country in which it was fought. It was the first of what became wars of stalemate or "limited wars" during the Cold War period—limited by necessity, given the catastrophic consequences of any broader conflict between the world's two nuclear powers. In fact, as far as we know the last serious discussion about using the atom bomb as adjunct to "conventional" warfare took place on the American side during the Korean War.[5] Moreover, the Korean War began the refinement of the euphemisms we now commonly use to obscure the reality of modern war and the effects of the terrible weapons developed in this the most warlike century in human history. The Korean War was a "police action" or a "conflict" in American news accounts. The Korean War witnessed the first extensive use of jet aircraft, mass use of napalm, and brought concepts like "wind chill, brainwashing, and surgical bombing" into our vocabulary. A total of 33,625 Americans, hundreds of thousands of Chinese and Korean (North and South) soldiers, and millions of civilians died in this brutal "police action."[6] Yet if asked to compare the Vietnam and Korean wars, few Americans nowadays would have the slightest sense of just how big a war it was.

This memory gap is stranger still, considering that the general contours of East Asian security arrangements today are still predicated on the inconclusive truce that ended the conflict in 1953 and drew a hard line between the two Koreas. The war began with a massive North Korean assault over the 38th parallel in the early dawn hours of June 25, 1950. For years a debate has raged as to who started the fighting. Some insist the invasion was premeditated and directed by the Soviet Union, another of Stalin's maneuvers to expand the socialist world. Others point more accurately to a more supportive role played by the Soviets, with Kim Il Sung taking the lead after gaining the half-hearted blessings of the Chinese and the Soviets, as well as tanks and heavy guns, in the winter and spring of 1950. There is also a conspiracy theory that insists that Syngman Rhee provoked the North Korean attack under preparation in May 1950 in order to force the United States into a larger war that would end in the conquest of the North. Whatever the precipitating event, it emerged out of the very tense military standoff along the 38th parallel that had grown into a border war of position during most of the nine months preceding the invasion. Both sides had placed their troops in defensive positions along the border; both sides had initiated attacks to refine their military advantage along the artificial line of division. And both sides had contingency plans for a larger conflict. Whatever the final conclusion about who started the war after all the archives are opened, the fact remains that the North had gained Russian material support in the form of tanks, guns, and advice and grudging Chinese acquiescence by May 1950. Their preparations completed, they pushed ahead with an all-out attack (whether provoked or by design) on June 25.

The North Korean blitzkrieg exposed the lack of preparedness and experience within the ROK military. In the months before the war, US analysts had considered the military balance of power on the peninsula to be in favor of the South, and the State Department worried Rhee might make good his threat to unilaterally invade the North and precipitate a broader conflict. The swift and decisive Northern progress, and the collapse of the Southern army, proved this calculation terribly wrong. The combination of Soviet-supplied heavy armor and battle-experienced North Korean troops proved to be unstoppable in the first weeks of the war. The North Koreans drove the ROK government and its military out of Seoul in two days. The first weeks of the war recorded disaster after disaster for the ROK troops and the few American combat troops who had arrived on short notice to help. The decision to come to the aid of the ROK was the first major test of the containment policy that became the lynchpin of American Cold War strategy to limit further spread of Communism throughout the world. The test came at a very bad time because the demobilizing US army had to scramble to find troops to dispatch to Korea, and it was uncertain how the US decision to defend South Korea would play in domestic politics.

The inexorable North Korean advance continued in mid-July as the North Korean army overran the key city of Taejŏn, capturing US Maj. Gen. William F.

Dean. Then the army forked, sending one group of troops southwest into the Cholla province while the other drove the main ROK and US forces southeast toward Korea's largest port and second largest city, Pusan. At this point the United States successfully petitioned the United Nations for a mandate to defend South Korea and roll back the invasion. The Americans won the Security Council vote because the Soviet delegate surprisingly departed the session in protest. A Soviet veto would have blocked UN action on the Korean crisis. The United States, therefore, turned the defense of South Korea into a UN "police action" that was under the command of an American general and in which 95 percent of the non-Korean, "international" UN force were US troops. The ROK army was put under UN command. Ironically, this major action by the United Nations hinged on the inadvertent mistake of a Soviet diplomat; for the rest of the Cold War, Security Council actions were stalemated by mutual vetoes of the antagonistic superpowers.

At the beginning of August the advance by the North Korean People's Army halted after it had occupied virtually all of South Korea. The US and ROK forces faced a determined and well-led fighting force that worked in league with guerrilla forces in the South. At the decisive battle in Taejŏn, 150 kilometers south of Seoul, the KPA worked with local peasants fighting on the flanks and rear of the retreating ROK and American forces. After Taejŏn the way was open to drive southeast toward Pusan. It was here that General MacArthur, leading the US First Marine Division, and ROK army, managed to organize a defense along a forty-to-fifty-mile arc known in military history as the Pusan perimeter. While the main KPA forces pushed southward along the Seoul–Pusan corridor, another North Korean army had already swept along the western coast, through the Cholla provinces, and then eastward along the south coast to threaten Pusan on its western front. From August until mid-September the North Koreans occupied South Korea and added a political front to their already effective conventional military and guerrilla conquest of the South.

During their roughly fifty-day occupation, the North Koreans attempted to replicate their northern revolution in the South, and many South Koreans joined them. Political cadres from the North began systematically to restore the disbanded people's committees in order to undo what they believed had been a reimposition of colonialism under the US occupation. Bringing their own lists of peoples' enemies, they began a purge of collaborators of all stripes. They emptied the ROK jails of political prisoners, unleashing a backlash of reprisals against the system that had incarcerated them. The North also immediately began a land reform in all occupied territories; while hastily accomplished and in the end temporary, this reform further undermined the social power structure in the South and added to the confusion and violence when the Northern forces retreated after mid-September.

The North Koreans attracted new supporters to their cause, but the occupation was short-lived, and in the confusion of this roughly fifty-day interval discipline was difficult to maintain and violence endemic. That mass killings and arrests were frequent was not surprising because the retreating ROK troops and their American advisors had committed their own atrocities. In the retreat and confusion during June and July, the desperate ROK and US troops, harassed by guerrilla and peasant irregulars, had turned on entire villages. Survivors of these atrocities rallied around the advancing KPA, urging reprisals against captured ROK forces; some were emboldened to seek out class enemies themselves. More so than during any other part of the war, the internecine terror and violence of this phase has remained obscured in the accounts that focused instead on the forward movement of troops and the main battles.[7] But for Koreans, the fateful decision of hundreds of thousands to support or not support the Northern troops remains woven into the fabric of postwar memory. This was especially so because the North Korean occupation and nascent revolution was temporary, and set off a new wave of violence when South Korean forces reoccupied the territory and began a new round of reprisals against all who might have rallied to the Northern cause. And for their part the North Koreans either killed or abducted to the North thousands of prominent South Korean politicians and intellectuals.[8] To this day entries in South Korean biographical dictionaries bare witness to this phase of the war in the death-day notation for hundreds of entries: "Birth date–1950?," "taken north *(nambuk)*, or simply "dates unknown."

The US intervention under UN auspices shifted the course of the war with a massive counterattack in late September. General MacArthur's now famous amphibious assault of the port city of Inch'ŏn on September 15 dropped an army to the rear of the North Koreans, effectively cutting their forces in two. The UN forces broke out of the Pusan perimeter to chase the collapsing North Korean army north. A month later the UN and ROK forces recaptured Seoul. With the enemy in seemingly full retreat, the idea of crossing the 38th parallel to roll back the North Koreans and perhaps reclaim the peninsula gained currency in Washington. MacArthur was eager to press the offensive and soon the UN forces drove northward, capturing P'yŏngyang, then proceeding toward the Yalu, in what became MacArthur's famous "reconnaissance in force." By late November forward units of the US Eighth Army reached the Yalu River in the northwest and ROK units captured the port city of Ch'ŏngjin in the extreme northeast.

We now know that US aerial reconnaissance had informed MacArthur that massive columns of Chinese troops had been seen moving into Korea over the preceding weeks. On November 27 reports of large-scale Chinese assaults in the rear of the US units heralded a disaster. MacArthur had allowed the Chinese to infiltrate the rear of his overextended columns and confident projections of total victory turned to reports of a "strategic withdrawal." In short, the Chinese and North Korean troops had cut up the forward elements of MacArthur's army and were chasing the UN forces pell-mell southward. By December 6 they had recaptured P'yŏngyang and by the end of December had overrun Seoul for the second time in the war.

Refugees fleeing south of Seoul. Source: SRC Peter Ruplenas, 7th Signal Corps, US Army.

Since the entry of the Chinese into the war was not a surprise to US army intelligence, why did MacArthur push to the Yalu in the face of certain danger? Scholars will debate the reasons, but it appears to boil down to MacArthur's conservative politics and his desire to reopen the war with China in the hopes of destroying the People's Republic of China (PRC) and thereby helping America's erstwhile allies, the defeated Nationalists on Taiwan, to regain control on the mainland. The Chinese entry into the Korean War created a heated debate in Washington. Policymakers considered all manner of options, including the use of nuclear weapons. But cooler heads prevailed, and World War III was averted.

Eventually the UN forces stopped and reversed the southward movement of the Chinese, recaptured Seoul, and drove the enemy northward to a line closely matching the current division between North and South Korea. For the next two and a half years, a bloody and, in retrospect, needless war of attrition ensued. This was the war chronicled in the popular antiwar film *M*A*S*H* and the long-running TV series of the same name. The war had stalemated along a line not much different from the status quo ante bellum, and the Soviets continued to avoid direct involvement.

During the stalemate the debate about rolling back the line by using nuclear weapons continued. MacArthur clamored for permission to reopen a broader

campaign against China and his flagrant insubordination forced President Truman to remove him from command. Beginning in the winter of 1951 and continuing after the start of truce negotiations in the summer, the United States mounted
a dreadful campaign of bombing against North Korea. In two years the US Air
Force destroyed every North Korean city, its industrial capacity, and its railroad
infrastructure; it leveled the major dams and hydroelectric plants and napalmed
villages suspected of harboring troops. By the end of their campaign, the US
bombers could find no meaningful targets at all and were reduced to bombing
footbridges or jettisoning their ordnance into the sea in order to land safely upon
return. The memory of this ghastly carnage remains at the heart of North Korean
enmity and distrust of the United States to this day.

The war of attrition on the front and the US bombing in the rear provided
a depressing backdrop to the deadlocked truce talks. For months the talks foundered on various issues. The final problem was how to repatriate the prisoners of
war held by each side. The United States insisted on voluntary repatriation of prisoners, meaning that North Korean prisoners would be allowed to choose either
to repatriate or to stay in the South. The North insisted that prisoners from both
sides must be repatriated to their country of origin. When the truce was finally
signed on July 27, 1953, the three years of fighting had solved nothing. The 1953
border was, with some modifications, the same as it was in June 1950. Seoul was
in shambles, having been fought through on four occasions, and the North lay in
ruins from the American bombing.

The Legacy of the Korean War

The war scarred Koreans for several generations. It tore the peninsula in two, dividing it with the heavily fortified DMZ, a two-to-three-mile swath traversing the peninsula for 120 miles from southwest to northeast. The more serious scars, however,
were psychological. Koreans have lived the last fifty years in a state of war. Because
of this the peninsula is one of the most militarized areas in the world today. The
war tore families apart and sent several million refugees from North to South. The
North Koreans' brief occupation left a guerrilla insurgency that fertilized the seeds
of distrust and discrimination against the region of South Korea where this movement was strongest, in the southwest Cholla provinces. The war polarized politics.
In the South anti-Communism became the litmus test for all in politics, the major
ideological justification for authoritarianism from above, and the reason for the
thirty-five-year intrusion of the ROK military into government.

The solidification of two separate Korean states hunkered down behind their
respective fortifications and minefields, ended any lingering hopes for creation of
an independent, unified Korean nation. And thereafter North and South Korea
embarked on very different paths of nation-building. For its part, North Korea
faced the tremendous task of rebuilding a smashed infrastructure and resuming

the construction of its vision of a socialist society. The rapid rebound of the DPRK in the next ten years was a testament to its tenacious will, determined leadership, and ability to organize its population through a centralized mass party to work hard and cleave to the will of the state. North Korea rebuilt its capital, P'yongyang, as a showcase of a worker's paradise. While doing so it began to burrow its defenses and strategic industries into Korea's ubiquitous granite hills and mountains. As they dug, the state and party, if not the general population, developed a bunker mentality, vowing never again to be vulnerable to a threat of such bombing. Fifty years later the North remains captive to this mentality and paranoid about continuing threats from without. In its mind it remains in a death struggle with its implacable foe the United States, but now, burrowed into the earth, it is threatening the world with its own nuclear weapons. From 1953 until the mid-1970s, the country had climbed the mountain of rebuilding and had created a semiflourishing socialist state and economy, but at that point its fortunes began to decline in direct proportion to its commitment to self-defense and autonomy above all else. Chapter Seven examines the development of North Korea's unique brand of socialism, turned into a solipsistic elaboration of its Juche ideology that in turn is built around an extraordinarily elaborate personality cult of the leader.

The South faced its own nightmare of poverty, a smashed economy, and the crushing demands of a population swollen by refugees and riven with political instability.[9] Korea's development until 1945 had been integrated within the Japanese yen bloc of Manchuria, Japan, and Korea. The end of the war had sundered its connections with Japan and China. The division between North and South shattered the natural economic division of labor on the peninsula itself. After the division, 80 percent of heavy industry, 76 percent of mining, and 92 percent of electricity-generating capacity lay in the North, while light manufacturing and agriculture dominated in the South. The North Koreans literally turned off the electricity in the South in 1948, but even before the Korean War the South had faced serious power shortages. Its agricultural production could not meet the food requirements of the population, and the country survived on bulk grain shipments from the United States into the 1960s. The South also inherited the remnants of a Communist insurgency. These were not auspicious beginnings for building a pluralist democracy. Chapter Six examines how the struggle to establish self-sustained economic development as well as a democratic society defined the political culture and social experience of the ROK in the coming decades.

POLITICAL AND ECONOMIC DEVELOPMENT IN SOUTH KOREA

옥

SOUTH KOREA HAD BARELY BEGUN the process of nation-building in the summer of 1950, when war threw the fledgling republic into chaos: first came the hasty evacuation of the government to Pusan, followed by the brief, but brutal North Korean occupation of 90 percent of its territory, the fight north, the second withdrawal after entry of Chinese troops, and finally stalemate along the original line of division. During the war the government necessarily ruled by emergency decrees, and there was scant room for the development of democratic institutions. After the war, the First Republic under the leadership of Syngman Rhee established patterns that formed the basis of South Korean political culture for the next thirty-five years. Established with an American-inspired constitution that stipulated three government branches, the nascent Republic now had to interpret the relationships between its administrative branch headed by the president, its National Assembly, and its judiciary. Under its strong-willed first chief executive, the presidency monopolized power by extending wartime emergency measures into the postwar era. To do this required creation of a large, intrusive police and internal security apparatus and manipulation of US military and economic aid. Until the late 1980s constitutional governance remained a façade behind which Rhee and later chief executives wielded authoritarian power in what was a barely masked dictatorship.

Leaders in power altered the constitution at various moments of crisis in order to protect or augment their authority, thereby giving birth to six separate republics.[1] Following the student revolution of 1960 the constitution was amended to reduce the power of the executive, but this experiment was short-lived. After the Military Coup of 1961, constitutional amendments were used to thwart formal political opposition, with each change blocking or substantially weakening the power of the opposition within the legal framework. Changes of the election law, a formal shift in structure from a premier to presidential system, and the latitude given the president to declare emergency powers all served at various times to preempt political opposition. A legal framework was constructed that foreclosed the possibility of a peaceful transfer of power to an electoral victor. With little hope of challenging the system, the public turned to mass protest and the politics of the streets. Thus changes at the top were accomplished not through an orderly process of constitutional transition but by unpredictable, often violent protest from below. The cycle of constitutional manipulation, building public tension, and mass protest made for considerable political instability, which dramatic economic and social change compounded. Caught between the memory of the catastrophic Korean War and a desire for better material conditions, the people in South Korea resigned themselves to authoritarian rule as the price of relative domestic peace and economic improvement well into the 1980s.

Syngman Rhee and the Politics of the First Republic

After 1953 Syngman Rhee consolidated his control by ruthlessly extending wartime emergency measures into the postwar era. At the base of his authority lay the powerful National Police and its internal security apparatus, whose power to arrest and otherwise intimidate Rhee's political opponents was legitimated by a vague and flexibly interpreted National Security Law.[2] This law, aimed principally at uprooting the remnants of Communist subversion or insurgency that had arisen during the war, provided numerous provisions for the arrest, interrogation, and imprisonment of elements in society opposed to the state. Indeed, during the war over 60,000 people had been arrested for collaborating with the North Koreans or under suspicion of being Communists. Its provisions were so notoriously vague that Rhee could arrest almost anyone by calling them Communists or persons or organizations whose activities were "deleterious of public order." The president could also declare a state of emergency, which allowed the executive to rule by fiat, providing even more latitude for the quasi-legal use of the security police. In many cases Rhee turned this power against the formal political opposition, once ordering the police to round up opposition lawmakers who had gone into hiding in order to ensure a quorum for legislation. The National Security Law also allowed Rhee to muzzle the Korean press with censorship or the outright arrest of reporters. During the 1950s the public grew to loath the abuses of the National Police, but few dared oppose this powerful force.

Syngman Rhee also built a new political party, the Liberal Party. Through a combination of intimidation and arrests of Rhee's political opponents, bribery and coercion of independents, and election fraud. In the summer of 1952 Rhee's party further amended the constitution to switch presidential elections from the National Assembly, as the constitution had originally stipulated, to a direct, popular vote. Rhee's Liberal Party gained a firm two-thirds majority in the National Assembly by 1954. This meant that Rhee could amend the constitution at will, which he proceeded to do the same year to remove the two, four-year term limit for the presidency. By the mid-1950s Rhee's power was absolute in legal terms, quite apart from his control of numerous extralegal channels of power.[3] Although Rhee was in his early eighties, he nevertheless intended to continue as president into a fourth term in 1960.

The president enjoyed enormous powers of political patronage within the

ROK political system. He appointed his cabinet and other high officials within the state bureaucracy, as well as provincial governors, mayors, and county magistrates. As a consequence, an enormous number of people became personally indebted to Rhee and amenable to his whims and orders. The poorly paid government bureaucracy itself was awash in corruption at this time; bribes and favors were necessary to pry any service, license, or approval from the government. Rhee and his cronies at the top of the government used state revenue—a significant portion of which was made up of US grant and guaranteed loans—to reward their supporters, support the government party, now called the Liberal Democratic Party, subvert the opposition, invest in private business deals, and generally insulate themselves from criticism or scrutiny from without. The rampant corruption of the Rhee years demoralized the population. As the years rolled by, the effort at rebuilding the economy and fostering economic growth lagged, burdened by government inefficiency and indecision as well as graft. Yet it was clear that some in society were doing very well, as the ruling class built mansions and lived lavishly within easy sight of the grinding poverty of those crowding into shantytowns in Seoul and the other major cities.

Statistical growth rates of the economy in the 1950s masked a number of serious problems. During that time the annual expansion of South Korea's gross national product (GNP) hovered between 4 and 5 percent, a respectable rate for any national economy. It was, however, measured from a very low baseline, so in real terms the expansion was not impressive, and most of it was generated by US capital infusions in the form of direct financial aid. Much of the early investment was in basic infrastructure and industries lacking in the South. The low level of actual production within the economy meant flat tax revenues for the government. Most government revenue even for operating expenses, as well as most capital for public investment came overwhelmingly from US economic assistance.[4] By the late 1950s, South Korea had yet to develop enough economic dynamism to create self-sustained growth and generate further investment. It remained dependent on US capital to the continual bafflement and distress of US economic advisors and US Agency for International Development (AID) officials.[5] Indeed, South Korea's stagnant economy became emblematic of the waste and futility of America's foreign aid programs in general—political capital for those in the United States who wanted to cut foreign aid to "basket cases" like South Korea.

Import substitution was the concept behind economic planning during the Rhee years. The idea was to focus investment in South Korea's internal capacity to generate the products and services it would need in the future and thus wean its economy from spending precious foreign exchange on nonproductive, consumable goods. In order for this to work, capital had to be strictly apportioned to develop strategic industries. The Rhee government, however, was undisciplined and unable to lead in the economic sphere. In addition, the massive amount of US food aid left little incentive to increase productivity in agriculture. This was a critical problem, given South Korea's booming population (see Table 6.1); without this specific US intervention, South Korea would have had to spend huge amounts of precious foreign exchange for rice imports just to feed its population. The only positive development at this time was the recovery and expansion of the textile industry, which had developed around Seoul during the colonial period. Although the war had damaged South Korea less than the North, in many substantial ways the South had further to go, because it had to compensate for what had been lost—namely, the bulk of Korea's pre-1945 industrial base and electric power-generating capacity.[6]

Economic performance was lackluster, but there were other areas of positive growth in the South. In 1948 the ROK began the process of creating a mass education system by supporting compulsory education for all through six years of primary school. This had long been a dream for Koreans, one never fulfilled during the colonial period. By 1960 South Korea's literacy rate was estimated at 70 percent, a threefold increase from 1945. More literacy meant an expanded press and public sphere, and while the press was severely controlled, more education and more news led to an increasing political consciousness in society generally.

Post-secondary education also expanded to meet a tremendous demand for college education that the pre-1945 colonial system never satisfied. The ROK created a national university system, one university for each of its eight provinces, which was centered on the old Japanese Keijō Imperial University, now renamed Seoul National University. A Presbyterian institution, Yonhui College (later Yonsei University), a private, secular institution, Posŏng College (later Korea University), and the premier women's institution Ewha College (later Ewha University) all emerged after the war to become major universities. Ultimately a hierarchy of universities came into being, with Seoul National, Yonsei, Korea, Sogang and Ewha universities forming the top tier. A number of newer, private schools were considered second tier, and finally, the poorly funded national universities in the prov-

Table 6.1 POPULATION OF NORTH AND SOUTH KOREA: 1945–2000

Year	South Korea	North Korea	Seoul
1950	20,845,771	9,471,140	648,432 (1951)
1960	24,784,140	10,391,902	2,445,402
1970	32,241,000	13,911,902	5,537,000
1980	38,124,000	17,113,626	5,433,198
1990	42,869,000	20,018,546	8,364,379
2000	47,351,083	21,647,682	10,627,790

Sources: North/South population: U.S. Census Bureau, Population Division, International Programs Center. Seoul: Seoul Metropolitan Government.

inces brought up the rear. The universities clustered in Seoul created a very dense population of politically conscious, idealistic students. By 1960 perhaps three-quarters of all college students (92,934) were concentrated there, and that number expanded geometrically in the coming decades.[7] The concentration of higher education in Seoul mirrored the overcentralization of everything in the capital. Throughout the postwar period to the present day, periodic attempts have been made to decentralize political, economic, and social power, but they have always failed. In 2002 President Rho Moo Hyun pledged to move the capital of South Korea to the more central North Ch'ungch'ŏng province, and this has engendered a fierce public debate.[8]

Western-style education had been the primary requirement for social mobility during the colonial period. College degrees became necessary for entry into the state bureaucracy and for employment in the modern sector. And the spread of education begun during the Japanese occupation accelerated after Liberation. By the end of the 1950s a basic elementary education was available to the entire population, and this, in combination with an entirely new universe of jobs in the modernizing economy, fueled a tremendous drive for college degrees. By the late 1950s the universities were producing many more graduates than there were suitable jobs for them, a problem that has periodically plagued South Korea to the present day.

The Student Revolution of April 1960

The presidential election in March 1960 became the epicenter of a national upheaval in April that destroyed the First Republic and ended the long tenure of President Syngman Rhee. Rhee's electoral support had waned in his third term, and there was considerable expectation that he would not survive the 1960 elections. However, the untimely death of Rhee's opponent, Cho P'yŏng'ok, three months before the election helped Rhee in spite of his growing unpopularity. Nevertheless, against everyone's expectations, Rhee and his party won in a major landslide. Reports of massive election fraud galvanized public protests led by university and high school students in Seoul. The demonstrations soon spread throughout the country. The National Police responded violently, and there were a number of deaths and injuries in the riots. At the height of the demonstrations a dead student was pulled from Masan harbor with a tear gas canister embedded in one eye, setting off a general public outcry over police violence. With the bloody suppression on April 19 of the largest student demonstration yet, the public, led by university professors, came into the streets. Although the government declared martial law and was intent on suppressing dissent, the situation had escalated beyond control. The ROK army refused to intervene, and, under heavy US pressure, Rhee resigned his presidency on April 26, 1960. Now eighty-five, Rhee left Korea for exile in Hawai'i, where he died in 1965.

The National Assembly elected Foreign Minister Hŏ Chŏng to head a caretaker government and charged him to organize a constitutional revision in anticipation of new elections. The National Assembly's amendments to the constitution altered the ROK from a presidential to a parliamentary system of government. This placed more power into the House of Representatives, for it would now elect the premier, the head of the executive branch. The revised constitution also provided for a ceremonial president, who would be elected by the upper house. The new system restored limited local autonomy by reinstituting elections of mayors and provincial governors. And finally, it provided for unrestricted freedom of speech and press, which led to a burgeoning of newspapers and periodicals. Chang Myŏn, head of a new faction of the opposition Democratic Party, emerged as the new premier, and with the inauguration of Yun Posun as president in August 1960, the Second Republic was born.

This transformation of governance was clearly a response to public desire for more freedom and elimination of the arbitrary presidential powers that had characterized the First Republic. The new government indicted a number of former officials for corruption and malfeasance, and it curbed the feared National Police. It was unable, however, to capitalize on its early mandate. The Democratic Party was riven by factions, had little practical experience in governing, and merely shuffled the cabinet in response to its own internal political problems. Meanwhile, emboldened by their successes in the streets, student organizations and labor groups continued to mount pressure for more radical reforms. The long-repressed

Students commandeer truck during April 1960 anti-government demonstrations. Source: Photo by former Associated Press reporter Kim Chonkil.

left wing emerged prominently in the public debates of 1960 and 1961. The new National School Teachers' Union, formed in May 1960 with 18,678 members, added its voice to the clamor for reform. Labor unions and student organizations put forth a number of what they termed "revolutionary" demands to punish former government officials, pro-Rhee politicians, school administrators and professors, and those who had committed crimes against students in March and April 1960. At Seoul National University a new student organization, the Student League for National Unification, proposed immediate reunification talks with their counterparts in the North. Other demands by the left included withdrawal of all foreign troops, political, economic, and cultural exchanges between North and South Korea, and the "permanent" political neutrality of a future unified Korea.

Premier Chang was caught between his own divided party, the growing leftist demand for more radical reforms, and conservative anti-Communist organizations, including his own military, that demanded the restoration of public order. As the first year of his premiership wore on, the feeling grew in the ranks of the ROK military, itself in the throes of reform, that the government was not in control of the streets or of a widening and increasingly radical public discourse. During the 1950s the ROK military had emerged as one of the most modern institutions in Korea, but at the end of the Rhee regime, it was still under the command of highly "politicized" generals who blocked the advancement of younger officers produced by the Korean Military Academy. A group of lieutenant colonels, all graduates of the academy's eighth class (1949), were promoting a purification movement within the military to remove corrupt officers at the top. In addition they were increasingly alarmed by the radical drift of demonstrations and what they considered to be Communist agitation within the ranks of labor and student groups. They began by petitioning the defense minister to start restructuring and reform of the military itself; in this, they were rebuffed and even punished for acting outside of the command structure. They did not quit, however, but carried their demands to the army chief of staff in September 1960. For this, they received court-martials.

The Military Coup of May 16, 1961

By spring of 1961 what had begun as a movement to reform the army had transformed into a more ambitious plot to overturn the government itself. The coup, led by Maj. Gen. Park Chung Hee and Col. Kim Chongp'il working with about 250 other officers, was carried out in the predawn hours of May 16, 1961. They used 1,600 marines to occupy Seoul, while the bulk of the army remained in their barracks, and the coup then organized the Military Revolutionary Committee. Determining that no support would be forthcoming from the US, President Yun Posun and Military Chief of Staff Chang Toyŏng had to acquiesce to the coup. The Military Revolutionary Committee announced a six-point plan to stabilize ROK politics based on an uncompromising opposition of Communism. It further resolved to observe the United Nations Charter and maintain relations with the United States, eliminate corruption and other social evils, attack poverty, and devote the entire energies of the government to economic development, and strengthen military power.

The Military Revolution Committee transformed itself into the Supreme Council for National Reconstruction and announced itself to be the supreme governing organ of the nation. The council suspended the constitution, dissolved the National Assembly, forbade all political activities, imposed press censorship, and banned student demonstrations. It then carried out a clean-up of the bureaucracy, dismissing over 40,000 civil servants, held trials of the super-rich for "illicit accumulation" of wealth, and began rounding up gangsters and hooligans. Lastly, it created a new internal intelligence agency, the Korean Central Intelligence Agency (KCIA) under the command of Kim Chongp'il. It was charged to counter Communist influences within the state as defined by the new anti-Communism law.

The coup represented a second major course correction in Korean politics and a return to authoritarian politics at the center. It also marked the intrusion of the military into civilian governance. For the next thirty-two years generals in mufti assumed the highest posts in the ROK government. The first of these, Park Chung Hee (1917–1979), led Korea from the moment of his appointment as chair of the Supreme Council for National Reconstruction in July 1961 until his death by an assassin's bullet in October 1979. Park was a complex individual, the creation of many different experiences. Born to a poor peasant family in North Kyŏngsang province, Park attended Taegu Normal School and became a primary schoolteacher in 1937. During the war he resigned his position and completed a two-year course at the Manchurian Military Academy; thereafter he served as a second lieutenant in the Japanese Imperial Army in Manchuria. And the experience in the Japanese military influenced Park's nationalist vision and the shape of his massive mobilization campaigns at the height of his presidency. After Liberation, Park became first a captain in the Korean Constabulary and later served in the new ROK army. At the end of the Korean War, in 1953, he was a brigadier general.[9] At the time of the military coup Park was a major general in command of Logistic Base Command in Pusan.

Little was known of Park when he assumed the chairmanship of the Supreme Council. In the next few years, however, he set the tone for a new politics in the South. The United States acknowledged the Supreme Council, but with the understanding that it would quickly return governance to civilian rule. In the midst of the Council's purge of the government and its society-wide purification campaigns, Park did make plans for the transfer back to a civilian government. However, the transition to civilian rule would mean yet another wholesale revision of constitutional order. Park resigned from the military in 1963 to become the leader of his own political party, the Democratic Republican Party (DRP). Concurrently, during the period of martial law, he moved to repress every possible source of resistance to his taking control when civilian rule returned. The new KCIA cut its teeth by arresting thousands of people as suspected Communists. Bureaucrats and university professors were purged through dismissals and forced retirements, and there was an absolute ban on political activity or discussion at this time. In the meantime Park packed the cabinet and the most powerful positions in the bureaucracy with his military colleagues. After his triumph at the head of the DRP in the 1963 fall elections, he assumed unchallenged authority in a new, once again presidential, system, although US pressure forced him to preserve a cosmetically democratic system between 1963 and 1972.

Park shared Syngman Rhee's virulent anti-Communism; however, unlike Rhee he had a clear vision and plan for the economic development of the country. He believed that development was the key to moving Korean society forward, but he also thought it the necessary basis for strong national defense. Thus from the beginning Park established national defense and economic development as the twin pillars upon which all his programs rested. As his presidency evolved, Park used both ideas to justify the severe limits on political freedom. In time the dramatic reversal of South Korea's economic fortunes under Park's stewardship, from economic stagnation in the late 1950s to the era of rapid growth that began in the mid-to-late 1960s, earned a grudging acceptance for the harsh tactics his government adopted to maintain political control and public order.

Export-Led Growth and the Miracle on the Han

By the 1980s popular consciousness about Korea in the West had changed from a general sense of Korea as a poor third-world nation and frontier of the Cold War to a model of economic growth and dynamism. This change was rooted in the dramatic economic turnaround that coincided with the authoritarian rule of Park Chung Hee. Scholars of development note that late capitalist development in East Asia has been associated with the intervention and leadership of a strong state.[10] In contrast with the lack of government will to enforce economic discipline during the Rhee era, Park directly applied his authoritarianism to the task of economic development. For the most part Park and his military colleagues lacked social or economic ties to entrenched interests in the society, so they were able to move forward with state-directed economic planning without being hampered by debts to such connections. Park's economic plan was not new; the Rhee government, together with USAID officials, had written, but never implemented a plan for export-led development. The Chang Myŏn government had dusted it off but collapsed before it could be implemented. Park, however, put the plan into action in 1962 with the first of a series of Five-year Plans.[11]

The dramatic expansion of the South Korean economy over the next twenty years was breathtaking. In 1963 the estimated per capita income was about $100; this grew to $6,614 in 1990 and more than doubled to $13,980 in 2004.[12] South

Korea's dramatic rise from third-world basket case and USAID junkie to middle-class industrialized world trading power gave rise to the expression, used by both Western development economists and Korean national boosters, "Miracle on the Han," Han referring to the river that flows through Seoul. It was, however, no miracle, with its condescending implication that for Koreans to build an industrialized economy was a miraculous event. Miracle better describes the speed and breadth of the development. The mechanics of the phenomenon are now well known. South Korea's rapid growth stemmed from creating a good plan and from the country's inexpensive, disciplined labor force and its entrepreneurial talent, both of which were strengthened by certain historical and cultural factors. Furthermore, open world export markets and certain fortuitous world events helped the economic program at several crucial moments. The reorganized, authoritarian state under Park Chung Hee was able to orchestrate, sometimes with considerable coercion, the planning process and ensure that investment was channeled into effective activities so that foreign exchange earnings were not frittered away in unproductive ways. The result manifested itself in an average annual 8.2 percent increase in South Korean GNP over the two decades between 1962 and the late 1970s—a very rapid rate of growth by any measure (see Table 6.2)

Table 6.2   Macroeconomic Indicators for Republic of Korea: 1965–2000

Year	GDP (2000 $)	% Growth of GDP	Per Capita Income (2006 $)	Exports (2006 $millions)	Trade Balance (as % of GDP)
1965	3,018		1,295	251	- 7.61
1966			1,426	381	-10.10
1967	4,703		1,478	518	-10.89
1968			1,615	731	-13.02
1969	7,476		1,803	067	-12.21
1970			1,912	1,213	-10.19
1971	9,851	8.2	2,027	1,475	-10.60
1972		4.5	2,075	2,081	-4.80
1973	13,691	12.0	2,279	3,927	-3.16
1974		7.2	2,395	5,141	-11.16
1975	21,459	5.9	2,489	5,769	-8.52

(continued on next page)

Table 6.2   Macroeconomic Indicators for Republic of Korea: 1965–2000

Year	GDP (2000 $)	% Growth of GDP	Per Capita Income (2006 $)	Exports (2006 $millions)	Trade Balance (as % of GDP)
1976		10.6	2,709	8,870	-1.99
1977	37,926	10.0	2,933	11,518	- 0.84
1978	51,126	9.3	3,158	14,528	- 3.73
1979	65,512	6.8	3,321	17,433	-7.05
1980	63,834	-1.5	3,221	20,468	-7.90
1981	71,470	6.2	3,367	24,452	-5.39
1982	76,218	7.3	3,558	25,324	-2.52
1983	84,511	10.8	3,884	27,865	-1.10
1984	93,211	8.1	4,147	31,103	-0.27
1985	96,619	6.8	4,385	30,891	-0.59
1986	111,305	10.6	4,807	39,672	-5.06
1987	140,005	11.1	5,290	57,582	-7.07
1988	187,447	10.6	5,797	68,271	7.14
1989	230,447	6.7	6,129	70,976	-2.05
1990	263,776	9.2	6,614	73,735	-1.07
1991	308,184	9.4	7,169	81,154	-2.65
1992	329,886	5.9	7,521	87,718	-1.15
1993	362,136	6.1	7,911	96,069	0.39
1994	423,434	8.5	8,510	112,793	-0.74
1995	517,118	9.2	9,159	149,076	-1.09
1996	557,118	7.0	9,707	155,371	-3.47
1997	516,283	4.7	10,063	167,237	-0.60
1998	345,423	-6.9	9,306	159,466	12.86
1999	445,399	9.5	10,117	173,989	6.68
2000	511,659	8.5	10,884	208,858	3.15

Source: WDI Online: http:www.libraries.iub.edu/scripts/countResources.php?resourceId=472293

The development plan had been there, but it was not until the 1960s that the state had the ability and commitment to implement it. The plan stressed South Korea's comparative advantage in cheap, educated labor as the basis for building an export-centered economy. Using US grants and guaranteed loans for its initial capitalization, Korea was, by the 1970s, itself successfully financing its economic expansion in the private global equities market. Given the ROK's strategic importance and the deep US commitment there, US banks willingly provided huge loans (Woo, 1991). The plan projected investment in labor-intensive export industries in its early phases; then as foreign exchange earnings increased, subsequent investment would continue to expand the economy while shifting to higher value-added exports and simultaneously slowly developing capacity in strategic industries such as steel, chemicals, and so forth. In order to reduce Korea's dependence on imports, each exporting industry was expected to create excess capacity to meet domestic demand. Under the plan South Korean exports and foreign exchange earnings increased and the basis for its highly productive steel, chemical, and electronics industries was laid.

The state did not become the administrator of large state-owned industries, as was attempted in other developing economies. It took the responsibility for planning, but the initiative for creating and implementing various industries depended on private entrepreneurship. This dynamic was crucial to the success of South Korean development; the few times that the state itself did attempt to organize large-scale industrial projects—as when it created a massive tool and machinery industry in the mid-1970s—it failed. Generally speaking, "guided capitalism" succeeded in South Korea, although it was not without its problems. The emphasis on light industry created an imbalance in the economy by the 1970s, and wage differences between the successful export sector and the domestic economy began to create a stratified labor market. Moreover, income in the neglected agricultural sector stagnated, requiring heavy subsidies to support rice prices.[13]

Important to the success of South Korea's export-led development was the existence of talented entrepreneurs. A small number of Korean entrepreneurs during the colonial period had been involved in the creation of large-scale industries. Some were from landed elite families who made the transition from rents to investment in modern commerce. There was also some continuity of personnel between the business boom during the Pacific War and the recovery years following the Korean War. In the 1960s there were talented entrepreneurs willing and able to work with government incentives and take the risks associated with business start-ups. During the first two Five-year Plans, a group of businessmen emerged whose successes in the early phases of development garnered them additional capital from the state. Ultimately the enormous business combines known as the *chaebŏl* grew from the continued state patronage of successful companies like Hyundai, Samsung, Daewoo, and Lucky Goldstar (Amsden, 1989; Eun Mee Kim, 1997). The state wielded a number of controls and incentives to get private entrepreneurs to work for and within the overall economic plan. Chief among the state's carrots was its control of capital (Woo, 1991). The state provided investment capital only for projects that fit its overall plan. In addition, businessmen who successfully fulfilled export quotas continued to receive favor and were thus able to expand their operations. The state also regulated business with an elaborate system of licenses and permits that defined and limited the scope of their activity. Any change in business activity had to receive proper permits from the responsible government agency. In this way the state was able to prevent wasteful duplication of effort and assure that businesses were making efficient use of capital relative to overall planning goals. The state also lowered income taxes, provided import tariff relief for exporters, and gave other tax subsidies to businesses that succeeded in executing the state's overall economic plan. Finally, the state cultivated business leaders as partners in the grand national project of developing the Korean economy by singling out for prizes and honors those who fulfilled or exceeded development plan goals.

South Korea possessed a considerable comparative advantage in its plentiful and inexpensive labor force. The development plan exploited this labor force by investing in labor-intensive semi-finished goods that required minimal capital investment but could earn foreign exchange on the open world market. Early export industries manufactured goods such as plywood, simple rubber items, wigs, textiles, and so forth, and the earnings from these early exports were ploughed back into the economy in the form of capital investment in higher value-added processes. The state enforced labor discipline throughout the era of rapid growth; this meant suppressing labor strikes and delaying as long as possible any natural rise in wages as economic productivity rose. The state also relied heavily on public campaigns to promote austerity and frugality, to reduce personal consumption in order to squeeze out all available funds for investment in the economy's productive capacity.[14] Moreover, the labor force was not only inexpensive; it was literate and well socialized for on-the-job training. Clearly, the strong, society-wide desire for and rapid expansion of mass education in the postwar era paid enormous dividends. Another aspect of South Korean labor productivity was its capacity for hard work. By the 1970s Korean workers sustained one of the longest hourly workweeks in the world, averaging about 54 hours per week across the entire manufacturing labor force (Koo, *Korean Workers,* 2001).

Much has been also said about the cultural and historical factors that lay behind the hard work of Korea's labor force and its acceptance of relatively low wages during the period of intensive growth. Of course, the state forbade by law the organization of industry-wide labor organizations, preferring a centralized union organization controlled at the top, with separate unions by industrial sector (textiles, transportation, etc.). Horizontal and independent union activity was also illegal. But the absence of independent labor unions does not explain the whole phenomenon. Some have pointed to the continuing strong resonance of Confucian values as a reason behind worker discipline. Such values enjoin children's loyalty and obedience to parents and parents' loyalty and duty to the lineage and the ancestors writ large. Abstracting broadly to the economy, Korean companies repeatedly played upon this concept to spur worker loyalty to the company. Thus the idea of reciprocity—the employer accepts responsibility for the welfare of the worker and expects the loyalty, hard work, and even gratitude of its employees in return—was a common theme in company ideology. Moreover, while wages in the new companies leading the export charge may have remained low, they were still relatively higher than comparable jobs in the "old" economy, and working conditions in the new plants were considerably better. Labor pressure—many people chasing fewer jobs—caused workers to bear with the long hours and feverish pace in the new plants.

Another factor in the continuing hard work and rising productivity of the Korean labor force was the state's mobilization of nationalist appeals. Park Chung Hee not only promoted the ideas of loyalty and duty embedded in Confucian values, but he also appealed to Korean nationalism. Korean workers were told they were working for the greater cause of national development. This idea was also reflected in company ideology; that is, the successful owners of the great *chaebŏl* continually insisted that their activities were motivated by national purpose, not the desire for individual gain. This argument deflected Confucian disapprobation at the amassing of great wealth through commercial activity at the same time that it appealed to workers to sacrifice for the greater good (Eckert, "South Korean Bourgeoisie," 1993). The state simply ignored the astounding wealth being accumulated by the new captains of industry as it mounted national campaigns to encourage frugality and savings among the general population in order to reduce consumption and channel more capital into the development push.

The Korean economic miracle benefited considerably from external factors the economic planners could not have anticipated. Perhaps most importantly, South Korea began seriously pursuing its development project precisely when world markets were generally open. Thus, in its early phases, Korean exporters had access to the important US market at a time of considerable prosperity. At the same time, Korea was allowed to protect its own economy from imports in the first few decades of its own export boom. Not until the mid-1970s did Korean exporters begin to face resistance from American companies, who complained to US trade authorities about Korea "dumping" textiles and other imports under cost and against GATT regulations.

South Korea's participation (1965–1973) in the Vietnam War as a US ally also provided an unexpected boost to economic development. The United States paid for the equipment, wages, and housing of the two ROK army divisions participating in the war and also provided lucrative contracts to Korean overseas construction firms for road, harbor, and airport construction—a billion dollars from 1965–1970. This brought additional infusions of foreign exchange into the Bank of Korea a critical moment in the start-up phase of the development. Finally, South

Korea managed to ride out the potential disaster to its development drive posed by the drastic rises in world oil prices during the 1970s (the first OPEC oil "shock" of 1972 and again in 1979) by contracting for major construction projects in the Middle East and later selling supertankers from its new shipbuilding industry to the oil-producing states there.

Democracy on Hold: The Yushin Constitution and the Fourth Republic

Park Chung Hee's first term as ROK president (1963–1968) brought order in the streets, but this came at a price. Park severely repressed the political activities of university students, insinuating covert agents onto campuses to subvert student political organizing. Arrests of radicals and suspected Communists during these early years filled the ROK prison system. Park also wielded the new anti-Communist Law and a bolstered National Security Law (NSL) to throttle the South Korean press. Thus the Military Coup in 1961 abruptly ended a brief era of relative freedom of the press, and debate in the public sphere became increasingly circumscribed. The administration used outright censorship and intimidation to direct public discourse away from Park's abuses of free speech and other basic rights and toward national unity for defense and economic development.

Park was, however, ruling within a system that provided some restraints on his power. Although his Democratic Republican Party (DRP) enjoyed a large majority within the National Assembly and could legislate almost at will, the opposition Democratic Party began to gain electoral strength by the end of the 1960s. When Park ran for his second term as president in 1967, the formerly divided opposition unified into a new coalition party, the New Democratic Party (NDP), but it could not defeat Park or significantly reduce the ruling DRP's majority in the National Assembly. Park continued to enjoy strong support in conservative rural Korea and grudging acceptance of the new stability in the cities. In 1969, however, Park forced a constitutional change to allow him to run for a third term. This move galvanized the opposition, and in 1971 the NDP candidate, Kim Dae Jung (Kim Taejung, 1925–) narrowly missed unseating Park in the closest presidential election in ROK history. Kim garnered 45 percent of the vote, and his margin of victory in the cities was 56 percent. His electoral success established him as a major opposition leader and made him the object of intense state suspicion.

The erosion of Park's power within the Assembly and the growing threat of an opposition victory in future elections came at a time of dramatic power realignments in Asia. Park's government was shocked and completely unprepared for President Richard Nixon's overtures to China in 1971 and his almost simultaneous announcement of a gradual US troop withdrawal from Vietnam. Park saw both moves as destabilizing to ROK security arrangements in the region. To counter the perceived security threat, he announced a National Emergency Decree to strengthen national defense. This precipitated a sit-in strike in the National Assembly by the opposition party and renewed antigovernment demonstrations by university students. For their part, Park and his supporters worried that, given the fluid international situation, a change of leadership would jeopardize the economic program and national security. He resolved, therefore, to restructure the government in order to continue in power.

The restructuring amounted to an internal coup d'etat. Park declared martial law, dissolved the National Assembly, abrogated the old constitution, had a new constitution written by an Extraordinary State Council made up of his appointees, and then legitimated the new structure in a national referendum in November of 1972. The result was the promulgation of the Yushin (Yusin) or "revitalization reforms" Constitution and the birth of the Fourth Republic of the ROK.[15] In effect the Yushin Constitution created a legal dictatorship for Park. Indirect election of

Tank guards the Capitol Building at the Kwanghwa during martial law period, 1972. Photo © Norman Thorpe 1972.

the president by a 2,359-member National Conference for Unification (NCU) replaced the old direct election system. One-third of the new electoral college was to be appointed by the president, thus virtually assuring the continuation of the incumbent in office. In subsequent National Assembly Elections, Park's DRP and a new allied party called the Yujŏnghoe captured a two-thirds majority. Park had secured control of selection of the president and an overwhelming legislative majority that would rubberstamp his initiatives.

The Fourth Republic saw growing tensions within Korean society. The rapid pace of economic change had fueled a massive exodus of people from the countryside to the new cities. Labor discontent grew as business continued to hold down wages and demand long work hours. Businessmen knew that when challenged, they could count on the support of the National Police. Student activism increased, and Park's attempt to stop it through expulsion and arrests drove many underground, where antigovernment activities became institutionalized and a professional, extralegal opposition was born. The government faced persistent demands for a new constitution, and the situation grew worse with a worldwide recession in the mid-1970s. Park narrowly escaped death in 1974 when an assassin's bullets missed him only to kill his wife, the very popular Yuk Yŏng-su. While the Korean economy continued to grow, the Fourth Republic became increasingly hostile and unstable in the years after Madame Yuk's death. Park became more reclusive, and the opposition increased its demands for a broadening of human rights and an amelioration of the plight of labor. Violent demonstrations on campuses became frequent. By the tenth National Assembly elections in December 1978, the opposition outpolled the DRP, but given the skewed nature of the electoral system, it still remained out of power.

Beneath the Miracle: Social Change and Discontent

From 1965 until the late 1970s South Korea experienced very high rates of economic growth and a continuing expansion of wealth. There was, moreover, a dramatic expansion of the urban middle class, largely white-collar workers in the expanding bureaucracies of commerce and government. Workers in the new export industries also experienced relative economic mobility, for they were earning wages hardly conceivable in the 1950s. But the dynamic expansion of the economy was also made possible by the efforts of an army of very poorly paid workers toiling in small- and medium-sized factories. Particularly in the textile industry, working conditions were horrible and dangerous. Since the workers had no recourse to labor organization, employers freely exploited them, replacing recalcitrant workers at will. The urban working class was crowded into substandard housing, in many cases company dormitories. During the early years of expansion, workers were more willing to put up with the difficult conditions for a chance to leave the countryside and establish themselves in the cities. Also inhibiting protest was the fact that a large portion of the growing labor force was fresh from the countryside and inexperienced with labor organization or they were young females working limited-tenure jobs and still under the sway of patriarchal controls, whether parents or the boss. But during the 1970s the growing gap between the consuming power and lifestyle of the white-collar middle class and the low wages and miserable conditions of labor became more obvious and intolerable. And year by year labor strife increased (Koo, 2001).

Just because the deck was stacked against labor organization and the full force of the government's considerable coercive machinery was deployed against it did not mean laborers were utterly cowed or quiescent during the economic boom years. Indeed there was always worker resistance, and labor actions increased after the fall of the Rhee government. Again in the late 1960s and early 1970s wildcat strikes and sit-downs were not uncommon. In 1970 a textile worker, Chŏn T'aeil, immolated himself in the East Gate Market, site of numerous textile sweatshops, protesting the treatment of young women in the industry. As the decade went on, this individual act became a rallying point for increasingly militant labor. Indeed, the Yushin system had been born, in part, out of the government's desire to curb labor unrest. At the same time, the more socially conscious and active segments of the Christian church, such as the Urban Industrial Mission, worked hard to keep the plight of labor in the public eye (Ogle, 1990).

In 1974 workers rioted at the Hyundai Heavy Industries shipyard in Ulsan. Less privileged women workers also began to organize to resist the oppressive conditions and low wages in the textile industry. In 1976 women workers of the Dongil Textile Company, who had been locked in their dormitory during a fraudulent takeover of their union by company-sponsored male workers, broke out and staged a sit-in in the union hall. By the second day the number of women in the strike had grown to 800. When the riot police came to forcibly break up the sit-in, women workers stripped naked, temporarily immobilizing all present with this extraordinary spontaneous act. Ultimately, however, the police set upon the naked women, and the strike was brutally suppressed. The Dongil struggle continued for over a year, with the women ultimately losing control of their union, but their sacrifice publicized the plight of workers and drew sympathy for their cause throughout the country. In 1979, during the second oil shock recession, police brutality toward women workers holding a sit-in strike at the YH Trading Company further exposed the workers' horrible conditions. The YH women ended up occupying the headquarters of the opposition New Democratic Party, where the police again attacked them, injuring dozens and killing one woman (Koo, 2001, chap. 4). The Dongil Strike and YH incident galvanized the labor movement by bringing together intellectuals, religious leaders, and students to publicize the plight of women laborers. In the fall of 1979 labor unrest began to spread to the Masan Free-export Zone, an area dominated by large manufacturing plants and relatively privileged male labor. Eventually the labor strikes in turn stimulated urban protest sparked by student demonstrators in Pusan and Masan. Troubles were deepening for the Park administration.

The End of the Fourth Republic

Park Chung Hee's end came when he was assassinated by his own KCIA director, Kim Jae Kyu (Kim Chaegyu), at a private dinner on October 26, 1979. That fall the deepening economic recession and simmering political crisis had stimulated a new outbreak of labor and student demonstrations. KCIA Director Kim had been locked in a dispute with Cha Chich'ŏl, chief of Park's personal security detachment. (Cha was killed along with Park that fateful evening.) The issue was whether to use paratroopers to put down the massive demonstrations in the Masan area, which had already been placed under martial law. Kim reportedly had argued for restraint, but Park, under Cha's influence, was getting ready to use the troops. Park's death shocked a nation in turmoil. The people mourned his passing with mixed feelings; he was at once the leader who had orchestrated Korea's great economic development, but he was also the major obstacle to genuine democratic reforms. During the months after Park's death there was genuine hope that the country could bring its politics in line with the remarkable economic and social developments of the last twenty years.

Public optimism was, however, premature. The interim government under Prime Minister Choi Kyu Hah (Ch'oe Kyuha) chose to continue the Yushin system. In December a new election was organized, and the NCU, using the old Yushin machinery, chose Choi Kyu Hah to be president. Choi made early moves to signal a major change in the political system. He pledged to carry out a national referendum on a new constitution, rescinded the hated Emergency Measure Nine, and released hundreds of political prisoners, including Kim Dae Jung, who had been under house arrest since leaving prison in 1978.[16] Early in 1980 Choi restored the civil rights of Kim and 700 other former political prisoners. Progress toward a new constitution, however, stalled in the midst of complicated power struggles between the National Assembly and the administration, between the government and the opposition parties, and within each party as well. The internecine political struggles were mirrored in the streets, as opposition groups of all stripes demonstrated for a return to democratic politics.

Early in 1980 the question of whether the military would stand aside and let the political transition continue was answered in the negative. On December 12, 1979, Gen. Chun Doo Hwan, head of the Army Security Command and lead investigator into Park's assassination, along with generals Rho Tae Woo and Chŏng Hoyong, carried out a bloody internal coup that placed the entire ROK military under their control. Without giving up his military posts, Chun assumed control of the KCIA in April 1980. Chun's self-appointment touched off furious demonstrations that renewed the call for the rapid abolition of the Yushin system and the lifting of martial law. Chun responded on May 16 by extending martial law, dissolving the National Assembly, closing all colleges and universities, banning labor strikes, and prohibiting all political discussion and activity. This set the stage for Chun's final moves to assume complete control that culminated in the fall of 1980 in his election by the NCU, packed now with his representatives, as president under yet another revised constitution. All this activity had taken place in a nation under martial law. The opportunity to open the South Korean political system to true democracy was lost in the spring of 1980. In the process of Chun's brutal seizure of power, ROK troops turned on the citizens of Kwangju, the provincial capital of South Cholla, in a bloody massacre that forever tainted Chun's Fifth Republic and that ultimately led to the ascendance of the forces of democratization in the summer of 1987.

The Kwangju Massacre and the Road to Democratization

The demonstrations in the middle of May 1980 that provoked General Chun's final crackdown and later seizure of the government were nationwide. In the southwestern city of Kwangju, the hometown of longtime opposition leader Kim Dae Jung, a small demonstration of Chŏnnam National University students demanding the end to martial law and the release of Kim Dae Jung was set upon by black-bereted paratroopers who indiscriminately beat and mauled, even using bayonets, demonstrators and spectators alike. After several days of such brutality the citizenry of Kwangju responded en masse and drove the Special Forces and police out of the city in what became a full-fledged insurrection. For a week Kwangju was cordoned off and isolated from the rest of the country while a citizen's council attempted to negotiate a truce with the army. They also appealed with no success to the United States to intervene. On May 27, regular troops invaded the city to reimpose martial law. Students who had armed themselves during the insurrection with abandoned weapons were slaughtered in the fight. When it was over, hundreds were dead and thousands injured. The official death toll was set at 200, but witnesses to the tragedy claimed many more had died in the fighting.[17] Chun's willingness to use the army against his own citizens demonstrated his ruthlessness. The Kwangju massacre, however, became the rallying point for a grassroots movement that would decisively alter the course of postwar Korean politics in the summer of 1987.

An important issue that swirled around the Kwangju incident was the presumed complicity of the United States in the massacre. In 1980, while there was token international representation, the UN command was comprised of the US Eighth Army, and the ROK Army under the command of a US general. It was assumed that the movement of ROK Special Forces to Kwangju was only possible through a complex system of orders within the UN forces under American control. Thus the public believed that any movement of regular ROK army units to Kwangju, and their subsequent participation in the events there, had been at

Students collect guns at citizens' rally May 1980. Photo © Norman Thorpe 1980.

least passively permitted by the UN commander. To this day the United States denies that it approved of any such troop movement by arguing that the ROK Army had freedom of movement within the structure of the UN command. Such legalistic explanations, however, of the difference between American command and the operational freedom of the ROK army to move its troops at will fell on deaf ears. The lack of any apology or statement of responsibility seemed proof of US complicity.

Chun's Fifth Republic followed the pattern of the 1961 military coup. He created a new party, the Democratic Justice Party (DJP). This party became his political base because the proportional electoral system allowed him to control the National Assembly with the votes of only one-third of the electorate. He packed the government with his supporters, mostly members of his Korean Military Academy class, the eleventh. He denounced government corruption, purged the bureaucracy, and announced his intention to be a one-term president (seven years). Unlike Park, however, Chun did not have the legitimacy of being the architect of economic development, nor did his personal behavior engender popular

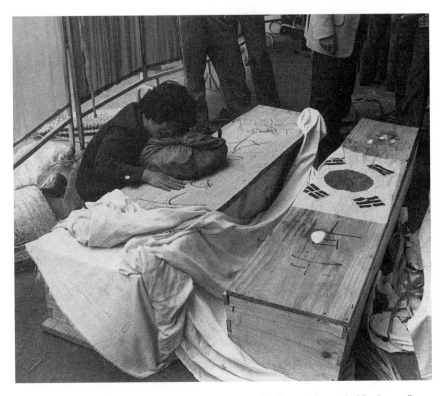

Woman grieves at the Kwangju morgue, May 1980. Draped coffin at right marked "unknown."
Photo © Norman Thorpe 1980.

respect. Far from the ascetic aura of Park, Chun enjoyed the regal trappings of the presidency, and his wife's family was viewed as corrupt and grasping. Of course, he was viewed as a usurper and responsible for the Kwangju massacre as well. He tried to compensate for his lack of legitimacy by allowing opposition parties more power, and he rescinded the ban on political activities of a number of opposition politicians, this, however, did not include Kim Dae Jung. Finally, Chun announced a number of new social policies; he ended the requirement for military-style uniforms and short haircuts for middle- and high-school students, and he also lifted the nightly curfew that had been in operation since the Korean War.

Chun never gained acceptance for his rule; try as he might, he was unable to distinguish his Fifth Republic from the Park's Yushin system. He had climbed to power on the deaths of soldiers in the December 12 internal coup, and he could never wash the blood of the Kwangju massacre from his hands. His government refused to accept responsibility for Kwangju and continued to charge that the insurrection had been a Communist plot. More importantly, however, Chun's hold on power was ultimately challenged by the massive socioeconomic changes that had transformed South Korea over the preceding twenty-five years. These changes were responsible for the challenge to the Yushin system after Park's assassination, and no amount of physical repression could put the genie back in the bottle. Chun tried in vain to augment the power of his coercive apparatus by adding tens of thousands of young conscripts trained in riot control to the National Police. In spite of their continual presence in the cities, he was unable to quell the swelling opposition and vocal street demonstrations that focused on the evils of his regime and demanded an end to the Yushin system and the continuing suppression of civil liberties and labor organization.

The nature of political opposition had transformed in the 1970s, and after the Kwangju massacre the student movement was pushed to the left, becoming more radical and uncompromising. The Yushin years also had created a large cadre of permanent ex-student organizers among those who had been expelled or jailed during the Park years. A widespread conviction of American complicity in the Kwangju massacre also turned students and other segments of the population against the United States. This added anti-Americanism to the complex mix of leftist, nationalist, and anti-Chun sentiments that expanded the public resistance to his rule. Liberal democracy was no longer the simple goal of the student movement. The issue became the legitimacy of the government itself—in the students' parlance, a government led by a usurper and supported by American neocolonialist power. Students also attacked the structural issues that were embedded in the original division of the country, once again bringing up the issue of reunification.

Another change in the nature of the student activism was a new interest in national identity. Students began to question how the rapid economic development and urbanization of Korea had distanced the society from its original cultural roots. This interest translated into what is now referred to as the Minjung movement, *minjung* meaning "the people" or "the masses." Students began to study folk traditions and organized summer programs to connect with people in the countryside. Here, it was thought, lay the authentic repository of Korean national identity. Farmers' music troops, masked dance clubs, drumming corps, and *p'ansori* became popular on campus. And this study of the folk was translated into the politics of the moment. Students augmented their demonstrations with creative uses of Korean folk rituals drawn from shamanism and appropriated traditional masked dance drama in order to turn its satirical force against what the students believed were the "false" national credentials of the government (Wells, *South Korea's Minjung Movement*, 1995).

By the mid-1980s student organizers were successfully beginning to create connections to a long-smoldering labor movement in Korea. Wildcat strikes and louder calls for a reformed labor law emanated from organizing workers from the myriad textile sweatshops. And these demands were seconded by increased unrest within the huge labor force of the giant *chebŏls*.

By 1986 these forces began to combine in ways that prevented their selective repression by the government. Moreover, the collapse of the long dictatorial rule of Ferdinand Marcos in the Philippines, which had been brought about by enormous public demonstrations, created a sensation in Korea. Ironically, the impending Summer Olympics of 1988 in Seoul also played a key role in bringing the opposition forces together. Korea had been awarded the Olympic venue early in Chun's rule, and the ROK had planned to use the 1988 Olympics as a stage from which to tout Korea's arrival on the world stage as a transformed industrialized nation. Preparations that included the construction of new subways, freeways, airport facilities, and other huge civic projects had disrupted life in Seoul for years. Now the increasing size and belligerence of the demonstrations threatened the successful staging of this coming-out party. Chun deflected the raised tensions in 1986 by acceding to discussions on constitutional revision in preparation for the election of his successor in 1988. But in April 1987, he reversed course and cancelled the talks. Two months later he anointed his colleague, Rho Tae Woo, head of the DJP and candidate for the fall presidential elections. These moves precipitated an explosion of protest.

The summer of 1987 witnessed the worst street fighting since the demonstrations of 1979–1980 following the assassination of President Park. As usual, students were in the lead, but as the situation worsened, it was clear that more and more ordinary citizens were joining in the fight. By June the demonstrations were pulling hundreds of thousands of people into the streets, and the National Police were being overwhelmed. Moreover, the demonstrations had spread to every city in South Korea and were drawing unprecedented numbers of people for what had usually been smaller secondary actions in the provinces. Unlike the situation in 1980, the United States did intercede; it sent Assistant Secretary of State for East

Asian Affairs Gaston Seigur to remonstrate with the Chun government, warning him of the dire consequences in ROK-US relations if he used military force to subdue the demonstrations. The combination of citizen participation, the lack of US support, and the sheer size of the demonstrations compelled the government to back down. On June 29, Chun's handpicked successor, Rho Tae Woo, unilaterally issued a "Declaration of Democratization and Reforms" (Eight Point Declaration) that promised a new election law, press freedoms, local elections of mayors and governors, restoration of civil rights for Kim Dae Jung and other political prisoners, and bold new "social reforms."[18] Two days later Chun accepted the proposal and the crisis passed. At long last and by the sheer force and breadth of public demand, a South Korean authoritarian regime had been forced to accept terms for a peaceful transition toward a new, more open pluralist democracy. The long struggle to democratize Korea had apparently ended in victory.

Chapter Seven

GOING IT ALONE
The DPRK 1953–Present

A NOW-FAMOUS SATELLITE PICTURE, published in February 2002 in the *New York Times*, shows a bird's-eye view of the Korean peninsula at night. The southern half is ablaze with light, its cities and highways easily visible, while north of the DMZ a perfect blackness outlines the landmass of the DPRK, a crisp black shadow, between the lights of the South and the China north of the Yalu River.¹ It is a stunning image of a nation in a downward economic spiral and alone in the world. Indeed, many contemporary observers of North Korea marvel that the country still exists. By all important measures of national well-being, the DPRK is a very sick society. Its economy has been stagnant or in negative growth since the mid-1990s. Its infrastructure is crumbling. Built with now outmoded Soviet technology in the 1950s, its electric grid barely functions, negating what had been a major comparative advantage for the North in the postwar period. When the power is on, less than one-half of the power produced from its many hydroelectric and coal-burning generators survives its course along the wires. The North's meager and now uncertain electric supply symbolizes the broad failure of the DPRK economy and the general decrepitude of its infrastructure.

A nation cloaked in darkness aptly describes the DPRK for at least the last two decades. North Korea was once connected by trade and at least minimal participation in the affairs of the socialist world economy, but since the collapse of this system, it has found itself alone in the world.² Even within the now-past world brotherhood of socialist states and economies, reclusive North Korea closely guarded entry into its physical space, let alone into its secretive decision-making processes. Over the years it has kept even its closest allies and benefactors, the Soviet Union and the PRC, in the dark about the workings of its society and politics. Indeed, while South Korea's insinuated itself wholeheartedly into the world system after the Korean War, the North set itself on a path that all but hermetically sealed off its borders to the outside world, thus begging for itself the old title of Hermit Kingdom that had been applied to Korea in the nineteenth century.

The very idea that North Korea survives long after the collapse of Communism sticks in the craw of triumphant, conservative Cold Warriors in the United States. By all accounts, the DPRK, with its collapsed economy and failed agricultural sector, should have disappeared along with all the other Eastern European socialist states and their Soviet mentor. Its continued presence, however, simply proves that

146

the DPRK was no satellite in the first place. Lumping North Korea together in American foreign policy with the larger problem of world Communism allowed US leaders to ignore the differences between the Soviet satellites in Eastern Europe and the unique historical context of the DPRK's genesis. Certainly, the imposition of the joint occupation after World War II created the original conditions for the flourishing of a North Korean state, but once established its claim to historical legitimacy was at least as valid as the South's, and it enjoyed the solid support of its own peasants and laboring classes. For decades the debates over Soviet involvement in the decision to attack the South and the ultimate participation of the PRC in the Korean War also masked, in the minds of Western Cold Warriors, the essential independence of the DPRK. In fact, even with Soviet aid after the war and continuing close economic ties with the PRC, the DPRK remained obdurately independent of the two socialist giants. This became even more so after the Sino-Soviet split in the early 1960s.

The DPRK's survival also baffles those that would remake the world in the service of American hegemony after the events of September 11, 2001. Reading US news accounts of the North Korean regime creates a bizarre picture. The North is characterized as irrational, demonic, and self-destructive. Its leader, Kim Jong Il, is routinely represented as crazy, unbalanced, reclusive, venal, and depraved. At one point US President George W. Bush slurred Kim as a "pigmy," arrogantly disqualifying Kim of any credibility or respect as a national leader, but such contempt can not make the North disappear. Actually in some ways the North's current fragility presents an even greater problem to its neighbors in Northeast Asia than it did as an economically more viable and bellicose presence in the 1960s and 1970s. Since the end of the Cold War, the idea that North Korea could be easily absorbed by the South, thus eliminating the problem, is now a dead letter. Moreover, solving the problems of the North's large dependent population, its crumbling infrastructure, and its technological backwardness would require enormous expenditures. Absorbing East Germany created serious economic and political dislocations within the Federal Republic that continue to this day. North Korea covers a larger territory, contains a more inert economy, and has a population equal to half that of the South; how could a South Korea less wealthy than Germany and ideologically more polarized handle such an enormous problem? And how would the PRC react to the massive refugee outflow and changing geopolitical environment that any sudden collapse of the North might cause?

Since the early 1990s, North Korea's program to develop a nuclear bomb has offered another major problem to the general cause of strategic realignment in Northeast Asia. The first nuclear crisis of 1992–1994 was averted only temporarily. Then came a decade of wrenching economic disasters, the collapse of North Korea's agriculture, and a horrible famine in the mid-1990s that left the North prostrate and, contradicting its resolute stance on economic autonomy, accepting emergency food aid. By 2002, the DPRK again startled the world with the announcement that it had continued its nuclear bomb program, precipitating another political crisis. By the beginning of the second Bush administration in 2005, the standoff with North Korea had no resolution in sight. The prospect of North Korea's membership in the nuclear club threatened the regional status quo in fundamental ways. Most notably, it challenged Japan's fifty-year commitment to pacifism; by 2004 Japan's Diet had passed a number of laws widening the acceptable areas for the use of Japan's defense forces. There have also been rumblings that Japan might join the nuclear club, an unthinkable idea only a decade ago. The very concept of a rearmed and militarily more aggressive Japan sends shudders throughout East Asia and destabilizes its relations with South Korea, China, and Taiwan.

Much of the consternation expressed by US policymakers over North Korea could be easily resolved by a better understanding of the DPRK's origins and early history. After all, North Korea did not suddenly emerge in the 1990s as an obstacle to realignment of geopolitical power relations in East Asia or as a threat to the nuclear nonproliferation regime. North Korea as it stands today, at the nexus of these important global issues, is the product of fifty years of political, economic, and social development. For a good portion of this time, from 1953 to the early 1970s, the DPRK was at least economically the equal, if not more, of a struggling South Korea. At the end of the Korean War, North Korea began to rebuild its society with Soviet technical and financial support and the helpful labor of hundreds of thousands of Chinese soldiers, the same soldiers who had saved North Korea by intervening in the war in December 1950. The nation's successful recovery from the war was followed by a rapid transformation of the economy, solidification of a totalitarian state, its own social revolution, and, finally, its immuring itself within its own ideology.

Korean Workers Party and the State

North Korea has evolved a rigorously centralized state apparatus as the principle means of implementing the policies of the Korean Workers Party (KWP). The KWP was formed in a merger of the North Korean Workers Party and South Korean Workers Party in 1949. It has since grown into an enormous institution; more than 12 percent of North Korea's entire population, perhaps as many as 3 million, are estimated currently to be members. From its beginning, the DPRK state was deeply penetrated at all levels by representatives of the KWP, for party bureaucrats held concurrent positions of leadership in both state and party bureaucracies. The higher one gazes on the organizational charts, the more one finds top party leaders occupying the most powerful government posts, a fact that makes the separation between the party and state bureaucracies meaningless at some point.

From the beginning of the DPRK, the KWP has spread out to organize the entire population. Party authority emanates downward from its core leadership, those who have risen to positions on the Political Bureau (Politburo) and its even more select Standing Committee. Below these organs stands the Central Committee of the party, the official overseer of the party bureaucracy. The published rosters of membership on the Central Committee, Politburo, and Standing Committee have been an important indicator of how the leadership has evolved over time. The party maintains committees that parallel all state administrative divisions (province, county, district), and over time it has come to create committees any place where there are a hundred party members: enterprises, factories, government offices, military units, and schools. All KWP members belong to the smallest party unit, a cell, where party organization activities are rooted in regular meetings. At the start, "good class origins" were perhaps the most important criteria for membership in the party. Since the 1970s, however, the party has stressed ideological and technical training; thus merit, competence, and above all, absolute loyalty to the leader, his Chuch'e (Juche) ideology, and the party have become the hallmarks of a good party cadre.[3]

The twin bureaucracies of KWP and state provide effective means to mobilize the entire population. Over time, the state also developed an extensive domestic security apparatus, augmenting the bureaucratic regimentation of North Korean society. Not content to involve all citizens within the interlocking organizations of the party and state, an enormous surveillance apparatus works out of the Ministry of People's Security (MPS) and the State Security Department to watch and report on citizen behavior. While the DPRK flag symbolizes the main groups in the population (workers, peasants, working intellectuals) upon which the state's ultimate authority rests, the security apparatus cuts the population into many more gradations.[4] The state maintains a political classification system that divides the population into three groups: the core class, the wavering class, and a hostile class (Oh and Hassig, 2000). Members of the KWP—poor peasants, revolutionary fighters, war veterans, workers, and soldiers—constitute the core class. The wavering class is composed of elements descended from pre-Liberation merchants, rich farmers, service workers, immigrants from South Korea, China, or Japan, and the relatives of people who went to the South after Liberation or during the Korean War. Finally, the hostile class are those whose forebears were Japanese collaborators, Buddhists, Confucian scholars, or Christians and anyone who has ever been hostile to the regime. Members of the core class are given advantageous treatment, better food rations, and other privileges. People in the wavering class are assumed to be educable and can work their way up in society as well as join the KWP. The hostile class, however, receives poor treatment and is given the least desirable housing and jobs; they are not eligible for party membership. The MPS also oversees an extensive penal system that houses as many as 200,000 people, many of them political prisoners; reports of these camps by defectors paint a picture of hideous conditions for those whose loyalty is suspect.[5] Propaganda and thought control round out North Korea's rigorous system. Constant attention is paid to

ideological matters and political education in the workplace, in mass organizations, and, of course, in party cells and government offices.

It is sufficient to say that the DPRK is one of the most intensely organized
societies in the world today. It became so because of its thorough restructuring of
society, a process that began even before the inception of the DPRK in 1948. The
North made its own revolution, and this point is often missed in the discussions
of its current malaise. There was a revolution in land policy: land belonged to
the tillers, which ultimately developed into a principle of state landholding and a
shift to cooperative farming. Industry and commerce were commandeered in the
name of the state. The revolution imposed the principle of collective life above the
individual. Almost every aspect of life is open to oversight by the state through the
party. The surrender of individual will, however, was an exchange for the establishment of broad socialist programs to which all in society were entitled. Education,
employment, and health care became the responsibility of the state. In the first
decades of DPRK rule, the state trumpeted its achievements in establishing basic
welfare for all and a leveling of access to resources for the vast majority (Armstrong, 2003). The socialist paradise described in North Korean propaganda has
roots in reality. We can quibble with what constitutes a "paradise," but compared
with the wretched conditions of the late colonial period and the horrors of the
Korean War, North Koreans were initially better off because of the revolution. This
was true particularly in the first decades of socialist construction between 1953
and the mid-1970s; the rigorous centralized organization, planning, and mobilization paid dividends in a rapid recovery and a forced march toward economic
development.

Postwar Recovery and Socialist Construction

North Korea had been devastated by over two years of US bombing. Perhaps as
much as 80 percent of its productive capacity and all its major cities lay in ruins.
In spite of this catastrophe, the North rebuilt its economy with surprising speed.
Its initial success was due to timely aid from the Soviet Union in the form of thousands of technicians and an estimated two billion rubles in direct grants. Between
1953 and 1956, it also received financial help from the PRC along with the labor
of remaining Chinese military units (Nahm, 1988). Other factors speeded the
recovery. It was less difficult to resuscitate an industrial base that had existed
before the war than to start one from scratch, and the North was able to rebuild
its electric power-generating capacity fairly quickly. Perhaps most significantly,
it commanded the loyalty of its population, ensured by the powerful controls of
a centralized mass party and a coercive state. It did not contend with the sort
of political turbulence that plagued the South. The state's ability to mobilize its
workforce and direct its labor with, at least initially, effective central planning led

to the successful jump start and early expansion of the North's industrial sector after 1956.

The period of rebuilding ended in 1956 with the classic Stalinist announcement of the first of a series of multiyear plans. Even discounting the often bogus reporting by party functionaries in command economies of filled or exceeded quotas, the early plans remained on track until the early 1970s and supported an impressive record of growth. Such assessments are by necessity relative because of the lack of reliable self-reporting or problems finding equivalent data with which to compare to other economies. Having begun nationalizing major industries by 1947, the Two-year Plan for 1949 and 1950 focused on rebuilding transportation infrastructure and food production. The plan reportedly raised industrial production by 3.4 times.[6] The first Three-year Plan (1954–1956) targeted production of basic necessities and rebuilding. It should be noted that Chuch'e, the central tenet of North Korean ideology, was announced during this planning period. Central planners then pushed heavy industry during the first Five-year Plan (1957–1961). This plan also consolidated collectivization of the agricultural sector and introduced mass-motivation campaigns such as the Chŏllima (Flying Horse) campaign and the Ch'ŏngsan-ni (agriculture) and Taean (industry) systems. The Chŏllima campaign of 1958 was no doubt influenced by the Great Leap Forward in China, but without its disastrous economic effects. The Ch'ŏngsan-ni and Taean systems were modifications to traditional command economics introduced by two of Kim Il Sung's famous "on-the-spot-guidance" visits, one to the Ch'ŏngsan-ni agricultural cooperative in 1960 and one to the Taean Electric Appliance Factory in 1961. In essence these systems directed managers to understand the needs of the people; the peoples' representative, the KWP, was to "go to the people," report back to the center, and integrate the masses' wishes into the economic and political planning process. Nominally, this engagement of "mass line" politics was probably related to the leadership's desire to overcome the bureaucratism that plagues command economies. But given the party's main job of mobilizing and indoctrinating the populace, we must wonder how much seeped up through party channels to the top (Oh and Hassig, 2000). By the end of the Five-year Plan what came to be the standard features of North Korean economic policy were in place: upholding the Chuch'e ideology of autonomy and self-reliance in all policies, a Stalinist emphasis on heavy industry first, and the use of mass-mobilization campaigns—all this with foreign technical and financial assistance lurking in the background.

The DPRK's planners followed the success of the first Five-year Plan with an even more ambitious Seven-year Plan (1961–1967). It continued the emphasis on heavy industry and aimed to roughly triple national income and industrial output. By 1967 the North Korean national income had increased by 8.6 times that of 1953 and had achieved an annual growth rate of 16.6 percent during the period. By the end of this planning period, however, it was clear that the more ambitious goals were not being met, and the plan was extended three years to 1970. One explanation for the extension is the precipitous drop in Soviet aid during this period because the North had aligned with the Chinese in the Sino-Soviet rift of the 1960s. By 1970 the North Korean economy began to show signs of strain; clearly the years of easy expansion based on central planning, worker mobilization, and foreign aid and technical assistance were over. Indeed, the proportion of foreign aid in North Korea's national revenues dropped steadily from a high of 31.4 percent in 1954 to only 1.9 percent in 1961 (Nahm, 1988, p. 390).[7] While this might be considered in line with the DPRK's insistence on autonomy and its avowed goal of economic autarky, the diminution of aid and, perhaps more importantly, foreign technology imports, clearly limited the economic expansion. Moreover, North Korea's military build-up took an increasingly larger share of the national budget, a yearly average of 24.3 percent during the period.

Over the 1970s the limits of the North Korean economic system became obvious. A Six-year Plan (1971–1976, extended to 1978) and a second Seven-year Plan (1978–1984, extended to 1986) both failed to achieve their ambitious goals. Increasingly the rhetoric of success was belied by the announcements of "adjustments" and delays in starting new planning periods. As a consequence of the first oil shock of 1973, mineral prices on the world market fell drastically and this constricted North Korea's most important source of foreign exchange earnings (iron ore, gold, magnesite, zinc, and tungsten). Caught in an income crunch, the DPRK defaulted on hundreds of millions of foreign loans, the largest of which were held by Japanese banks, which precluded any continuing access to international capital. Initially the debts were rescheduled, but by 1985 the North ceased payments to all its creditors. Classic problems endemic to command economies emerged in the 1970s: bottlenecks and inefficient distribution of materials, failure to upgrade technology, and lagging worker productivity. The state's "prestige spending" compounded this problem. It lavished enormous amounts on festivals and the construction of monuments for Kim Il Sung's sixtieth (1972) and seventieth birthdays (1982). Such spending continued even as the economy faltered in the 1980s. Rebuffed in its appeal to jointly stage the 1988 Olympics with the ROK, the North spent $4.5 billion building facilities and staging an international socialist athletic event, the Thirteenth World Festival of Youth and Students in 1989.

The initial success in industrialization between 1953 and the early 1970s was accompanied by the gradual collectivization of agriculture. After the initial land reform of 1946, farmland was reorganized first into small cooperatives in 1953–1954, then through a "mass production phase" in 1954–1956, until arriving at a so-called collectivized stage in 1958. This staged collectivization gradually increased the size of collective farms to an average of 300 households working approximately 1,225 acres; there were 3,843 such farms by 1960. In the 1970s even larger state farms were organized to continue the "rationalization" of agricultural production. Land reclamation was also an agricultural priority, as was the expansion of irrigation and increased use of insecticides and chemical fertilizers. By 1970 the DPRK trumpeted the fact that 60,000 indigenously produced tractors were working vastly expanded acreage. It is clear that at the peak of North Korea's economic success in the mid-1970s, its chronic food shortages had been eased. However, rice production at its high point of eight million tons was still insufficient for the country's needs. As we shall see later, the agricultural techniques and policies of this period led to catastrophe in the mid-1990s, when severe soil depletion, natural disasters, and chronic shortage of inputs led to the total collapse of agriculture and a disastrous famine. But as long as the state could afford to import its residual needs and was careful with rationing, a fixture in the North from the beginning, the food supply was secure if not bountiful.

North Korea's economic expansion initially exceeded that of the South, particularly in heavy industry. Even the American Central Intelligence Agency (CIA) estimated that production in the North was ahead of the South in almost every sector of the economy in this period (McCormack and Lone, 1993). Not surprisingly, the late 1960s was perhaps one of the tensest periods in North-South relations.[8] Perhaps the economic success encouraged North Korean aggressiveness and hostility toward the still economically fragile and politically volatile South. But by the 1980s the limits inherent in autarkic growth were manifest. North Korea's isolation from the world economy meant no access to foreign capital in the form of export earnings, and their default on early loans foreclosed continued borrowing. Lack of foreign exchange meant scant means for obtaining new technology, which in turn drove the economy back on its own resources and less productive processes. As its economy grew, it exceeded the limits of effective central planning. Command economics put political calculations and often wishful thinking ahead of common sense, and the system produced falsified or misleading economic information that compromised central planning. Socialist ideology also appeared to be a poor motivator for workers both in industry and on the large cooperatives and even more massive state farms. What was the effect on workers' morale after decades of shrill state exhortations to stem growing economic shortfalls and declines in productivity? Finally, while the economy was able to carry the heavy burden of tremendous military expenditures, which equaled 25 percent of GDP in the early decades, this burden retarded growth in the 1980s as the North Korean economy faltered.

The Cult of the Leader

After 1945 Kim Il Sung emerged as the single leader of the North Korean revolution, and a personality cult has been spun around him that has few equals in the twentieth century. The cult began to emerge at the time of Kim's return to Korea with the Soviet troops of occupation. In his first years back, Kim established himself as the embodiment of the Korean nation itself and his anti-Japanese struggle in Manchuria as the genesis of the Korean revolution (Armstrong, 2003, pp. 222–229). Over the next decades the cult came to attribute seemingly every aspect of life itself in North Korea to the thought and actions of Kim, who became to be known as Suryŏng (great or supreme Leader). And ultimately the cult expanded to include his son Kim Jong Il as legitimate successor to what may be described as a Kim dynasty.

While Kim Il Sung had the advantage of arriving with the Soviet forces, he was not the unchallenged leader until the mid-1960s. Before the Korean War, Kim had to maneuver among other factions within the KWP. Four main groups shared power: the domestic faction—Korean Communists from the colonial period led by Pak Hŏnyŏng; the Yenan faction—formed of Korean Communists active in China before and after the Chinese civil war; the Soviet faction; and Kim's own Manchurian guerrilla group, also known as the Kapsan faction. Using the disaster of the Korean War as a pretext, Kim purged Pak Hŏnyŏng and the domestic faction; in 1956 there was a showdown between Kim and Kim Tu-bong, leader of the Yenan faction, with the latter purged completely from power. It is generally recognized that Kim's power was consolidated by the time of the Fourth Party Congress in 1961 because at this point Kim assumed most of the top posts and his oldest colleagues from the partisan days dominated the Politburo and army. As the first Seven-year Plan ran into trouble, however, Kim selectively purged remaining alternatives to his leadership, first the Soviet faction, then disloyal members among his own followers, and finally, military and economic officials between 1967 and 1969. By 1972 and the promulgation of an amended constitution, Kim Il Sung had assumed total control of all central nodes of power. He held all the top posts in government, the KWP, and the North Korean People's Army. Thus Kim's leadership of the North, whether in collaboration with others or as unchallenged hegemon, lasted forty-nine years until his death on July 7, 1994.

The importance of Kim's long rule cannot be overstated because over this time he placed his personal stamp on every aspect of life in North Korea. The cult that was built around him surpasses in grandiosity and sheer hyperbole the well-studied cults of Stalin, Mao, and Hitler, not to mention those of less important twentieth-century dictators such as Mussolini, Tito (Yugoslavia), or Nicolae Ceausescu (Romania). Ceausescu was reported to have been deeply impressed during his visits to the North by the enormous architectural tributes to Kim.

The cult of Kim, however, did not appear overnight. Kim was born Kim Sŏng-ju to peasant parents in 1912 and spent most of his early years in Manchuria where he was ultimately expelled from school in the eighth grade, his only formal education.[9] He fell among anti-Japanese activists in his late teens and ultimately became a leader of a guerrilla band that worked in association with the Chinese Communists in Manchuria, where the Chinese Communist Party (CCP) dominated organizational activity in the 1930s. It was at this time that Kim adopted the pseudonym Kim Il Sung. Beginning in 1932, the Japanese began a series of major military campaigns (1932, 1934, and 1937) to destroy the guerrilla resistance. In response the CCP reorganized eleven separate military units then operating in Manchuria into a Northeast Anti-Japanese United Army. Kim's unit numbered between 50 and 300 men and worked within this organizational frame, although it had its own operational independence.

Korean detachments within this army carried out a desperate and ultimately losing battle against the Japanese pacification campaigns. Kim's group carried out a number of raids in Manchuria and twice conducted successful raids into Korea itself. His guerrillas existed on forced contributions from wealthy farmers, impressed peasants into his force, and had to endure the defection of leaders not only from his ranks but from those of other principally Korean units. While never a major threat to Japanese control in Manchuria or the colony itself, Kim's force was still a major problem. His successes singled him out as a special target for capture, and Korean Communist defectors were enlisted to help hunt him down. In early 1941, Kim crossed with his remaining followers into the Soviet Union, where they spent the rest of the war in training camps in the Khabarovsk area with other retreating Korean partisans. Here he married and had children. It was in such modest circumstances that Kim Jong Il was born, not on the slopes of sacred Mount Paekt'u, and certainly without the whirlwinds and thunderbolts above the crater lake at its summit as is now portrayed in contemporary paeans to the current leader.

This capsule summary of Kim's Manchurian guerrilla experience sketches the bare and verifiable facts. It is important to recognize that Kim was one of the most successful and resolute anti-Japanese fighters. He never capitulated, nor was he ever defeated. From this modest record of achievement, however, North Korean propagandists have created an incredibly elaborate history of Kim's leadership of the entire anti-Japanese resistance in Manchuria. This story, a story elaborated over the decades, also reaches back in time and establishes Kim's family—his father, uncle, wife, and children—as leaders of a continuous Korean resistance to encroachment on the sacred soil of the fatherland. The virtual deification of Kim and his family began in the 1960s and expanded over time to anticipate the dynastic succession from father to son after Kim's death in 1994. The fact that Kim arrived after Liberation with Soviet troops is long forgotten. After all the sole purpose of the narrative was to establish Kim's credentials as a resolute, successful leader in the nationalist resistance, a brilliant military tactician, and a genius ideologue, whose Chuch'e thought forms the basis of the one true idea for world revolution. This has become especially important since the collapse of the Soviet and Eastern European Communist regimes and the discrediting of their foundational ideology.

The cult seems to hinge on two important assumptions: the leader is the father of the people, and his Chuch'e idea is the organizing principle of society. Kim's position as a father of the people flows naturally out of Korea's Confucian

Monumental bronze statue of Kim Il Sung erected in celebration of the Great Leader's sixtieth birthday. Photo by Ruediger Frank.

tradition. At the apex of the great North Korean family, the leader commands the filial loyalty of his officials and the people. Filial piety combines authority with affective, reciprocal duty and loyalty. Thus loving and nurturing the family is the father's obligation, while absolute loyalty and obligation to the father is the responsibility of his children. The concept is deeply rooted in Korean society, and the evolution of Kim's leadership drew extensively from it to augment his total power within the political system. The familial bonds between the leader and the people could be seen everywhere: in the leader's affection for and devotion to Korean children ("the kings of the country"), in the fatherly advice Kim would dispense during frequent "on-the-spot-guidance" visits to factories and farms, and even in the fatherly gaze from his ubiquitous portrait, hung over infants in their nurseries, students in classrooms, and adults in offices and at all work sites. The Kim family came to embody national independence and the revolution. And finally, Kim successfully established his son as successor, thus ensuring continuity of the Great Leader's bloodline in the new leader. There is much of the Confucian "sage king" in the attributes manufactured around Kim—he is the exemplar of virtue, all-knowing, and benevolent in his interest and compassion for his subjects. Kim was obviously not the ideal passive Confucian monarch, but was drawing upon this deep reservoir of family values to intensify the power of his image and legitimate his assumption of total power at the apex of society.

Kim's extraordinary personal charisma allowed him to act the part of the all-powerful, all-seeing, all-knowing leader. His above-average height for Koreans, his robust physicality, and his obvious ease with people combined with his intense personal drive and political acuity set him apart from others. But to create such a grandiose cult and draw so much power to himself also indicates a powerful narcissism and megalomania nurtured by unique historical circumstances. By the time of Kim's *hwangap* (sixtieth birthday celebration) in 1972, the language used to describe him and his qualities approached deification. Massive celebrations and the unveiling of a colossal bronze figure of Kim in the center of P'yongyang marked this event. A decade later, with Kim in semi-retirement, his son dedicated the world's tallest stone monument, the Tower of the Chuch'e Idea, to commemorate the Great Leader's seventieth birthday. By then, the vast stage set that is P'yongyang was also gathering another layer of architectural tributes to Kim Jong Il. Such an absurd level of veneration for a mere mortal political leader can be alternately comical and repugnant to most outsiders, a parody of itself. For the twenty-two million North Koreans, however, this is deadly serious business. Their fate within this system depends entirely on total loyalty to the Great Leader—and now the Dear Leader—whose image and symbols saturate all visual space in the country.

Kim Il Sung began preparing the succession for Kim Jong Il in the early 1970s. Kim Jong Il became a member of the Politburo in 1973 and head of the Organization and Guidance Department (Propaganda and Surveillance). Soon he was being referred to as the "party center," and ideological tracts began to appear under his name that established him as a major interpreter of Chuch'e. During the 1970s Kim rose in the party hierarchy as his father's older comrades died or were pushed aside. By the Sixth Congress of the KWP in October 1980, Kim Jong Il was listed as number two in the eighteen-member party Secretariat, number four on the five-member Standing Committee of the Politburo, and number three on the ten-member Military Commission. Placing people loyal to him in key positions as he rose in power, Kim Jong Il, it is assumed, was the day-to-day manager of the country by the mid-1980s. The younger Kim does not have his father's physical stature, and certainly none of the charisma. His relative youth and lack of military service made gaining control of the army his most difficult task. By 1991, however, he had become "Marshall" and Supreme Commander of the People's Army.

With succession assured, father and son were joined in the cult of the leader. The honorific Suryŏng, Great Leader, was reserved for Kim Il Sung and the younger Kim was given the curious sobriquet Dear Leader (Chinae hanŭn chidoja). After his ascension, the cult made efforts to paint the son with genius-like qualities equal to those of his father.[10] North Korean propaganda incessantly portrays the seamless interaction between the Great Leader and his genius son. A propaganda film on the construction of the great Nampo Barrage provides a vivid example. The plot and characterizations of the film may be paraphrased as follows: Kim Il Sung, from the deck of a cruiser, traces with outstretched arms the line of what will be a great wall across the estuary of the Taedong River. The Great Leader's lieutenants are astounded by the acuity of this brilliant inspiration—the dam will simultaneously in one great project provide energy by harnessing the tides and reclaim land from the sea to boost agricultural production. The People's Army (surrogates for the North Korean people) proceed to begin the project with unbounded enthusiasm and indomitable will. But at a crucial moment a design problem blocks completion of the great dam. Kim Jong Il enters the picture. With a flash of prescient insight, Kim the younger provides the People's Army with specific, detailed technical advice that overcomes the problem. The People's Army redoubles its efforts and completes the project ahead of schedule.[11] The father's inspiration and the son's technical prowess complete a metaphor for the revolution itself. The film also neatly recapitulates the changing of the guard, with the new generation bringing new skills and technical knowledge to advance the revolution and complete the creation of a workers' paradise.

The "Great Chuch'e Idea"

The North's successful quasi-Stalinist economic development did not mean that North Korea adopted the particular blend of Marxism-Leninism developed under Stalin in the 1930s. On the contrary, if the North's ideology resembled any socialist experiment, it was closer to the Chinese model. In retrospect, it is now clear that

North Korea actually developed an independent ideological line from the beginning. Perhaps because of its early close association with the USSR and the PRC, the North continued to parrot a line of Marxism-Leninism, but from Kim Il Sung's first formal elaboration of Chuch'e thought in a 1955 speech, Marxism-Leninism progressively declined as a formal category of thought in the North. In hindsight, it is difficult to see how the North's economic and social revolution had anything at all to do with Marxist antecedents. Since the collapse of the Soviet Union and its Eastern European satellites after 1989, North Korea quickly disassociated itself from Marxism altogether. Moreover, the development of Chuch'e thought in tandem with the rise of the cult of the leader has provided the North with a ready explanation for the survival of its revolution even after the collapse of the Socialist world order.

Not only do North Korean ideologues assert they have leaders such as the world has never seen before, they also have an ideology that completes their self-image as the center of a world revolution. This ideology revolves around the seminal idea of Chuch'e. Chuch'e is a Sino-Korean compound formed from Chinese characters for the words "subject" and "body." Together they adumbrate the concept of "autonomy" or "self-reliance." In its most straightforward use, Chuch'e can denote one's independence and autonomy from any external control or manipulation. Therefore, one core meaning of Chuch'e resonates in society-wide contexts to describe an autonomous, independent, and self-reliant nation. The *ch'e* in Chuch'e is the same character used in *kukch'e*, often translated as "national body" or "polity"(see below). Here it can also carry the connotation of the "national face," as in self-respect. Thus an independent and autonomous nation's face (honor) must not be besmirched or denigrated.[12] This core definition goes a long way to understanding the intense emphasis in North Korean ideology on their independence, whether in terms of their national integrity, their position earlier in the global socialist revolution, or their autarkic economic policies. The nationalist connotations of Chuch'e developed in the late nineteenth century, when it was used as an antonym of the concept of "serving the great" *(sadae)*, a term used originally to describe the interstate relationship between Korea and China during the Chosŏn period. In the twentieth century, *sadaejuŭi* (the "ism" of *sadae*) became synonymous with being subordinate to another, with being a toady. To have *sadae* consciousness means to worship the outside world while denigrating one's own culture. Chuch'e thus had come to mean an independent stance, in mind and in body, and in nationalist context it means to uphold the independence and integrity of the nation.

Chuch'e was a useful concept in creating distance with the early Soviet presence in North Korea, and later, during the time of extensive Soviet assistance in the rebuilding and first Five-year Plans, it was deployed to signal North Korean independence. The term, first elaborated by Kim Il Sung in 1955, moved to its central position during the 1960s as Kim maneuvered between his giant socialist neighbors during the Sino-Soviet split. By the 1970s Chuch'e thought had become so linked to the genius of the Great Leader that it literally became the "ism" of Kim Il Sung, as in "Kim Il Sung-ism."

In the polemical warfare between the two Koreas, the North's Chuch'e stance gave it an advantage over the South, especially in the first decades of division. The South was an economic dependent in the 1950s, and until the mid-1960s it relied heavily on American military protection. Although the North was also relatively dependent on the PRC and USSR in the early years, foreign troops withdrew after the Korean War, leaving the North to defend itself. To the North Koreans, the continuing presence of the US Eighth Army in the South has been proof of the ROK government's "slavish" dependence on outside power.[13] The Chuch'e argument continued to resonate with opposition forces in South Korea into the 1980s, since they had from the start questioned the legitimacy of the ROK government and they railed against the continuing US military presence in the South. They pointed to the contrasting stance of the North and its resolute emphasis on autonomy. Whatever the facts may have been with regard to the North's actual independence, its consistent propaganda and its emphasis on national independence reminded all South Koreans of Korea's historical humiliations at the hands of imperialist and colonial powers.

Chuch'e has become the principle behind all government policy in the North, which, of course, has significant implications for economic policy. Indeed, in keeping with a strict adherence to independence in all matters, North Korea has developed perhaps the most autarkic economy in the world. Economic achievements are touted as successes based on self-reliance, and great pains were taken to seek internal solutions to economic problems. The story of the creation of the synthetic fiber "vynalon" by North Korean scientists using indigenous raw materials (in this case limestone) became an often-repeated morality tale of technological self-reliance in state propaganda. Where indigenous capital was scarce or other inputs unobtainable inside the country, the state resorted to exhortation and mobilization of the innate creativity of the masses. Thus all problems, technical or otherwise, are solvable if the people retain a staunch consciousness of Chuch'e. Such a stance inhibits overtures to the outside world for the economic or technical assistance the North now desperately needs to solve its economic woes. With the principle of Chuch'e inviolate, the state finds itself in its own straitjacket. And as we will see below, the new policies that have created zones for foreign investment, initiatives to find foreign capital, and, most obviously, accepting foreign food aid during the 1995 famine are issues that must be justified in terms of the unitary logic of self-reliance.

At its most abstract, Chuch'e operates as a code word for North Korean identity itself. Thus holding a consciousness of Chuch'e is to have a North Korean subjectivity. Some speculate that Kim Il Sung developed the idea in reaction to the vague and virtually indefinable concept of *kokutai* (*kukch'e* in Korean) used to evoke "national essence" in Japanese ideology before 1945 (Cumings, "Corporate State," 1993). All North Koreans are enjoined to hold Chuch'e in their minds and hearts, as only in so doing will their actions be appropriate. Since Chuch'e is the leader's core inspiration, all his subjects carry the leader in their hearts when they hold fast a consciousness of Chuch'e. Just as the emperor embodied the essence *(kokutai)* of the nation in pre-World War II Japan, so does the leader, now Kim Jong Il, embody the very essential principle that guides all thought and action in North Korea today.

Falling Behind in the 1980s

By the end of the second Seven-year Plan in 1984, it was abundantly clear that the power balance on the peninsula had tipped in favor of South Korea. The meteoric rise of the ROK economy and its growing importance in world trade placed the somnolence of the DPRK economy in stark relief. While the military balance on the peninsula remained a standoff, it was increasingly obvious that North Korea was not keeping up with its dynamic southern neighbor in terms of economic and technological development. This had, of course, implications for any future reconciliation or reunification on the peninsula. As a consequence perhaps, there was a notable shift in the relations between the two Koreas. If the North Korean attempt to assassinate President Chun Doo Hwan in Rangoon in October 1983 marked a low point in relations, by the end of the decade, the two Koreas were enjoying a major "thaw" in the seemingly endless rounds of enmity and recriminations that had characterized their relations for the three decades after the Korean War.[14] President Rho Tae Woo's policy of *nord politik,* in which South Korea normalized relations with North Korea's closest allies, USSR (1990) and the PRC (1992), also fundamentally altered North-South relations. Thus by the end of the 1980s, North Korea found itself in a fundamentally different position internationally.

The international realignments that led to North Korea's increasing isolation in the world began with China's new economic policies that emerged in the wake of Deng Xiaoping's "Four Modernizations" in 1977. The Chinese abandonment of command economics led to increased diplomatic, economic, and cultural contacts with the global community. The end of Maoist isolationism brought them into formal relations with the North's sworn enemy the United States decisively complicating the North's relationship with one of their main economic and political benefactors. By 1989 and the fall of the Berlin wall, the collapse of the socialist world order that had begun with rebellion in the Baltic states several years earlier was a virtual certainty. North Korea found itself alone in its adherence to socialist economics. And South Korea's expanding economic ties with the Soviet Union were a harbinger of worse things to come. The Soviet's search for hard currency and Western technology that began during the halting economic reforms of the Gorbachev era changed the long-standing economic relationship between its old socialist trading partners. Even before the fall of the Soviet Union in 1991, the Russians had begun to demand payment in foreign exchange for its oil and other crucial exports to North Korea. With little or no foreign exchange, North Korea suddenly could not afford the strategic imports it had once relied upon and had obtained on easy terms or for barter within the old system. Thus the ending of the Cold War meant not only the loss of a fraternal community of socialist states but also full exposure of North Korea's economic weaknesses to the harsh realities of the capitalist world system.

The second Seven-year Plan ended ambiguously in 1984. While announcing the plan a great success, the government also called for a period of adjustments and delayed the start of the third Seven-year Plan until 1987. A new foreign investment law and the recognition by DPRK economic planners that increased foreign contacts would be favorable to further economic success was a part of the "adjustment" announced in 1984. As the decade wore on the gap between government announcements of triumph in the economic arena and the grim reality of dwindling food supplies, scarcity of fuel and energy, the crumbling of an outmoded infrastructure, and the absence of consumer goods became impossible to bridge. By the beginning of the 1990s it must have been increasingly difficult to listen to the doublespeak of the annual New Year's message that would laud the great successes of the preceding year and promise an even better year to come—this in the face of scarcity and deprivation. How could the people think an even better new year was in the offing? Indeed, the North Korean people must have felt like Alice in Wonderland given the total lack of correspondence between public pronouncements and the reality of life on the ground (Oh and Hassig, 2000, p. 76).

There were also changes in the North Korean stance toward contact with the global economy. While continuing to trumpet the ideological victories of Chuch'e economics in the face of contrary reality, the North quietly began to introduce new experiments into their economic orthodoxy. The previously mentioned 1984 law on foreign investment had not encouraged foreign firms to invest in the North Korean economy. Trying another tack, North Korea opened its first Foreign Trade Zone on the remote northeastern coast at Najin-Sŏnbong in 1991. This zone emulated the successful export zones established by the PRC on their southeast coast in the early 1980s. The Najin-Sŏnbong complex was established in part to take advantage of a UN-designated development area at the border confluence of Russia, the PRC, and North Korea around the Tumen River estuary. And its remoteness made it an ideal spot for experimentation because any foreign political or cultural influences that would come with investment in the zone would be far away from any North Korean population center. However, problems with poor communications and weak infrastructure discouraged investment. In 2002 another special economic zone on the PRC-DPRK border at Sinŭiju was established, but corruption and scandal within its management has hindered its growth. More hopefully, a joint ROK-DPRK investment zone was established in the precincts of the old

Koryŏ capital, Kaesŏng, only miles north of the DMZ; it is now linked to the south by a reopened railroad line.

North Korea matched its new economic experiments with a brief diplomatic opening in the late 1980s and early 1990s. Spurred in part by President Rho's *nord politik*, the North softened its normally rigid closed-door policy regarding visitors and contacts with the West. Rho's successful diplomatic offensive not only challenged the North's lack of relations with the United States, but with Japan and the major European nations as well. Normalizing relations with the United States and Japan was impossible, given the North's precondition that US troops withdraw from the peninsula and, in the case of Japan, unresolved issues of reparations for the colonial period, but informal contacts opened in the mid-1980s and increased toward the end of the decade. Groups of South Korean emigrants resident in the United States were allowed to visit their relatives in the North, and cultural and academic exchanges began. Most dramatically, however, relations with South Korea actually improved at this time. Red Cross contacts led to an exchange of family reunification visits in the late 1980s. And in 1991 the signing of a South-North Basic Agreement that acknowledged reunification to be the goal of each government created another breakthrough. This was quickly followed by a Joint Declaration of Denuclearization of the Korean Peninsula in 1992.

Nuclear Confrontation, Famine, and Summit

This seemingly hopeful period abruptly ended with a confrontation between North Korea and the United States over the North's nuclear program. In their 1992 agreement with the South, P'yongyang had signed on to an inspection regime as part of their agreement to accept International Atomic Energy Agency (IAEA) safeguards. The North had also become a signatory to the Treaty on the Nonproliferation of Nuclear Weapons. In February 1993, however, the North Koreans refused to allow special inspections by IAEA officials of two disputed nuclear sites. Having received the first censure ever from the IAEA for violating the treaty, P'yongyang was, two months later, threatening to pull out of the treaty altogether. This precipitated new discussions with the South as well as talks with the United States. The United States, as leader of the nonproliferation movement, was particularly concerned that the North would reprocess their considerable stock of spent nuclear fuel into weapons-grade plutonium. By April 1994 diplomatic efforts to coax the North back into compliance had failed, and the US administration began to discuss the destruction of the DPRK nuclear facilities by military means. This escalated tension to a point where North Korea announced it would consider the imposition of further sanctions by the international community an act of war. At the eleventh hour, in June 1994, former President Jimmy Carter visited the North and achieved a breakthrough by getting P'yongyang to agree to talks with the United States in Geneva scheduled for July 8, 1994. However, the sudden death of Kim Il Sung on

July 8 caused the cancellation of the Geneva talks as well as a planned North-South summit. The Geneva talks were rescheduled, and an agreement was formalized when North Korea and the United States signed a protocol of understanding, the Agreed Framework, in Geneva in October 1994.

The signing of the Agreed Framework began an unprecedented period of engagement between the United States and North Korea. In exchange for the North's freezing of their nuclear program and not reprocessing its stock of spent nuclear fuel, the United States agreed to supply the North with bunker oil to fuel alternate sources of electricity. The agreement also brought South Korea and Japan into a consortium with the United States to help the North pay for and construct safer, non-plutonium-producing, light-water reactors to fill the void created by the shutdown of the North's existing nuclear plants. The Agreed Framework was an imperfect solution to the problem, and some time later it was discovered that all parties had either equivocated on or actually broken its essential provisions, but it supplied the first and longest-lived mechanism for US-North Korean diplomatic contacts. Despite the absence of any formal diplomatic recognition, the Agreed Framework continued to function until the outbreak of a second nuclear crisis—which is not yet resolved at this writing—in the fall of 2002.

The Great Famine

While the world breathed a sigh of relief with the resolution of the first North Korean nuclear crisis, a profound internal economic and humanitarian crisis was brewing in the DPRK. The North's economy had been showing signs of severe problems by the late 1980s, and by the time of the first nuclear crisis, it was in stagnation. In the summer of 1995, North Korean agricultural production was battered by severe floods, and it collapsed following a drought the next year. This precipitated a catastrophic famine, the full extent of which was known to the world only several years later. Agricultural production was already in decline because of inadequate electricity for running irrigation pumps, a steep decrease in the use of chemical fertilizers (which now had to be purchased on the world market), and a history of poor land management—particularly the clear-cutting of slopes for timber that had led to severe problems with erosion.

The floods of 1995 destroyed the rice crop, but more importantly, mud slides and unchecked runoff from the denuded mountains ringing the North's most productive rice land caused silting in large parts of this area. Food rationing had been in effect for years, so the loss of the 1995 rice crop created a truly desperate situation. In addition, freak hailstorms in 1996 destroyed over 70 percent of the corn crop. Despite the DPRK's normally tight control of information about its internal affairs, by 1996 there were isolated reports of massive malnutrition among the children of the North. The next summer what had been only rumors of massive starvation were confirmed when the North finally permitted humanitarian groups to help with the distribution of food aid. Aid workers reported that the conditions they observed in North Korea were equal to the notorious famines in Ethiopia and Somalia. As many as one million people perished in what now ranks as one of the most destructive famines of the twentieth century (Haggard and Noland, 2006).

Through sheer incompetence—or more likely extreme paranoia and secrecy regarding its internal affairs—the North Korean government exacerbated the disaster by not appealing for aid in a timely manner. Even after the world effort to channel food aid to the North began, government officials hampered aid workers by insisting on distributing the food themselves and barring access to the areas hardest hit by the disaster. Only after private relief organizations and the UN World Food Programme entered the North and demanded direct access to the hungry did a better sense of conditions emerge. Since 1997 the major donors of food aid have been South Korea, Japan, the PRC, and, ironically, the United States. Food was funneled through neutral channels such as the World Food Programme, and by 2000 the worst of the famine was over. Since 2000, however, North Korea has continued to depend on food aid from the world community. The famine also drove hundreds of thousands of refugees into Manchuria. By agreement the Chinese were supposed to return all refugees ("defectors," in the parlance of the North), but the scale of the problem and Chinese unwillingness to police the agreement meant most of the migrants could continue in their uncertain refuge as illegal immigrants. This large underground population of North Koreans in Manchuria represents a continuing problem in Chinese-North Korean relations.

Road to a North-South Summit

The famine obscured hopeful signs of rapprochement between the North and South. In 1997 South Koreans elected longtime opposition leader Kim Dae Jung as president. Kim had to face the economic turmoil caused by the Asian financial crisis in his first year in office. Nevertheless, he ambitiously inaugurated a diplomatic offensive aimed at North Korea under the name of the Sunshine Policy. Buoyed by increased contacts on the economic front and South Korean humanitarian intervention in the famine, diplomats began working on the difficult project of arranging a summit meeting between the leaders of the two Koreas. But on June 13, 2000, Kim Dae Jung boarded a plane and was warmly greeted by Kim Jong Il himself at P'yongyang's Sunan International Airport. For the next several days the two Kims held meetings and staged photo sessions in a variety of venues that were eagerly transmitted to the world media—over 15,000 journalists covered this unprecedented event.

The summit was a public relations triumph for Kim Jong Il. His solicitous deference to the South Korean president, who is his elder, particularly impressed southerners viewing the ceremonies on television, and Kim Dae Jung reciprocated with traditionally appropriate behavior. Long sequestered and seldom visible in public, let alone in the world spotlight, Kim projected an image of an agreeable ruler who was interested in improving relations between the two Koreas. It was impossible to gauge what the spectacle of the two presidents side by side in their limousine meant to the thousands of ordinary North Koreans who had been mobilized to line P'yongyang's normally empty boulevards for the presidential motorcades. Did they feel pride at the sight of the southern president coming north into the center of their workers' paradise? Did they harbor secret dreams that the prospect of reunification might finally end their long era of deprivation and hardship? Whatever their thoughts, they had to return to their work, food rationing, dark homes, and uncertainty following this public display of Korean unity. And within another two years, their leader was once again committing them to a facedown with the entire world in a new round of nuclear politics (see Epilogue).

Chapter Eight

DEMOCRATIZATION IN SOUTH KOREA
1987–2000

THE SUDDEN CAPITULATION of the Chun government in the face of the
massive demonstrations of June 1987 marked a major turning point in the
evolution of South Korean democracy. Many viewed it as the beginning of true
democracy in the South. Less optimistically, it might be more apt to consider it
only the beginning of a process of democratization. In 1987 Korean society had
yet to work out how a truly open, pluralist democracy might function. After all it
is difficult to find any period in the history of South Korea when the democratic
procedures and rights embedded in the often-amended constitution had not been
overridden by authoritarian abuses perpetrated by both civilian and military dictators. But the exhortations of authoritarian governments for the population to
exercise discipline and accept limits on their democratic freedoms in the name of
economic development and national security had ceased to resonate long before
1987. With the death of Park Chung Hee in 1979, there emerged a broad-based
conviction that the time had come to create an open democracy and to curb the
excessive powers of the executive. This hope had been shattered by the military
coup in late 1979 and the rise of Chun Doo Hwan to power in 1980. It was a testament to the power of authoritarianism that it took another seven years for the
popular will, so evident in 1980, to manifest itself again.

It is significant that democratization began at the behest of the government
itself. Rho Tae Woo made enormous concessions in his Eight Point Declaration
because he had to, but in doing so, he made sure that those in power would have a
role in shaping how democratization would evolve. The nationwide crisis subsided
rather quickly after his June 29 declaration. The concessions to introduce direct
elections, a new press law, local autonomy, etc. satisfied the basic demands of the
relatively conservative urban middle class that had tipped the balance in favor of
popular reform. The more radical demands of students and labor leaders were
relegated to the background. Negotiation between elites, of both the government
and opposition parties, ensued over procedural issues for instituting direct elections and the restructuring of the Yushin constitution. Quickly the spotlight was
directed toward a constitutional referendum and the promise of an open, direct
election of a new president in the fall of 1987.

But what of the demands for the freedom to organize labor, the institution of
distributive justice, the elimination of the National Security Law, and the creation

of a social welfare system that had also been a part of the protest agenda since the 1960s? How the new constitution and electoral procedures would serve the process of broader reform was still a question as the election of 1987 drew near. Procedural democracy does not necessarily mean that the goals of social justice will always be served. If the legal transfer of power through free and fair elections is democracy, then South Korea had democratized. But if democracy means a true sharing of power between all major constituencies in society, then South Korea was still in the process of democratizing. In the years remaining before the new century, the political process in South Korea matured. Society became much freer and political debate more open, but the drive to create a truly inclusive politics remained a work in progress. Over the next three administrations, those of Rho Tae Woo (1988–1993), Kim Young Sam (1993–1998), and Kim Dae Jung (1998–2003), the struggle to create a truly representative democracy continued to evolve.

The struggle played out in a Korean society vastly transformed by thirty years of economic growth, massive urbanization, and new global influences. While conservative anti-Communist sentiment continued to resonate, new ideas—and new cultural influences in particular—also moved to center stage. In addition, a new debate emerged in the 1990s as a consequence of the rapid creation of wealth in South Korean society. How had successful economic development altered the lifestyles, but more importantly, the values of the average Korean? This question was compounded by the effects of South Korea's complete insertion into global economic and cultural flows over the last thirty years. Indeed, globalization, the "World to Korea, Korea to the World," as one government slogan expressed it, stimulated more questions about South Koreans' social and cultural identity.[1]

The Elections of 1987 and the Formation of the Sixth Republic

Following his now-famous Eight Point Declaration, Rho Tae Woo seized the initiative in the negotiations over a new constitution. Since he had given in to the main demands of the opposition, Rho instantly gained some legitimacy as a candidate. He also restored Kim Dae Jung's civil rights, thus liberating Kim for a run at the presidency.[2] These moves began the process of isolating the students and more radical elements of the opposition from mainstream politics. Rho then entered into negotiations with representatives from the main opposition parties over the shape of the new constitution. One issue was the length of the presidential term: the government proposed a six-year single term and the opposition favored a four-year single term. Compromise produced a five-year single term. The government made another major concession by agreeing to drop the power of the president to dissolve the National Assembly. More wrangling fixed the voting age at twenty, not the eighteen years of age favored by the opposition in order to create more student voters. The new constitution was ratified by the National Assembly and then approved by 93 percent of the electorate in a national referendum in October 1987.

For the first time in decades the way was clear for the opposition to gain the presidency in the fall elections. While Rho had salvaged some legitimacy for the ruling Democratic Justice Party, his party faced an uphill battled against an invigorated opposition. But the two major opposition leaders, Kim Dae Jung and Kim Young Sam, were unable to agree on one single candidate whom both could support, and each entered the election as head of a separate party, so the election boiled down to a three-way race between Rho's Democratic Justice Party, Kim Dae Jung's Party for Peace and Democracy, and Kim Young Sam's Reunification Democratic Party. The public was sorely disappointed that the opposition had failed to settle on a single candidate, and indeed, Kim Young Sam and Kim Dae Jung split 55 percent of the total vote, which allowed Rho to win the presidency with a bare plurality of 37 percent.

The election highlighted the joining of regional loyalties to the national electoral process. Regionalism in Korea had simmered in the postwar era. Over the decades of authoritarian rule, beginning with Park Chung Hee, the lion's share of government investment in development had fallen along the Seoul-Pusan corridor. The government had favored its leaders' home districts in the southeast Kyŏngsang provinces, with major development projects such as the Pohang Steel Complex, oil refineries, and the largest free export zone in Masan. The communications infrastructure (double tracking the railroads, the first superhighway, port development, and so forth) was first upgraded along the Seoul, Taegu, Pusan corridor. Of equal importance was the fact that people from the Cholla provinces in the southwest, also known as Honam, were systematically excluded from government leadership positions. Over time, people in the poorer, predominately agricultural Honam region felt progressively discriminated against. In addition, they had long felt a strong personal bond with Kim Dae Jung, a native of the South Cholla port city of Mokp'o, and his political prominence in the opposition provided them a spokesperson. Attacks on Kim were perceived as attacks on them. Then, after the Kwangju massacre, general discrimination transformed into active repression. The government blamed the Kwangju uprising on Communist instigation, thus by implication smearing Honam people as "sympathizers."

Regionalism emerged as an important factor in the open electoral politics of the Sixth Republic after 1987. Voting patterns in the three-way race for the presidency neatly coincided with each candidate's home district. Kim Dae Jung swept the vote in Honam, Kim Young Sam carried his home area around Pusan, and Rho Tae Woo's voters came from the Kyŏngsang region. Another factor crucial to the emergence of such strong regional identifications was that postwar South Korea lacked a history of issue-based politics. The range of acceptable ideological difference tolerated in its political culture had been extremely narrow, a product of the national division, the Korean War, and the emergence of anti-Communism as the one preoccupying concern. Moreover, the pattern of controls concentrated in the presidency personalized authority around the president and his handpicked leadership. The opposition parties represented simply opposition, not an array of different ideologies, policies, or ideas for reform; they were not linked to a social base or any interest group such as labor. Machinations within the elite leadership in the parties determined who would lead. And the opposition's only stance was a desire to gain power, while the party in power was motivated only to maintain their hold on power. There was little or no accountability to public opinion (Choi, *Democracy*, 2005). Thus it was not surprising that at the start of the new era of open electoral politics, the process continued to be highly personalized and regional affiliation played a major role.

As Rho Tae Woo's administration moved into its second year, however, it was clear that politics in South Korea had changed. The opposition parties did considerably better in the 1988 National Assembly elections. In a stunning turnaround, the DJP won only 87 of the 224 constituencies, the rest being divided up among three opposition parties and a few independents. Since the National Assembly had gained power in the new constitution, the government party had tremendous difficulties with only 87 seats. Any policy initiatives required coalition-building with the opposition parties, who were not particularly willing to cooperate, because each was waiting for the next presidential campaign. The political process stalemated for the next several years, but within the government there were important developments.

The Rho administration did not have a strong mandate for reform, but it was able to initiate change through executive fiat. In spite of being closely associated with the military clique of the Fifth Republic, Rho began the process of returning the Korean military to the barracks, although a full purge of the military clique of the Fifth Republic would come later. During the summer of 1987 controls over labor organization were removed, and this led to a burgeoning of labor unionization and labor actions. Between June 1987 and June 1988 some 3,400 labor disputes, strikes, or lockouts occurred, the vast majority of which were over wage disputes (Ogle, 1990). In the next years most such disputes led to long-delayed increases in wages, often averaging 25 percent or more. While working conditions continued to be problematic, and Korean laborers still worked perhaps the longest average hours per week in the industrialized world, the rapid increase in wages, so long delayed, was welcome. That the government stepped back and let this occur was very significant, and did much to mollify labor's discontent. It also decoupled labor from the more radical opposition forces.

As the 1990 National Assembly elections approached, Rho Tae Woo was searching for a way to break the deadlock between the executive and the highly fractious legislature. For his part, Kim Young Sam was attempting to consolidate support for the next presidential election in 1992. Their meeting of minds produced the stunning creation of a grand coalition party in which Rho's DJP merged with Kim

Young Sam's RDP and the smaller National Democratic Republican Party of Kim Jong Pil to form a new majority party called the Democratic Liberal Party.[3] This was a hugely cynical move on the part of Kim Young Sam, who had long been associated with opposition politics. In effect Rho, Kim Young Sam, and Kim Jong Pil had created a party very similar to the long-ruling government party in Japan, the Liberal Democratic Party (LDP).[4] This marriage of convenience had been made behind closed doors and represented the personal ambitions of major political figures, not important reform issues. The bargain created a viable government party and at the same time provided for a controlled transfer of power in the next election. Kim Young Sam took his chance, seeing that there was no other sufficiently powerful politician in line for the government party presidential nomination. Regaining control of the legislature after the 1990 elections emboldened Rho to be less tolerant toward the opposition, and political arrests increased during 1989 and 1990. Rho also responded to the business lobby by cracking down on labor union activity, asserting that further rises in labor costs would end Korea's comparative advantage in global trade.

Settling Accounts: The Kim Young Sam Presidency

Kim Young Sam's gamble paid off. He won the 1992 presidential election, defeating his old rival Kim Dae Jung with 41.4 percent of the national vote and becoming the first civilian president to occupy the post since 1963.[5] Significant as well was the fact that although he had been in opposition for his entire career, he was now head of the government party. And in spite of his calculated opportunism, the public was optimistic at the beginning of his term; he enjoyed a 92 percent approval rating in polls taken in early 1993. Given this strong mandate, expectations ran high that significant reforms would be possible and a new era of politics had begun in South Korea.

Kim's presidency began with several major and very popular decisions. He removed the last of the so-called TK faction (Taegu-Kyŏngsang group) from the sensitive positions they had dominated during the Chun and Rho years.[6] He also made a number of popular appointments of intellectuals and prominent dissidents in his administration, some of whom were important figures from the Honam region. He restructured the dreaded KCIA in order to reduce domestic surveillance and make it accountable to the public. Expanding on Rho Tae Woo's limited amnesty, Kim restored the civil rights of thousands of dissidents. And in a surprise move, he pushed through a Real Name Law that made it illegal to hold bank accounts and property in fictitious names. The use of fabricated names for such purposes was customary and widespread, and it made hiding income to avoid taxes or any government scrutiny very easy. The law declared that after a short grace period, all accounts had to be declared under a legal name. Many accounts were abandoned; politicians and government bureaucrats were particularly threatened, for it became more difficult to hide bribes and slush funds. This law was part of a general anticorruption and clean-government campaign undertaken by the Kim Young Sam administration. In the first year of his administration dozens of high-ranking bureaucrats, including military officers, were indicted and punished for unethical and illegal activities.

Kim came to power as the Korean economy was in the throes of readjustment. The heady years of 8 to 10 percent increases in GDP were long gone, and the government came under pressure from competing economic interests. Big business lobbied for more labor controls because they were worried that foreign investors would leave Korea for cheaper labor markets in Southeast Asia or Indonesia. The public wanted the administration to create a social welfare safety net and address the long-term effects of the last twenty-five years of economic expansion, particularly the dismal state of environmental quality in South Korea. The pension system begun in 1988 was scheduled for full implementation by the end of 1996, and Kim's administration added a new program of unemployment insurance in 1995. Nevertheless, environmental improvement and social welfare remained seriously underfunded.

Before he was halfway through his term, Kim Young Sam's administration was bedeviled by a number of problems. Many of his early reforms and announced intentions failed to be translated into concrete form either in new institutions or programs. Critics charged the administration with excessive favoritism in appointments and an "imperial" style of unilateral action and lack of consultation. By 1995 the anticorruption campaign had unearthed a number of irregularities within campaign finances, notably the existence of huge slush funds amassed by Rho Tae Woo during his administration.[7] The campaign implicated other politicians as well, notably Kim Dae Jung, who admitted to accepting, ironically, some two billion won ($2.5 million) from Rho Tae Woo in the 1992 elections. During Rho's trial for corruption, the president was dogged by rumors that he himself would ultimately be implicated in the widening scandal. And in 1996, Chang Hak Ro, one of Kim Young Sam's top aides, was indeed arrested and charged with collecting millions of dollars in bribes from Korean businessmen.

Late in 1995 the Kim administration reopened the lingering wound of Kwangju by passing special legislation to punish members of the military coup responsible for the carnage. Within a month of this move, Kim had former presidents Chun Doo Hwan and Rho Tae Woo arrested to stand trial for their roles in the military coup as well as their responsibility for Kwangju. In March 1996 the nation watched with mouths agape as the joint trial of the two former presidents opened. Their bribery and malfeasance had been handled in separate trials, but both men were now in the dock to be tried for mutiny and sedition. On August 26 the court sentenced Chun to death (later commuted to life imprisonment) and Rho to twenty-two-and-a-half years in prison for mutiny, treason, and corruption in office.[8] The spectacular trials in some sense resolved public outrage at the worst excesses of the authoritarian state. In no small way they also signaled a strengthening of the judiciary and the concept of the rule of law in South Korea.

The trials of the former presidents did not, however, deflect public dissatisfaction with Kim Young Sam's administration. By 1997 his approval rating had sunk to a dismal 4 percent, which in large part reflected unhappiness with the legislative deadlock, the scandals continuing to swirl around the Blue House, and persistent signs of an economic slowdown. The public and Kim's political opposition had been outraged by the tactics he used to ram through a controversial labor law in late 1996. In addition, several of Kim's closest aides were implicated by revelations of corruption and bribery that surfaced in the wake of the sudden collapse of the Hanbo Steel Company, a subsidiary of one of the largest *chaebŏl*. Making matters worse, it was revealed that Kim's son, Kim Hyun Chul, had solicited illegal political funds from Hanbo. Kim's personal reputation was now destroyed, and he progressively lost control over his own party, renamed in 1995 the Korea National Party, as its leaders struggled to secure the nomination as candidate in the 1997 elections. With Kim's administration in such widespread disrepute, the stage was set for a wide-open election in 1997, and interest was especially high because Kim Dae Jung had returned to politics after a brief retirement between 1992 and 1995.

The Asian Financial Crisis and the Election of 1997

A far more serious crisis than partisan politics loomed in the economic arena, as South Korea fell into a severe recession following the 1997 Asian Financial Crisis. This crisis erupted in mid-1997 with a speculative attack on the Thai baht that led to sharp declines in currencies, stock markets, and other asset prices in a number of Asian countries. When the crisis spread to South Korea, the world's eleventh largest economy, the possibility of Korea defaulting on its huge international debt obligations raised a potential threat to the international monetary system. For South Korea, the economic downturn and the massive layoffs that followed was a trauma of the first order.[9] It came at a high point of Korean confidence and financial expansiveness and was a sober reminder of the fragility of economic and social well-being in South Korea. Throughout the summer and fall, cascading loan defaults exposed the financial weakness of many overleveraged Korean companies. The government was slow to respond to the crisis, and labor remained inflexible, unwilling to lose any of its hard-won gains. Interest rates rose precipitously as everyone scrambled for hard currency. At their highest point, 30 percent, interest rates caused massive bankruptcies as they exacerbated companies' debt-service burdens. In 1998 some 20,000 firms went bankrupt. The Korean won *(wŏn)* devalued, reaching an all-time low of 1,640 won to the dollar in January 1998. Unemployment soared to almost 9 percent in December of that year. And Korea's growth rate, a public obsession for decades, slid to a negative 5.8 percent in 1998 (Doowon Lee, "South Korea's Financial Crisis," 2000).

The Korean government was forced to go to the International Monetary Fund (IMF) for a bailout. One editorial termed the day these negotiations became public a "day of national humiliation" and a "loss of economic sovereignty," and the press lamented that Korea had come into a new era of "IMF trusteeship" (Byung-Kook Kim, 2000). This sense of national humiliation was particularly understandable given South Korea's passionate nationalism and colonial history. Moreover, the $57 billion rescue package came at the price of mandatory reforms. It dictated changes in government economic policy, reform of banking and accounting practices, and the restructuring of industry—a clear intrusion by international economic interests in Korea's affairs. Hurt nationalist sensibilities notwithstanding, the real pain was felt by the tens of thousands of middle-class managers and office workers who would lose their jobs in the subsequent bankruptcies and downsizing of many of Korea's largest corporations. An even greater disaster lay in store for as many as a million laid-off or fired workers in the dark years of 1998 and 1999.

The Asian Economic Crisis came in an election year. By the fall of 1997 the full extent of the crisis was manifest, and with the government party in disarray, the election seemed wide open. Once again it was a three-way race. Lee Hoi-Chang ran as candidate of what was left of the ruling party. Under the banner of the New Party for the People, a newcomer to national politics and former governor of Kyŏnggi province, Rhee In Je, promised to sweep away the old generation of leaders. A reinvigorated Kim Dae Jung ran by forming a new party, the National Congress for New Politics, in coalition with his old arch nemesis, Kim Jong Pil.[10] The expectation that Lee Hoi-Chang would carry the election with Kim and Rhee splitting an opposition vote was dashed by revelations that Lee's two sons had evaded military service by falsifying their health records. This devastating smear on Lee's integrity caused his ratings to nosedive. Similar attempts to besmirch Kim Dae Jung's by pointing to his record of creating political slush funds surprisingly had no effect on his public standing. Kim Dae Jung eked out a narrow victory in the December 18 elections, garnering 39.7 percent of the national vote to Lee Hoi-Chang's 38.2 percent and Rhee In Je's 18.9 percent, respectively.

Kim Dae Jung's victory and the establishment of his administration in 1998 marked the first peaceful transfer of power between government and opposition parties in the postwar history of South Korea. This momentous event, however, was overshadowed by the economic crisis and concern about Kim's abilities to manage the government, particularly the task of implementing the major reforms contained in the IMF bailout agreement. This would be no mean task because the reform package demanded the restructuring (downsizing) of the major economic engine of the Korean economy, the politically powerful *chaebŏl*. It also required major concessions on the part of labor because layoffs were necessary for the *chaebŏl* to reduce excess capacity and shed losing business ventures. Layoffs were also a precondition of the financial reform, namely, the acquisition and recapitalization of insolvent banks by foreign interests who would only do so if they could shed excess employees. Kim established a Tripartite Committee, a presidential advisory group that was charged with creating a plan to mediate the crisis. Ultimately a package deal emerged. It required "concessions on job security from labor federations in return for reform of the corporate-governance structure by the *chaebŏl*, strengthening of labor unions' political rights, and welfare programs for discharged workers" (Byung-Kook Kim, 2000, p. 40). This entire drama emanated an aura of unreality. The plan called for Kim Dae Jung, long known for his populist politics, to oversee what was in essence a neoliberal downsizing that would ask much from the long-suffering Korean laboring masses. Yet the grand compromise settled most of the outstanding policy issues. Employers would be able to lay off workers, labor unions could engage in political activities, the *chaebŏl* would have to reform reckless financial practices, and banks would hold businesses to higher standards of performance and financial probity. While not all of the new policies were implemented, the package outlined a route out of the crisis and started a process that would place the Korean economy on a sounder footing by the first years of the new millennium.

The IMF crisis was more than a financial threat to the stability of international financial markets or the bottom line of Korean corporate or state balance sheets. The massive layoffs, income reduction, and asset depreciation that attended the economic disruption created a profound "social crisis" in South Korea. The financial crisis disrupted the lives of millions of Koreans. While an unemployment rate of 8 percent may not be considered unusual in the United States during a recession, this rate meant two million Koreans were out of work in a society accustomed to full employment and decades of economic expansion. The crisis not only meant privation, even disaster, for hundreds of thousands of working-class families, it also actually shrank what had been a burgeoning middle class.[11] One survey taken during the crisis estimated the overall income reduction in Korea at 20 percent, with about 90 percent of the population experiencing some level of reduction. The Korean Development Corporation estimated that the number of households under the poverty line ($500 per month) rose to 12 percent of total households.[12] Of course the economic shocks were not felt evenly throughout the population; the poorest households suffered the worst (Gi-Wook Shin and Chang, 2000).

The social crisis shocked the South Korean population psychologically. Few were prepared for the crisis, and many had never experienced such dislocation. Unemployed men were cut from their social networks at work, and the social and economic hardships strained the basic social institution in Korea, the family. The divorce rate increased 34 percent at the height of the crisis in 1998. The family, however, remained the core resource for coping. The crisis necessarily stimulated an expansion of government programs to improve the nascent social safety net put in place but not fully implemented in the early 1990s. But in the end, the extended family provided the major source of aid for relatives affected by the layoffs. Families provided the "sharing of housing, guarantees for loans, cash lending, day care, role switching" that sustained members in distress (Gi-Wook Shin and Chang, 2000, p. 85). Looking back over the turbulent postwar period, it had always been this way. Perhaps the key to the resilience of Korean society itself has always been the strength, cohesiveness, and adaptability of the family unit no matter how assaulted by the enormous forces of change that have swept through South Korea over the last half century.

A Transformed Society: Korea in the 1990s

By 1990 fully 75 percent of the South Korean population lived in cities of more than 50,000, completely reversing the demographic profile of 1960, when the country was still 75 percent rural. And the megalopolis of Seoul, South Korea's capital, dominated this urban culture, for more than a quarter of the entire population lived within its environs.[13] Urbanization had developed hand in hand with the expansion of the middle class, which, in terms of income, measured over 50 percent of the population by the late 1990s; in terms of perception, surveys reported that over 80 percent of the population thought of themselves as belonging to the middle class.

By the 1990s education through the equivalent of high school was universal, and higher education had expanded to satisfy an enormous demand for college degrees, even postgraduate training. South Korea's education system created a virtually universally literate population, and many point to this fact when considering the productivity, adaptability, and drive of the Korean workforce. Society is awash in publications. South Korea's publication rates per capita rival Japan's and greatly exceed those of the United States, an older and more affluent democracy. Moreover, South Korea's rise as a middle-class, urban society coincided with the communication revolution of the late twentieth century. Around the time of the IMF crisis, South Korea was well on its way to becoming one of the most "wired" societies in the modern world (see Epilogue).

Urbanization, rising wealth, changing consumption patterns, increased literacy—all hallmarks of modernization—have altered behavior and values in Korea. Throughout the postwar period there have been periodic public debates over how traditional values and culture have been stressed, altered, or obliterated by the aggregate changes brought about by this great transformation. The more conservative elements in society have decried the breakdown of traditional familial roles and the movement of women into the workplace. Indeed, women have gained rights long denied them within patriarchal family law. Throughout the postwar period the fight over the legal constitution of the family acted as a metaphor for the larger debate over traditional values and identity in Korea. In the 1950s family law was codified to reassert the ideal of the Confucian traditional family that colonial policies were believed to have altered. But by the 1970s there was increasing pressure to make family law conform to more modern ideas about the position of women in society. Spurred by the rise of an organized women's movement as well as the political opening in 1987, a breakthrough occurred with the third revision in the family law in 1989. This revision abolished articles that discriminated against women in the areas of inheritance and custody rights but upheld the patriarchal idea of the man (husband or sons) as legal head of the family. In the 1990s women challenged the provision in the law that banned marriage between individuals with the same surname, but the courts ruled against them. More rights within the family and marriage have coincided with a rise in the number of divorces, a statistic often lamented and blamed on women's liberation by conservative forces within Korea. But the fact remains that while it has taken a long time, women were moving aggressively to gain gender equality in society and to remove patriarchal constraints from their lives (Ki-Young Shin, 2006).[14]

In the 1980s Korea had evolved from a developing to developed economy. Along the way the country had been physically transformed by decades of construction projects, both public and private: new superhighways, gleaming skyscrapers, endless rows of apartment blocks, a massive underground for the capital of Seoul, and new stadiums and parks for the 1988 Olympics and later the 2002 World Cup. A cornucopia of consumer products unimaginable to the prior generation were available. Perhaps no better index measures how economic change spurred changes in behavior than the rise of the automobile as an integral part of Korean life. By the 1990s the automobile had gone from being a luxury scarcely obtainable by the upper middle class to household necessity for the entire middle class. The availability of automobiles and their affordability was made possible by the general shift in the economy in the 1980s from a reliance on exports as the engine of growth to a greater emphasis on the power of the domestic market. Indeed, the combination of overcapacity and falling sales of automobiles abroad caused the automobile manufacturers—Hyundai, Kia, and Daewoo—to market their cars at home. There a tremendous latent demand coupled with enough disposable income created an explosion of automobile ownership that accelerated through the 1980s and continued into the 1990s.[15] The numbers of cars on the streets of Seoul and other major cities soon overwhelmed the roadways, and as a consequence enormous amounts of public funds have been spent on new roads, highways, bridges, and tunnels. When planners laid out the vast new area of Seoul south of the Han River called Kangnam, much of which developed only after 1970, planners clearly had automobiles in mind when they built broad avenues and laid the endless rows of apartment blocks on a coherent grid.[16] Building codes required one parking space per apartment, yet by the 1990s cars were spilling onto the streets. having long since overwhelmed available parking capacity.

It became socially significant whether one drove a Hyundai Grandeur at the top end or a Kia Pride at the bottom end of the brand hierarchy; and as time went on many gradations developed in between. Car ownership mirrored social status and respect for age—a younger middle-class individual did not want to buy above a socioeconomic equal of more advanced age, for instance (Nelson, 2000, p. 100). Korea had become a consumer society, and their new habits contradicted traditional values of restraint as well as thirty years of government exhortations to save, be frugal, and work hard for the national cause of development.

Government-directed economic development in the 1960s and 1970s had relied heavily on exhortations for public discipline and frugality. Such behavior had become an expression of national patriotism. The values of hard work, frugality, and deferred gratification also resonated with traditional Confucian values that were strongly imbedded in the public mind. Yet in the early 1980s, when import barriers to what had been classified as unnecessary luxuries were removed, the new middle class (per capita income reached $10,000 in 1995) went on a spending spree. Almost immediately, however, the new consumption was criticized as self-indulgent, unpatriotic, even threatening to Korea's fragile economic success.

In the early 1990s this challenge took the form of a debate over "excessive consumption" *(kwasobi)*. Editorials decried as an abomination the competition among the wealthy to put on the most extravagant weddings, complete with fabulous gift-giving (Kendall, 1996). Other critics focused on the obscene amounts of money spent in the salons and nightclubs of Kangnam or lamented the waste and self-indulgence exhibited within the youth culture. Did young people not understand that the present good times were built upon the hard work and sacrifice of a previous generation? Worse yet, were they completely ignorant of the horrible deprivations suffered by their parents and grandparents during the Korean War and its aftermath? *Kwasobi* critics expressed what was a widespread ambivalence about the meaning of wealth and just what might constitute "proper" or "appropriate" consumption. Just as college students of the 1980s had looked to the rural countryside and *minjung* culture for inspiration in developing a new national identity, intellectuals and critics of the new consumerism were reflecting on how the new materiality was affecting core traditional values. What was the relationship between wealth and social status? Did consumer greed signal a loss of communitarian values? And would Korea lose sight of its past values in favor of the untrammeled pursuit of personal pleasure(Nelson, 2000; Lett, 1998)?

Approaching the Twenty-first Century and the North-South Summit

Another issue that consumed public attention in the 1990s was a problem that had in many ways defined life in the South since 1948—North Korea. During his election campaign in 1997, Kim Dae Jung signaled his interest in pushing forward with reconciliation with the North, and his opposition attempted to play Kim's long-standing commitment to dialog with the North against him. But Kim's victory demonstrated that the playing the national-security or North-Korean-sympathizer card was no longer completely effective in Korean politics. Indeed, since the end of the Cold War, overall South Korean policy toward the North had shifted decisively toward engagement.

The roots of the new policy can be traced to the Rho Tae Woo administration, when its policy of *nord politik* sought a general engagement with the nations of the former Soviet Bloc. Rho established diplomatic ties with both the Soviet Union and the People's Republic of China in the early 1990s, and this had placed considerable pressure on North Korea. Rho also engaged North Korea in direct dialog, and, after a series of preliminary negotiations, the North and South announced a Basic Agreement in 1991.[17] It affirmed the principles of nonaggression and reconciliation and created exchanges, both cultural and economic, between the two Koreas. This was the most important state-to-state meeting between the two Koreas since the South-North Communiqué of 1972 that had established the first "hot line" between the countries. The Basic Agreement also contained the North's first formal recognition of the South Korean state. Implementation of the Basic Agreement stalled, however, after the outbreak of a crisis over the North Korean nuclear program in 1992, and the death of Kim Il Sung in 1994 also created a major diversion.

The North Korean famine provided a new chance for inter-Korean cooperation with South Korean offers of food relief in 1995. While the Kim Young Sam administration was criticized for its poor handling of Kim Il Sung's death and a general inattention to the North Korean issue, it did negotiate the shipment of 150,000 tons of food aid to the North. The famine also changed the way that many in the South viewed the North. By the time of Kim Dae Jung's election, North Korea was no longer the automatic "Other" in South Korean political discourse. It now played alternately as the main enemy or the dialog partner, a military threat or a desperate, isolated failure (Snyder, 2002). North Korea was now an issue about which various political stances could be openly expressed. Politicians could speak of positive engagement with the North and not automatically be labeled an enemy of the state or a Communist sympathizer.[18] Conservatives still feared rapprochement and engagement as a danger to security, and they generally believed that any economic relief simply rewarded bad behavior on the part of the North. But moderates like Kim Dae Jung insisted that engagement with and even economic assistance to the North could be a "win-win" proposition, bringing the North out of its shell, providing humanitarian assistance, and generally reducing tensions and thereby strengthening national security.

Kim Dae Jung announced his intention to reinvigorate dialog with North Korea at his inauguration. The Sunshine Policy was based on a concept of open-ended engagement with the North. It set no formulas for reunification, declaring that issue to be one for future generations to decide. Nonaggression, exchange, and cooperation were the fundamental tenets of the policy, and Kim made the initiative a priority. In April 1998 he opened state-to-state talks with the North, the first since the 1991 General Agreement. Kim was limited in what he could offer the North officially, and the talks foundered, but a private overture by Chung Ju-Yung, chairman of the Hyundai Corporation, produced an agreement that allowed Hyundai to established tourist visits to the Kumgang mountains on the eastern coast of North Korea in return for yearly payments of foreign exchange to the North. While the tours were highly controlled and there was no people-to-people interaction, the program was an unprecedented joint venture. Hyundai paid the North $330 million between 1998 and 2001, but could not sustain what was a money-losing project. The program demonstrated that the North Koreans would respond to financial incentives, but it also stimulated considerable controversy in the South over what was "appeasement" and what was "true" cooperation in such dealings.

The Sunshine Policy faced another test during the West Sea crisis in the summer of 1999. This crisis originated from North Korea incursions below the Northern Limit Line, a line never recognized by the North, that extends the DMZ into the West (Yellow) Sea off South Korea's northwestern coast. The North Korean navy began escorting their crab fishing fleet south of the line, and after several weeks of incursions and growing tension engaged in a significant firefight with the South Korean navy, in which the technologically superior South Korean ships defeated the aging Northern escorts. This was the most significant military confrontation between the two sides since the 1970s. Kim Dae Jung's willingness to respond to military provocation strengthened support for his Sunshine Policy, which had been vulnerable, as he had been, to charges of being weak on security issues (Olsen, 2002).

On April 10, 2000, three days prior to the National Assembly elections, Kim Dae Jung announced that he would visit P'yongyang for face-to-face meetings with Kim Jong Il. As the first-ever meeting between the heads of state of North and South Korea, the announcement created a sensation. Opposition politicians charged Kim with timing the announcement in order to affect the elections, and everyone wondered just how such an unprecedented summit meeting might unfold. In fact, Kim's announcement did not provide a positive bump for his party: the Millennium Democratic Party did poorly, and the main opposition party, the Grand National Party, fell only a few seats short of a majority in the Assembly. This augured poorly for Kim Dae Jung's legislative program in his final years as president, but for the next months all attention in the South focused on the meeting scheduled for that summer.

On June 13, 2000, when Kim Dae Jung arrived in P'yongyang, he was unexpectedly greeted at the airport by Kim Jong Il and immediately taken on a joint inspection of assembled troops from the Korean People's Army in parade dress. Before the summit South Koreans had speculated how the reclusive Kim Jong Il would behave; after all, South Koreans had been regaled with stories of his dissipation, depravity, and villainy for decades. But Kim Jong Il acted the gracious host. The live video coverage created a sensation in the South, as it showed Kim Jong Il's courteous and traditionally deferential treatment of the elder Kim Dae Jung. On the ride into the city from the airport, Kim Jong Il insisted that the southern president take the "power seat," and his self-deprecating jokes bespoke of a gracious, accomplished statesman. Years of vilification of the North Korean leader as a dangerous and mercurial tyrant were erased in the first hours of the summit. And Kim Dae Jung reciprocated the warmth, creating a remarkable set of images of how reconciliation could sweep away decades of enmity and bitterness. Certainly, this unexpected display by both leaders raised an entirely new prospect in the minds of people in the South.

While the imagery and symbolism of the summit was perhaps its most important achievement, it also produced a Joint Declaration on areas of common agreement: it stated that the two Koreas would solve the issue of reunification independently, it recognized common elements in previously discussed reunification formulae, it resolved to settle humanitarian issues by establishing visits between separated relatives, and finally, it declared the principle of balanced development of the national economy through cooperation and exchange.[19] Of course how to implement these areas of common agreement was the real issue. But at least in the first year of the new millennium the two Koreas had met face-to-face and had seen a glimmer of what relations might become.

The summit was the high point for Kim Dae Jung's presidency, and for engineering this first North-South summit and his lifetime commitment to the cause of democracy he was awarded the Nobel Peace Prize in 2000. He finished his term, however, amidst political controversy and personal embarrassment. His presidency disappointed many of his longtime supporters because he was unable to act substantially on many of his reform ideas. And during his last year in office he was hobbled by scandals that involved his sons' business dealings and influence-peddling. The habits of corruption within the top circle of power in South Korean politics remained seemingly intractable. And public disaffection with the political system remained high. But as with the Kim Young Sam regime, political gridlock and public anger with the process might also be seen as a symptom of the democratization process. Authoritarian regimes may have been more efficient, but they suppressed all voices of dissent. The more open politics after 1987 brought a certain amount of procedural democracy, but the process had yet to give expression to all voices in Korean society. Nevertheless, the army remained in the barracks, and the way was still open for a continuing evolution of Korean democracy. Already alternative voices are being heard from the thousands of nongovernmental organizations (NGO) working in all arenas of public life. The political parties may lack a social base, but NGOs—both great and small—have appeared either to lobby the government on issues or to solve independently the myriad problems of social welfare, gender equality, environmental quality, corruption, transparency in government, distributive justice, labor reform, and all the other problems any complex, modern society faces.

Epilogue

UNTYING THE KOREAN KNOT

THE POLITICAL AND ECONOMIC ARRANGEMENTS on the Korean peninsula at the beginning of the new century represent both the postmodern future and an anachronistic Cold War past. South Korea joined the community of industrialized states in the 1990s by becoming a member of the World Bank and net exporter of capital in global markets. Its exports are well known throughout the world, and its manufactures are no longer limited to low-end products or semiprocessed goods. Like Japan before it, Korea has advanced on the product cycle and now focuses on value-added products: computers, LCD displays, processing chips, and so forth. Its rise to middle-class status within the nation-state system has been copiously documented, first as a model of third-world development and more recently as a harbinger of the future. A 2004 ROK Ministry of Information and Communications survey noted that 86 percent of the population had access (wired or wireless) to the Internet, and 72.8 percent over the age of six used the Internet at least once a week (NIDK, 2004).

South Korea is, however, more than an economic and technological success story. The popularity across East Asia and beyond of the so-called Korean Wave (Hallyu) of cultural products such as films, TV productions, and popular music in audio disc form, was unprecedented in postwar Korean development. Long considered an imitator and follower in cultural terms, Korean film directors, TV producers, actors, and singers are now trendsetters. Entertainment exports are not only big money, they are also changing South Korea's regional and global image. This is highly ironic given that until 1998 ROK authorities had banned the importation of Japanese popular cultural goods out of a fear that it would have a bad influence on Korean youth and corrode traditional values. South Korea is no longer just a piece in the strategic puzzle of Northeast Asian security, nor an increasingly troublesome importer into the US economy. Moreover, the fact that it now has multidimensional relationships, economic, political, *and* cultural, with the region and the world has altered decisively its relationship with the United States, its old security partner and economic guarantor.

In contrast North Korea finds itself diplomatically and economically isolated from the world community. After the collapse of the Soviet Union and fall of the iron curtain, North Korea's economic arrangements with the Communist international system collapsed. This plunged its economy into a free fall from which it has yet to recover. With almost no foreign exchange earnings based on exports, North Korea has been forced to rely on its own devices. Indeed, while this is compatible with its Chuch'e philosophy of self-reliance, it prevents acquisition of the new technology and ideas it needs to rebuild and grow its economy. As a hermit in the world system, North Korea also has no access to global capital markets. By the year 2000, however, North Korea was recovering from the worst of the devastating famine, and small cracks seem to be appearing in its walls of isolation. For the two Koreas at least, the unprecedented North-South summit meeting gave credence to the possibility of change in North Korea.

In 2000, however, a different mood prevailed in the United States. Before his inaugural address George W. Bush announced a thorough reevaluation of the country's policy toward North Korea. This anticipated a reversal of the Clinton policy of engagement represented in the Agreed Framework of 1994. In his 2002 State of the Union speech, President Bush identified North Korea, Iran, and Iraq as members of an "axis of evil"—rogue states that he considered the greatest threat to stability in the new world order. In so doing, he began a crisis in US-North Korean relations that escalated to the point of nuclear confrontation by the spring of 2003. When, following the World Trade Center bombing, he declared America's right to unilateral pre-emptive military action, sent troops into Afghanistan to remove the Taliban regime, and invaded Iraq in the Second Gulf War, he confirmed in the minds of North Korea's leaders that their regime is under threat from America. For North Koreans, this justified breaking the agreements embedded in the Agreed Framework and accelerating its nuclear weapons program.

Fortunately, the People's Republic of China was abandoning their earlier reticence in world affairs, and they organized six-party talks to defuse the crisis that brought together the major players in the region—the United States, China, South Korea, Japan, North Korea, and Russia. A nuclear North Korea is perhaps the biggest single threat to the stability of the region; it threatens Japan to the point where Japan might shift its defensive military stance and develop its own nuclear capability. Such a change would send frightening signals throughout Asia, given the long-standing resentments that still linger from World War II. South Korea is committed to a nuclear-free peninsula, but how long they will tolerate the North's continuing nuclear ambitions remains unclear.

Clearly the two Koreas find themselves occupying very different positions in the world community as the new millennium begins. South Korea stands as an evolving pluralist democracy with an increasingly sophisticated postindustrial economy and an exploding consumer and popular culture. By contrast, North Korea is locked in a dance of death with its own failing economic fortunes and seeks to guarantee its sovereignty and future by playing the dangerous game of nuclear politics.

South Korea in the Twenty-first Century

The Kim Young Sam and Kim Dae Jung administrations that guided Korea through most of the 1990s were plagued by problems seemingly endemic to South Korean political culture. Each president continued a process, begun haltingly at the end of the 1980s, to address the problem of corruption surrounding the centers of power. Yet each administration ended awash in corruption scandals that implicated the very leaders conducting the anticorruption campaign. If the government was not solving the problem, a strong private movement led by NGOs to foster transparency in government emerged in the mid-1990s, and while corruption continues in the high levels of power, the NGO campaign against corruption continues. Moreover, as the trials of Rho Tae Woo and Chun Doo Hwan demonstrated, the South Korean president was no longer immune from prosecution. The continuing problem of corruption among the president's powerful personal advisors and secretaries has raised the question of how to reform the institution of the overpowerful executive itself. Only time will tell whether safeguards to preserve the probity of political leaders will be institutionalized.

The public remained disaffected from the rancorous, ineffectual behavior of political parties during the 1990s, and the continuing lack of a strong social base for political parties has meant that important issues continue to be lost in the process. As a consequence, direct action remains an important mechanism for addressing political issues. Again, the thousands of activist NGOs are taking up the challenge of addressing the outstanding social, economic, and cultural issues and lobbying the South Korean government to take action. Such organizing behavior augurs well for the continuing evolution of pluralist democracy in South Korea.

New electoral procedures started the process of democratization, and just as importantly stronger guarantees of free speech and the new press law widened debate and created a new, more open space for cultural construction. This was most perceptible in the freer discussion in the 1990s of South Korea's authoritarian past and issues related to North Korea. In 1995 one particularly influential television series, *Moraesigye (Hourglass)*, provided in melodramatic form a reckoning of social and political fissures in 1980s Korea. Its characters represented all the archetypal figures: student activists, salarymen, government officials, business tycoons, police, and laborers—all the players, mostly antagonists, in the political drama of postwar Korea. Normal daily activity virtually stopped as people tuned in for the latest episode. It was a national purging of the past that finally opened a public discussion of the trials, tribulations, pain, and suffering caused by the repressive politics, social and economic inequities, and cultural uncertainties in Korea's rapidly changing society in the 1970s and 1980s.

The new openness also permitted change in the way in which North Korea was portrayed in film. Two films, *Swiri* (1999) and *Joint Security Area* (2000), offered new, sympathetic representations of North Korea and North Koreans.

Swiri was the largest-grossing Korean film ever made until that time, its audience even exceeding the viewership in Korea for the global megahit *Titanic,* released the same year. Taking its title from a small fish indigenous to the DMZ—a fish that crosses to either side without reference to ideologies—the movie presented a mix of good and bad characters who were a novelty to South Korean audiences used to predictably "evil" North Koreans. *Joint Security Area* went further by establishing sympathetic relationships between North Korean and South Korean soldiers who work together to solve a mysterious death in the DMZ.

The overtures to North Korea begun during Rho Tae Woo's administration and deepened since have helped to foster a new candidness about the problem of national division. Indeed, as the Bush administration's increasingly hostile stance toward Kim Jong Il became manifest in 2002, South Korea's North Korea policy progressively moved on a divergent path, reversing decades of close coordination between South Korea and the United States regarding policy toward the North.

The most recent ROK administration, under president Rho Moo Hyun, elected in 2002, has continued the Sunshine Policy toward the North, and therefore found itself increasingly in conflict with the United States. This was particularly so after 2003 and North Korea's sudden revelation about continuing its nuclear weapons program in contravention of the Agreed Framework. In spite of the resulting heightened tensions on the peninsula, the South has continued its negotiations with the North over the rebuilding of railroad and motor road links across the DMZ to new economic zones. It also has continued to work independently of the United States in discussions with other participants in the six-party talks seeking resolution of the crisis. Some analysts attribute Rho's narrow margin of victory in the 2002 elections to a last-minute email campaign by a new, younger generation of voters. In part, these voters were motivated by waves of anti-American feeling that had swept Korea following the IMF crisis as well as later incidences involving the US army.[1] Clearly, the United States can no longer count on South Korea's long-standing conservatism and anti-Communism to provide support for its policies toward North Korea. Thirty-nine percent of the respondents in a 2004 poll chose the United States as the "greatest threat to peace on the peninsula," while only 33 percent chose North Korea; of respondents in their twenties, 58 percent identified the United States as the "greatest threat" to 20 percent choosing North Korea. In 2005, a Defense Ministry white paper reclassified North Korea as a "military threat" rather than the heretofore canonical "main enemy," in keeping with attempts on both sides of the DMZ to lower the level of belligerent rhetoric.

At the start of the twenty-first century South Korea is charting a more independent course in its diplomacy, economic relations, and internal politics. In the increasingly pluralist environment old alignments are fading, and a new generation has begun to assert itself and change the terms of political and social debates. The so-called cyber-generation of young Koreans under thirty have grown up experiencing neither the poverty nor the insecurity that dominated the lives of the first postwar generations. They do not calculate their political positions around an older nationalism defined in terms of economic development or a vigilant security against a threatening North Korea. Although they seem indifferent as well to the *minjung* populism of the 1980s, they have expressed a fierce nationalist commitment to Korean independence in economic and international affairs. When this generation takes leadership, they will do so as more self-confident global citizens unfettered by entrenched enmities or automatic gratitude for US security guarantees. But they will also have to solve the anachronism of Korea's division in order to guarantee the safety and stability of their future.

North Korea in the Twenty-first Century

Kim Jong Il's public relations coup at the 2000 summit meeting with Kim Dae Jung gave the North a needed lift in world opinion. But shortly thereafter the Bush administration turned US policy away from the limited engagement with the North that the Clinton administration had fostered, spoke with increasingly hostile rhetoric about the North as part of an "axis of evil," and invaded Afghanistan and Iraq, actions that gave North Korea reason to fear an attack as well. In the fall of 2002 the North Koreans candidly announced to startled US envoys that they were actively processing uranium into weapons-grade material.[2] The new nuclear confrontation still remains unresolved. Following the surprising announcement of its uranium program, the North abruptly expelled International Atomic Energy Agency (IAEA) inspectors and withdrew from the Nuclear Non-Proliferation Treaty, becoming the only nation ever to do so. Shortly thereafter, the United States charged the DPRK with breaking the Agreed Framework and terminated the pact; this ended fuel shipments to the North and halted construction (barely begun by 2002) on the light-water reactors.

The collapse of the Agreed Framework was a foregone conclusion. US conservatives had long chafed at the Clinton policy of engagement with the North; emboldened by the shifting political climate in Washington after the 2001 World Trade Center disaster, they seized the opportunity to put North Korea on the list of dangerous regimes that should be isolated, not supported by active engagement. For its part, North Korea took very seriously the Bush administration's advocacy of its right to unilateral "regime change" in its war on terror.

North Korea has always felt encircled and threatened, and at considerable burden to its failing economy it maintains one of the largest conventional armies in the world. Even with this enormous (if aging) military capacity, the North had clearly been moving toward obtaining nuclear capabilities for several decades.[3] The plutonium program halted in 1994 had been in development for years, and a parallel program of missile development had begun during the 1980s. In 1983 North Korea successfully test fired its first medium-range ballistic missile (MRBM), the Rodong *(nodong)* 1 with a range of 500 miles. By 1998 it had perfected the Taepodong *(taep'odong)* 2, a missile with a range of 2,500 miles, and they shocked the region with an unannounced test firing over Japan and into the Pacific in 1998.

The prospect of North Korea combining its missile and nuclear capabilities destabilizes strategic relationships throughout East Asia. It is even theoretically possible that a North Korean missile could hit US territory, which remains one of the principle justifications, however tenuous, of the US multibillion dollar anti-missile defense program. Since the 1998 test firing, Japan has passed several laws redefining the uses and rules of engagement for its defense forces. After the start of the Second Gulf War, Japan further revised its military policies in order to dispatch troops to Iraq as part of the "Coalition of the Willing"—this to the disquiet of the entire region. While the North Koreans may be considered paranoid by some, they are convinced that these programs are necessary for survival of their regime.

The nuclear crisis has overshadowed the continuing malaise of the North Korean economy and society. Since the terrible famine, the North has made a number of moves to restructure its economy and to boost food production. In the mid-1980s farmers were allowed to cultivate private plots, and sell their produce from these plots at occasional local markets. By the late 1990s, however, these markets were operating on a daily basis and had begun to offer a broad range of goods priced more or less according to free market forces. Since the famine and the flight of North Koreans into Manchuria, there has also been a regular cross-border trade in food and consumer items, with border guards bribed to look the other way or actively participating in the trade. Since 2002 the government has started to allow more market-based pricing for goods and services. In order to do this, the government determined that salaries should be raised to provide cash to use in the market place, and the old ration card system was suspended. The overvalued North Korean won was also devalued from 2.2 to 150 won to the dollar. With these moves, the official distribution system has all but broken down, a tacit admission by the government that the people must take care of themselves. This is different from a true commitment to market-based economics, as has been the case in China. Having not yet decided what to do, North Korea has simply begun letting informal market mechanisms fill the gaps in the economy, particularly in food production, thereby placing the burden of scrounging for a livelihood on the people themselves.

From reports within North Korea, it is clear that four economies are in operation. The least important is now the old primary economy. There is also an economy centered on the military establishment. The army has first call on government resources, supports a huge pool of its own labor, and maintains factories and agricultural production under its exclusive purview. The current exhortation of "rich nation, strong army" is at least half correct. The army is the key to regime survival, and as long as Kim Jong Il remains firmly in control of this key sector, he will remain in power. The third economy has been called the "court" economy of the North Korean nomenclature (Oh and Hassig, 2000, p. 66). The ruling elite—broadly defined as a class of about a million people—have their own stores, foreign trade organizations, and private bank accounts. They have first call on government resources, access to goods outside Korea, and, most importantly, are not accountable to the economic bureaucracy. This is the North Korean regime that is ready to do anything for its own survival, including sacrificing its own citizens to the vagaries of the black market. A large and complex black market forms the fourth economy of North Korea. Having its origins in the farmers' markets, the black market functions now as the market of the people. The formal state distribution system having failed, the black market is the last resort for food supplies. Almost anything can be bartered for on the market, and in recent years the range of commodities has widened because of the breakdown of controls on the Chinese border (Oh and Hassig, 2002).

North Korea has changed from the socialist economy and strict social control system presented in Chapter Seven. It seems possible that internal controls may be wavering also. There is still no sign of political dissent, not to mention overt rebellion, but there is clearly more movement within the country and more people crossing back and forth over the Chinese border. Whether this means ordinary North Koreans will start to receive more information about the outside world is an open question. Now, however, the regime seems intent on doing anything necessary to guarantee its survival. Observers in the South are hoping that their continued engagement with the North will encourage a broader opening to the world. Whatever happens, the two Koreas remained locked within their system of division, and this division holds the entire region hostage, preventing significant restructuring in any new world order.

Untying the Korean Knot

A new world order will not appear in East Asia unless the fifty-year truce that halted the Korean War in 1953 is transformed into a genuine peace. Indeed, the division of Korea is now the last remnant of the Cold War and lingers as a reminder of superpower nuclear confrontation and a bipolar struggle between Communism and Capitalism. The world has moved on since the collapse of Communism, but no genuine set of agreements guarantee a collective peace. Ironically, what was the Hermit Kingdom in the late nineteenth century is now where the major powers of the world are congregated, tied in a knot by their inability to find a new paradigm for stability in Northeast Asia. How the knot will be untied will determine in great part how power arrangements in a "new world order" will evolve. It is significant that China has stepped to the front and proposes to lead the world away from the most recent crisis. Even more significantly, Japan and South Korea have broken ranks with the United States; this signals the maturation of both and their desire to move out from under the Cold War defense umbrella of the United States and the limited initiatives in foreign policy it demanded of both nations. Clearly the US role in East Asia has been diminished by the increased self-confidence of Japan, South Korea, and China.

North and South Korea represent two nation-states that are contesting the leadership of one people. How reunification may be accomplished remains an international conundrum. It is my hope that this book will help readers understand the background for the present situation and how they may help their nations untangle the knot. This is especially important for Americans because we bear some responsibility for the genesis of the problem.

NOTES

· · · · · ·

CHAPTER 1
A New Century and the End of an Era

1. The Tonghak movement's charismatic founder, Ch'oe Cheu, had been executed in 1864. The religion had spread since the 1840s and stressed an eclectic mix of quasi-Christian, Buddhist, and indigenous beliefs. Central to the faith was the concept of *innaech'on* (God in Man); this included women, who worshiped with the men in Tonghak meetings, a radical departure from the strict segregation of the sexes that was characteristic of Neo-Confucian ritual. In the 1890s Tonghak followers tried unsuccessfully to rehabilitate their martyred founder by petitioning Kojong directly. Kojong's rebuff added to the economic and social discontent that lay at the roots of the rebellion of 1894. In the first decade of the twentieth century, Son Pyŏnghŭi, the religion's third patriarch, changed the faith's name to Ch'ŏndogyo (Church of the Heavenly Way) and aligned it with the growing nationalist movement.

2. Russia, France, and Germany jointly demanded cancellation of the lease on the Liaodong peninsula, which had been part of Japan's spoils following its victory in the Sino-Japanese war. This action has come to be known as the Triple Intervention.

3. Kojong's father, Yi Haŭng, is known to posterity by his court title, Taewŏn'gun. He controlled the government as an informal regent from 1864 to 1874 and promulgated a number of controversial reform measures intended to restore prestige and power to the throne. For an account of Taewŏn'gun's rule, see Palais, *Politics and Policy, 1975.*

4. *Han'gŭl* is celebrated in modern South Korea with a national holiday. North Korea moved quickly to rename the alphabet as *Chosŏn'gŭl* to avoid the use of the *"han"* that appears in "Taehan minguk," the official name of South Korea. Mixed script—the mixing of Chinese characters and Korean letters—is still used in the South, but Chinese is rapidly disappearing. North Korea eliminated the use of Chinese characters in 1949; see Schmid, 2002, pp. 256–260.

5. The quid pro quo was worked out in July in a secret agreement between Japan and the United States (the Taft-Katsura Agreement) before the signing of the Portsmouth Treaty in September. The English also renegotiated their alliance with Japan to acknowledge Japan's rights for "guidance and control" in Korea.

6. Itō's assassin, An Chunggun, has been elevated to the status of national hero in the post-colonial nationalist hagiography of South Korea.

7. The term Righteous Armies is of very old provenance in Korea. It was used to describe the irregulars mustered by local *yangban* during the Hideyoshi invasions in the

1590s. It could be more recently traced back to the "Protect the Righteous, Expel the Heterodox" *(wijŏng ch'oksa)* advocates who opposed the opening of Korea during the debates in 1876; see Schmid, 2002, p. 30. And Chŏn Pongjun, leader of the Tonghak rebellion also styled his armies thus.

CHAPTER 2
Colonial State and Society

1. Well over half of the entire GGK bureaucracy, local and central, was made up of Koreans. The proportion was higher for local administrative posts. In the central government in Seoul, Koreans made up 32 percent of the middle-ranking officialdom but only 18 percent of the highest-ranking posts.

2. The overwhelming majority of place names were rendered in Chinese characters. In these cases Japanese could use the Chinese and "read" them in Japanese pronunciation. The Japanese readings remain on many older maps where place names were rendered in roman letters. In Seoul and other cities new Japanese names replaced many traditional street names.

3. The capitol was finally razed in 1995. There had been a protracted debate about what to do with this huge structure. It was used as the first capitol of the ROK after 1948, and later it housed the Korean National Art Museum. Eventually public sentiment called for its removal and after a huge rally and ritual decapitation of the building (the removal of its cupola) on the fiftieth anniversary of Liberation (August 15, 1995), the building was demolished.

4. A poignant example of one such student returning and commenting on the contrasts between the metropole and Korea was written by Yi Kwangsu on a journey home from school in Tokyo. He left an account of such a trip in his essay "From Tokyo to Keijō (Seoul)" (Tokyo esŏ Keijō kkaji), *Ch'ŏngch'un* (Youth) no. 9 (1916): 73–80.

CHAPTER 3
Class and Nation in Colonial Korea

1. In its inaugural edition the *Tonga ilbo* had announced its intent to speak "for the masses *(minjung)*," but this was subsequently changed to "nation" *(minjok);* surprisingly, the Japanese tolerated both characterizations.

2. Productivity increases were not due to mechanization, but rather to increased labor inputs, better use of fertilizers, and expansion of land devoted to rice cultivation through land reclamation projects.

3. *Creation (Kaebyŏk), New Life (Sinsaenghwal), Eastern Light (Tongmyŏng), New World (Sinch'ŏnji),* and *Light of Korea (Chosŏn chigwang)* were examples of such journals. The political orientation of these journals ranged from conservative to fiercely leftist.

4. The Colonial Police created a new department to censor the increasing number of films, both imported and domestically produced, that were drawing large audiences by the late 1920s.

5. The *paekchŏng* occupied the lowest rung in Chosŏn's status conscious society. They were a stigmatized minority comparable to the "untouchables" in India or the *burakumin* in Japan. These people were associated with traditionally "unclean" professions such as butchering, leatherwork, and night-soil collection. See Joong-Seop Kim, 1999, pp. 311–335

6. "The Treatise on National Reconstruction" ("Minjok kaejoron") first appeared in the Ch'ŏndogyo journal *Creation (Kaebyŏk)* in its May 1922 issue.

7. Leftists used the term *minjung* (translated as "the people" or "the masses") during this period as a substitute for proletariat. Because there was only a very small class of industrial labor, the proletariat was reconceived to encompass all laboring elements (industrial labor and peasantry) in Korean society. *Minjung* also provided a name to the self-conscious movement to realign Korean national identity with the history and experience of the "masses" in postwar South Korea during the late 1970s and 1980s; see Chapter Eight.

8. Yi Kwangsu was able to study in Japan because of support from the Ch'ŏndogyo church, the modern religious form of the old Tonghak movement. The GGK also offered a limited number of scholarships for promising students from poor backgrounds.

9. The December Thesis was a formal directive from the Comintern to the Korean Communist Party that had criticized it for failing to distinguish between revolutionary and national reformist movements and for being isolated from proletarian elements in society.

CHAPTER 4
Colonial Modernity, Assimilation, and War

1. *Zaibatsu* were huge, often family-owned, financial and industrial combines that emerged during Japan's modernization in the Meiji period. The Chinese couplet *zai* (finance) *batsu* (group) is pronounced *chebŏl* in Korean. Similar companies (Hyundai, Samsung, Daewoo, etc.) appeared during South Korea's economic expansion after 1960. The South Korean *chebŏl*, while they were originally dominated by one family, did not grow from financial bases such as banks, as had been the case with *zaibatsu* in Japan.

2. The GGK created JDOK in 1927. Originally it broadcast in both Korean and Japanese. Then in order to encourage radio use, JDOK created an all-Korean-language station in 1933. Thereafter, radio sales increased dramatically.

3. *Kisaeng*, female entertainers, were intensively trained in literary arts, music, and dance. They were patronized by the upper-class men of Chosŏn Korea. This institution was similar in some respects to the better known *geisha* of Japan. By the colonial period the *kisaeng* tradition had been considerably debased and the term was often code for a prostitute.

4. The first public stories told by victims of the sexual slavery system led to an extraordinary international movement to gain redress for the victims, attack all forms of sexual servitude, and force a formal apology from the Japanese government for these war crimes. In 1995 the Japanese government established an Asian Women's Fund from private donations as a means for informally compensating victims. While some of the victims have accepted these payments, many have refused.

5. A memorial was created for the Korean victims of the Hiroshima bombing in 1970, but it was outside the Peace Park. Only after a concerted campaign for inclusion was the memorial moved inside the park in 1999. It is estimated that nearly 20,000 (around 10 percent) of the victims at Hiroshima were Korean.

CHAPTER 5
Liberation, Civil War, and Division

1. There was a short spate of trials of prominent collaborators after the emergence of the ROK in 1948. The issue then smoldered through the authoritarian period. Most recently, during the Rho Moo Hyun government (2002–), an investigative commission to revisit the issue under the guise of reconciling history was established.

2. See Cumings, *Origins of the Korean War*, 1981, chap. 8, for the best analysis of the formation and dynamics of the peoples' committees.

3. The largest such youth corps had been organized by the ultrarightist Yi Pŏmsŏk, who wielded considerable power both during formation of the ROK and afterward.

4. Kim Young Sam, a veteran opposition leader, was elected in 1993, but he had merged his opposition splinter party with the former government party in order to achieve his electoral victory. This left to Kim Dae Jung the honor of being the first member of the opposition to be elected president.

5. In 2003, during the run-up to the second war in Iraq, champions of the new doctrine of US unilateral use of force in world affairs began a discussion of the creation and use of small tactical nuclear weapons.

6. Modest estimates cite 1.3 million South Korean civilian and military casualties; the number for North Korea is 1.5, out of a population one-third the size of the South's.

7. Half a century after the war, Associated Press reporters in South Korea exposed an incident of July 1950 where retreating American forces killed several hundred civilians near the village of Nogunri about a hundred miles south of Seoul. According to interviews of US soldiers who had been on the scene, orders for the massacre were justified by reports of North Korean infiltrators disguising themselves as fleeing refugees.

8. South Korean sources claim that over 84,000 South Koreans were forcibly taken North, and 200,000 South Korean youths were forcibly drafted into the North Korean army. The confusion cut both ways, with the North going after its enemies in the South and, later, the South taking reprisals in the North during the month-long UN army occupation as they drove to the Yalu in November and December of 1950. The conflict between Christians and Communists in Hwanghae province is the subject of a controversial novel by Hwang Sok-Yong, *The Guest* (2005).

9. South Korea sustained a much larger population on a smaller land mass (37,060 sq. miles) than then North (48,420). The advantages conferred by its better climate for agriculture and more habitable land was nullified by its population density. The population of what became South Korea (1944 Japanese census) was 15,944,000. By 1953 it was probably much higher, swollen by a net migration South during the war. The population of what became North Korea was 9,170,000 in 1944.

CHAPTER 6
Political and Economic Development in South Korea

1. The Republics, determined by major constitutional changes, are dated as follows: First, 1948–1960; Second, 1960; Third, 1963–1972; Fourth, 1972–1980; Fifth, 1980–1987; Sixth, 1987–present.

2. The first National Security Law was passed during the first year of Syngman Rhee's presidency. Since that time some variant of this law has been in operation in South Korea. Even since the democratization of South Korean politics, the law has remained on the books; it is a source of considerable controversy.

3. Before and during the war Rhee had encouraged the formation of violent youth groups who used strong-arm tactics to break up opposition rallies and otherwise attack his opposition. One such group that emerged during the ROK government's stay in Pusan went by the intimidating name, the Skeleton Corps (Paekkoldan).

4. Between 1953 and 1961 US aid financed about 70 percent of Korean imports and accounted for nearly 80 percent of its capital formation, mainly in the areas of transportation, manufacturing, and electric power

5. Between 1945 and 1971 the United States supplied a total of $12.6 billion in economic and military assistance to South Korea.

6. The issue of Korea's economic history during the Rhee years is extraordinarily complicated. US political and economic interests, Rhee's disinterest in reviving trade with Japan, Cold War politics, and the enormous problems of rebuilding after the war all compounded planning. For the best short discussion of the political economy of the Rhee regime, see Woo, 1991, chap. 3.

7. Growth in enrollment at post-secondary educational institutions in the ROK between 1945 and 1980 was dramatic: 1945 7,819; 1960 92,934; 1970 201,436; 1980 611,394; see Nahm, *Korean Tradition,* 1988, p. 501.

8. Rho gave several reasons for his proposed move of the capital: reduction of crowding in Seoul, redistribution of wealth, and removing the threat of North Korean bombardment. A site at Kongju-Yongi in Ch'ungch'ŏng province, a hundred miles southeast of Seoul, has been selected for the new capital. The plans are very controversial, and the entire matter has been referred back to the National Assembly for further study.

9. Park is usually thought of as an uncompromising anti-Communist, but he had been arrested for joining insurgents during the Yŏsu Rebellion in the fall of 1948. This led some at the time to suspect him of being a Communist sympathizer.

10. In this view the strong state takes initiative in shaping the broad directions of the national economy. In the case of Korea the state does not directly control the economy but guides the actions of private entrepreneurs through a variety of incentives and coercive actions. See Haggard and Moon, 1993; Woo-Cumings, 1999.

11. The first four Five-year Plans followed the following timetable: First, 1962–1966; Second, 1967–1971; Third, 1972–1976; and Fourth, 1977–1981.

12. In 2004 the ROK was ranked thirty-second in the world in terms of its per capita income, the measure created by dividing the population into the sum of goods and services produced by the national economy.

13. This account of rapid industrialization in South Korea and the export-led industrialization program draws heavily on the more extended account in Eckert et al., 1990, chap. 20.

14. Perhaps the most famous of these campaigns was the New Village Movement (Saemaul undong) of the 1970s. Park organized the entire rural countryside into work teams based on village residence for "self-help" projects to create roads, waterworks, and other improvements. The villagers provided the labor, and the government the materials, organizational training, and exhortation.

15. Curiously, *yushin* is the Korean pronunciation of the Japanese *isshin*, translated as "restoration" when it is used to describe the restoration of the Meiji emperor to the center of Japanese politics in 1868.

16. Emergency Measure Nine of 1975 made it illegal to criticize the president or to criticize the Emergency Measure itself.

17. The Injured People's Association (a Kwangju victims' association) places the death toll at 284 (154 who died at the time, 83 who died later, and 47 missing). But this number does not include noncivilian deaths; nor does it calculate the thousands of injured; see Lewis, 2002, p. 70.

18. The Declaration said that constitutional reform should include direct election of the president, a new election law, and local elections of provincial and county heads. It further stated that political prisoners guilty of no other crime should be released, Kim Dae Jung's political rights should be restored, human rights respected, and freedom of the press allowed. Moreover, educational institutions should be self-regulating and full political party activities encouraged. Rho Tae Woo had been a senior general who supported Chun's takeover of the army in December 1979. He had risen to be Chun's successor, and in addition to being head of the DJP, he was also president of the Seoul Olympic Organizing Committee.

CHAPTER 7
Going It Alone

1. Numerous versions of this image are in circulation; perhaps its broadest publication came in a *New York Times* article in February of 2002. The photo can be found in the "Military" section of the Internet website Globalsecurity.org; see: http://www.globalsecurity.org/military/world/dprk/dprk-dark.htm

2. North Korea received aid from Eastern European Communist nations and the Soviet Union, and it did have trade relationships, but North Korea never joined the world Socialist Council of Mutual Economic Assistance (COMECON) and even timed its central plans to frustrate linkage with other fraternally allied socialist states.

3. *Juche* is the official North Korean romanization of the Korean word. It is rendered *chuch'e* in the McCune-Reischauer transliteration system used by Korean Studies scholars.

4. The state draws its sovereignty from three social groups: workers, peasants, and working intellectuals. The DPRK flag symbolizes the unity of these groups by adding a writing brush (intellectuals) to the familiar socialist hammer (worker) and sickle (peasants) logo made famous by its use on the flag of the Soviet Union.

5. In recent years a number of descriptions have been published by survivors of the camps in North Korea. One widely read memoir, that of Kang and Rigoulot, 2005, describes ten years at the Yodok labor camp.

6. Doowon Lee, "North Korean Economic Reform," 1996, pp. 317–336.

7. It should be noted here that during roughly the same period, direct aid to the ROK from the United States was also declining; the South Koreans, however, were able to replace this source of capital with loans from global capital markets.

8. In 1968 North Korean commandoes broke through the DMZ on a mission to assassinate the ROK president and were stopped only miles of their objective. The DPRK seized the US spy boat *Pueblo* and shot down an American EWC reconnaissance plane in the same year. In the early 1970s a number of tunnels under the DMZ were discovered.

9. The authoritative biography of Kim Il Sung is Suh Dae Sook's *Kim Il Sung*, 1988. This analysis best disentangles Kim's actual biography from the escalating claims of the massive hagiography of the cult of the leader.

10. Dear Leader could be also translated Kyŏngae hanŏn chidoja. This terminology was used in combination with Suryŏng and other titles for the father as in "Beloved and Respected." The Korean language provides many opportunities to make status distinctions because of its reliance on honorifics and the importance of different words and structures used in addressing people of varying statuses. After the death of Kim Il Sung, "Dear Leader" in reference to the son gradually disappeared.

11. This plot summary is drawn from my own field notes, made when visiting the Nampo Barrage in the fall of 1992.

12. I am indebted to Gari Ledyard for this insight. For a discussion on the etymology of *chuch'e* and *kukch'e*, see the archive of Korean Studies Listserve at Koreanstudies@koreaweb.ws. (June 2002).

13. The US Eighth Army has been stationed in South Korea since the Korean War. Over time there have been troop withdrawals, most notably during the Carter administration. The current troop level now is just under 36,000 men.

14. North Korean agents exploded a bomb at a ceremony to be attended by the ROK president and several of his major cabinet ministers. Twenty-one people perished, including seventeen high ROK officials, the ambassador to the United States, the foreign minister, the head of the Economic Planning Board, and the minister of Commerce and Industry. Chun Doo Hwan arrived at the ceremony late and thus escaped.

CHAPTER 8
Democratization in South Korea 1987–2000

1. Globalization *(segyehwa)* was made an explicit government policy during the Kim Young Sam administration. The administration embraced internationalization, but sought to ensure that while Korea was open to all international cultural and economic forces, it would also strive to inject Korean ideas, cultural habits, and values into the international community.

2. Kim Dae Jung had been hounded by the KCIA throughout his political career. While

living in Japan, Kim Dae Jung was kidnapped in Japan and returned to Korea in 1973, where he spent the rest of the 1970s under house arrest. In May 1980 he was again arrested, charged and convicted of responsibility in the Kwangju massacre. His death sentence was suspended, however, and he was allowed to go into exile in the United States in 1982. He returned to Korea in 1985, but his civil rights were restored only in 1987.

3. Kim Jong Pil had been prominent in the 1961 Military Coup and was later Park Chung Hee's right-hand man and prime minister. He reappeared in Korean politics on the strength of his conservative credentials, his name recognition, and the solid backing from his home province of South Ch'ungch'ŏng.

4. The LDP ruled Japan between 1955 and 1993. Successive prime ministers chosen within the party passed the top post among various "factions" within the party without any public nominating process. The party's large majority in the Diet created, in effect, one-party rule by a permanent government party, which faced an institutionalized permanent opposition.

5. This is excepting the brief "acting" presidency of Choi Kyu Hah in late 1979 and early 1980.

6. Many of these officials, including Chun and Rho, were members of a secret society, the Hannahoe (Unity Society), which was composed of military officers and others, almost all from the Kyŏngsang region. The Hannahoe was formally disbanded in 1993.

7. This was no small fund. Rho admitted on national television that between 1988 and 1993 he had accumulated a secret fund of $650 million. It was also revealed at Chun Doo Hwan's trial for corruption that his secret political fund contained hundreds of millions of dollars.

8. Chun and Rho each served a year in prison, but were pardoned by newly elected President Kim Dae Jung as a gesture of national reconciliation.

9. Six months before, in December 1996, South Koreans had taken great satisfaction in being admitted to the Organization for Economic Cooperation and Development (OECD).

10. This marriage of convenience was a startling turnaround for Kim. Kim Jong Pil had served as head of the KCIA, Kim Dae Jung's longterm nemesis, and prime minister under Park Chung Hee. Kim Dae Jung purportedly had offered to make Kim Jong Pil prime minister in a reformed parliamentary government he was to propose in the future.

11. Gi-Wook Shin and Chang, 2000, p. 87, provide figures from one survey showing that middle-class households with incomes of more than 2 million won ($1,700) per month, which made up 58 percent of the population in 1996, decreased to 45 percent by the end of 1998.

12. The Korea Development Institute uses 803,000 won per month as the poverty line. At 1600 won per dollar (the lowest point of won value) this equaled $502 per month.

13. The core city of Seoul has 9.9 million people and the greater Seoul metropolitan area (Inch'ŏn and Kyŏnggi province) 22.5 million, out of the total ROK population of 48.8 million. The population density is 16,500 people per square kilometer, 1.3 times greater than Tokyo and twice as dense as New York City.

14. In 2005 the National Assembly revised the Civil Code to allow women to hold the position of family head; it also abolished the ban against marriage between people of the same surname.

15. In 1971 there were only 26,806 registered private automobiles in Seoul: in 1981 there were still only 108,072, even though this was a 400 percent increase. This number increased by another 800 percent, to 883,415, at the end of the decade; the number has continued to increase almost geometrically since then; see Seoul, *Statistical Yearbook*, 1991.

16. The Kangnam area of Seoul grew from paddy fields south of the Han River that were undeveloped in the 1960s. As Seoul grew, an entirely new city of 5 million people rose in Kangnam, now the center of the new middle class as well as the location of some of the most exclusive housing in Seoul. Residents now refer to Seoul as bifurcated into Kangbuk (north of the Han River), and the newer Kangnam (south of the Han River).

17. This declaration was formally known as The Agreement on Reconciliation, Nonaggression, Exchanges, and Cooperation.

18. The National Security Law was still on the books, although it was used in only very select cases. The fact remained, though, that it was still against the law to aid North Korea, travel to North Korea without permission, and so forth.

19. These are common elements of reunification formulas, first proposed in the 1970s, that outline possible forms of governance for a reunited Korea. The North proposed a confederation of two separate governments; the South a single government that worked on the principle of federation.

EPILOGUE

1. In the summer of 2002 an US army tank on maneuvers struck and killed two young female students on their way to school. The US army's refusal to turn the tank crew over to Korean authorities for indictment inflamed anti-American sentiment during the presidential election campaign.

2. US Assistant Secretary of State James Kelly went to North Korea in October 2002 to confront them with evidence of their uranium enrichment, but he was totally unprepared for their open and public admission that they were indeed enriching uranium.

3. Just as this manuscript reached its final stages, North Korea startled the world with the detonation of a small nuclear bomb on October 9, 2006. After successful negotiations with the PRC, a US-sponsored UN Security Council resolution was passed that placed further financial constraints as well as an embargo on the export of missiles, nuclear material and equipment, and other heavy ordnance by North Korea. North Korea's successful test of a nuclear device clearly highlights the necessity for solving once and for all the continuing security problems on the Korean peninsula.

BIBLIOGRAPHY

· · · · · ·

Ablemann, Nancy. *Echoes of the Past: Epics of Dissent.* Berkeley: University of California Press, 1996.

———. *The Melodrama of Mobility: Women, Talk, and Class in Contemporary South Korea.* Honolulu: University of Hawai'i Press, 2003.

———. "Women's Class Mobility and Identities in South Korea: A Gendered, Transnational, Narrative Approach." *The Journal of Asian Studies* 56, no. 2 (1997): 398–420.

Ablemann, Nancy, and John Lie. *Blue Dreams: Korean Americans and the Los Angeles Riots.* Cambridge, MA: Harvard University Press, 1995.

Allen, Richard C. *Korea's Syngman Rhee: An Unauthorized Portrait.* Rutland, VT: Charles E. Tuttle, 1960.

Amsden, Alice H. *Asia's Next Giant: South Korea and Late Industrialization.* Oxford: Oxford University Press, 1989.

Anderson, Benedict. *Imagined Communities: Reflections on the Origin and Spread of Nationalism.* New York: Verso, 1991.

Armstrong, Charles K. *The North Korean Revolution, 1945–1950.* Ithaca, NY: Cornell University Press, 2003.

Asia Watch Report. *Human Rights in Korea.* New York: Asia Watch Committee, 1985.

Baldwin, Frank. "The March First Movement: Korean Challenge and Japanese Response." Ph.D. diss. Columbia University, 1969.

———. *Without Parallel: The American-Korean Relationship since 1945.* New York: Pantheon Books, 1973.

Bedeski, Robert E. *The Transformation of South Korea: Reform and Reconstruction in the Sixth Republic under Roh Tae Woo 1987–1992.* New York: Routledge, 1994.

Bunge, Frederica M., ed. *North Korea: A Country Study.* Washington DC: US Government Area Handbook Series, 1994.

———. *South Korea: A Country Study.* Washington DC: US Government Area Handbook Series, 1982.

Ch'ae Man-Sik. *Peace Under Heaven.* Trans. Kyung-Ja Chun. Armonk, NY: M. E. Sharpe. 1993.

Chandra, Vipan. *Imperialism, Resistance, and Reform in Late Nineteenth-Century Korea: Enlightenment and the Independence Club.* Berkeley: Institute of East Asian Studies University of California, Center for Korean Studies, 1988.

Choi, Chungmoo. "The Discourses of Decolonization and Popular Memory: South Korea." *Positions: East Asia Cultures Critiques,* no. 1 (1993): 77–102.

———. "Korean Women in a Culture of Inequality." In *Korea Briefing 1992,* edited by Donald Clark, pp. 97–116. Boulder, CO: Westview Press, 1992.

———. "Nationalism and Construction of Gender in Korea." In *Dangerous Women: Gender and Korean Nationalism,* edited by Elaine H. Kim and Chungmoo Choi, pp. 9–31. New York: Routledge, 1998.

Choi, Jang Jip. *Democracy after Democratization.* Seoul: Humanitas, 2005.

———. *Labor and the Authoritarian State: Labor Unions in South Korean Manufacturing Industries, 1961–1980.* Honolulu: University of Hawaiʻi Press, 1990.

Chung, Chin Sung. "The Origin and Development of the Military Sexual Slavery Problem in Imperial Japan." *Positions: East Asia Cultures Critiques* 5, no.1 (1997): 219–254.

Clark, Donald N. *Living Dangerously in Korea: The Western Experience 1900–1950.* Norwalk. CT: EastBridge, 2003.

Clifford, Mark L. *Troubled Tiger: Businessmen, Bureaucrats, and Generals in South Korea.* Armonk, NY: M. E. Sharpe, 1994.

Cole, David C., and Princeton N. Lyman. *Korean Development: The Interplay of Politics and Economics.* Cambridge, MA: Harvard University Press, 1971.

Cumings, Bruce, ed. *Child of Conflict: The Korean-American Relationship, 1943–1953.* Seattle: University of Washington Press, 1983.

———. "The Corporate State in North Korea." In *State and Society in Contemporary Korea,* edited by Hagen Koo, pp. 197–230. Ithaca, NY: Cornell University Press, 1993.

———. *Korea's Place in the Sun: A Modern History.* New York: W. W. Norton, 1997.

———. "The Origins and Development of the Northeast Asian Political Economy: Industrial Sectors, Product Cycles, and Political Consequence." *International Organization* 38 (Winter 1984): 1–40.

———. *The Origins of the Korean War.* Vol. 1: *Liberation and the Emergence of Separate Regimes 1945–1947.* Princeton, NJ: Princeton University Press, 1981.

———. *The Origins of the Korean War.* Vol. 2: *Roaring of the Cataract 1947–1953.* Princeton, NJ: Princeton University Press, 2000.

de Bary, Wm. Theodore, and JaHyun Kim Haboush, eds. *The Rise of Neo-Confucianism in Korea.* New York: Columbia University Press, 1985.

Deuchler, Martina. *Confucian Gentlemen and Barbarian Envoys.* Seattle: University of Washington Press, 1977.

———. *The Confucian Transformation of Korea: A Study of Society and Ideology.* Cambridge, MA: Council on East Asian Studies, Harvard University, 1992.

Deyo, Frederic C., ed. *Beneath the Miracle: Labor Subordination in the New Asian Industrialism.* Berkeley: University of California Press, 1989.

Dong, Won-Mo, "Japanese Colonial Policy and Practice in Korea 1905–1945: A Study in Assimilation." Ph.D. diss. Georgetown University, 1965.

Duncan, John B. *The Origins of the Chosŏn Dynasty*. Seattle: University of Washington Press, 2000.

Duus, Peter. *The Abacus and the Sword: The Japanese Penetration of Korea, 1895–1910.* Berkeley: University of California Press, 1995.

Duus, Peter, Ramon H. Myers, and Mark R. Peattie, eds. *The Japanese Informal Empire in China, 1895–1937.* Princeton, NJ: Princeton University Press, 1989.

Eckert, Carter. *Offspring of Empire: The Koch'ang Kims and the Colonial Origins of Korean Capitalism 1876–1945.* Seattle: University of Washington Press, 1991.

———. "The South Korean Bourgeoisie: A Class in Search of Hegemony." In *State and Society in Contemporary Korea,* edited by Hagen Koo, pp. 95–130. Ithaca, NY: Cornell University Press, 1993.

———. "Total War, Industrialization, and Social Change in Late Colonial Korea." In *The Japanese Wartime Empire, 1931–1945,* edited by Peter Duus, Ramon H. Myers, and Mark R. Peattie. Princeton, NJ: Princeton University Press, 1996.

Eckert, Carter, Ki-baik Lee, Young Ick Lew, Michael Robinson, and Edward W. Wagner. *Korea Old and New: A History.* Cambridge, MA: Korea Institute, Harvard University Press. 1990.

Eder, Norman. *Poisoned Prosperity: Development, Modernization, and the Environment in South Korea.* Armonk, NY: M. E. Sharpe, 1996.

Em, Henry. "*Minjok* as a Modern and Democratic Construct: Sin Ch'aeho's Historiography." In *Colonial Modernity in Korea,* edited by Gi-Wook Shin and Michael Robinson, pp. 336–362. Cambridge, MA: East Asia Council Publications, 1999.

Fenkl, Heinz Insu. *Memories of My Ghost Brother.* London: Anchor Books, 1997.

Foot, Rosemary. *The Wrong War: American Policy and the Dimensions of the Korean Conflict, 1950–1953.* Ithaca, NY: Cornell University Press, 1985.

Friedman, Edward, ed. *The Politics of Democratization: Generalizing East Asian Experiences.* Boulder, CO: Westview Press, 1994.

Fujitani, Takashi. *Splendid Monarchy: Power and Pageantry in Modern Japan.* Berkeley: University of California Press, 1996.

Gragert, Edwin H. *Landownership under Colonial Rule: Korea's Japanese Experience, 1900–1935.* Honolulu: University of Hawai'i Press, 1994.

Grajdanzev, Andrew J. *Modern Korea.* New York: The John Day Company, 1944.

Haboush, JaHyun Kim. *A Heritage of Kings: One Man's Monarchy in the Confucian World.* New York: Columbia University Press, 1988.

Haggard, Stephan, and Chung-in Moon. "The State, Politics, and Economic Development in Postwar South Korea." In *State and Society in Contemporary Korea,* edited by Hagen Koo. Ithaca, NY: Cornell University Press, 1993.

Haggard, Stephan, and Marcus Noland. *Famine in North Korea: Markets, Aid and Reform.* New York: Columbia University Press, 2007.

Hamilton, Clive. *Capitalist Industrialization in Korea*. Boulder, CO: Westview Press, 1986.

Han, Jongwoo, and L. H. M. Ling. "Authoritarianism in the Hypermasculinized State: Hybridity, Patriarchy, and Capitalism in Korea." *International Studies Quarterly* no. 42 (1989): 53–78.

Han, Sungjoo. *The Failure of Democracy in South Korea*. Berkeley: University of California Press, 1974.

Harvey, Youngsook Kim. *Six Korean Women: The Socialization of Shamans*. St. Paul, MN: West Publishing Company, 1979.

Henderson, Gregory. *Korea: The Politics of the Vortex*. Cambridge, MA: Harvard University Press, 1968.

Howard, Keith. *True Stories of the Korean Comfort Women*. London: Cassell, 1995.

Hulbert, Homer. *The Passing of* Korea. New York: Doubleday, 1906.

Hwang, Kyung Moon. *Beyond Birth: Social Status in the Emergence of Modern Korea*. Cambridge MA: Harvard University Asia Center, 2004

Hwang Sok-Yong. *The Guest*. Trans. Kyung-Ja Chun and Maya West. New York: Seven Stories Press, 2005.

Itō Takeo. *Life along the South Manchurian Railway: The Memoirs of Itō Takeo*. Trans. Joshua A. Fogel. Armonk, NY: M. E. Sharpe, 1988.

Jacobs, Norman. *The Korean Road to Modernization and Development*. Urbana: University of Illinois Press, 1985.

Jager, Sheila Miyoshi. "Women, Resistance and the Divided Nation: The Romantic Rhetoric of Korean Reunification." *The Journal of Asian Studies* 55, no. 1 (1996): 3–21.

Janelli, Roger. *Ancestor Worship and Korean Society*. Stanford: Stanford University Press, 1982.

———. "The Origins of Korean Folkore Scholarship." *Journal of American Folkore* 99 (1986): 24–49.

Janelli, Roger L., and Dawnhee Yim. *Making Capitalism: The Social and Cultural Construction of a South Korean Conglomerate*. Stanford: Stanford University Press. 1993.

Kajiyma, Toshiyuki. *The Clan Records: Five Stories of Korea*. Trans. Yoshiko Dykstra. Honolulu: University of Hawai'i Press, 1995.

Kang, Chol-Hwan, and Pierre Rigoulot. *The Aquariums of Pyongyang :Ten Years in the North Korean Gulag*. New York: Basic Books, 2005.

Kendall, Laurel. *Shamans, Housewives, and Other Restless Spirits*. Honolulu: University of Hawai'i Press, 1985.

———. *Getting Married in Korea: Of Gender, Morality, and Modernity*. Berkeley: University of California Press, 1996.

———, ed. *Under Construction: The Gendering of Modernity, Class, and Consumption in the Republic of Korea*. Honolulu: University of Hawai'i Press, 2002.

Kihl, Young Whan. *Politics and Policies in Divided Korea: Regimes in Contest.* Boulder, CO: Westview Press, 1984.

Kim, Byong Sik. *Modern Korea: The Socialist North, Revolutionary Perspectives in the South.* New York: International Publishers, 1970.

Kim, Byoung-Lo Philo. *Two Koreas in Development: A Comparative Study of Principles and Strategies of Capitalist and Communist Third World Development.* New Brunswick, NJ: Transaction Publishers, 1992.

Kim, Byung-Kook. "The Politics of Crisis and a Crisis of Politics: The Presidency of Kim Dae-Jung." In *Korea Briefing: 1997–1999,* edited by Kongdan Oh. Armonk, NY: M. E. Sharpe, 2000.

Kim, C. I. Eugene, and Han Kyo Kim. *Korea and the Politics of Imperialism.* Berkeley: University of California Press, 1967.

Kim, C. I. Eugene, and Doretha E. Mortimore, eds. *Korea's Response to Japan: The Colonial Period 1910–1945.* Kalamazoo, MI: The Center for Korean Studies, Western Michigan University, 1977.

Kim, Choong Soon. *The Culture of Korean Industry: An Ethnography of Poongsan Corporation.* Tucson: University of Arizona Press, 1992.

———. *Faithful Endurance: An Ethnography of Korean Family Dispersal.* Tucson: University of Arizona Press, 1988.

Kim, Elaine H., and Chungmoo Choi. *Dangerous Women: Gender and Korean Nationalism.* New York: Routledge, 1998.

Kim, Eun Mee. *Big Business, Strong State: Collusion and Conflict in South Korean Development.* Albany: State University of New York Press, 1997.

Kim, Hyung-chan, with Dong-kyu Kim. *Human Remolding in North Korea: A Social History of Education.* New York: University Press of America, 2005.

Kim, Illsoo. *New Urban Immigrants: The Korean Community in New York.* Princeton, NJ: Princeton University Press, 1981.

Kim, Ilpyong J., and Young Whan Kihl. *Political Change in South Korea.* New York: Paragon House Publishers, 1988.

Kim, Joong-Seop. "In Search of Human Rights: the Paekchŏng Movement in Colonial Korea." In *Colonial Modernity in Korea 1910–1945.* Edited by Gi-Wook Shin and Michael Robinson, pp. 311–335. Cambridge, MA: East Asia Council Publications, Harvard University, 1999.

Kim, Key-Hiuk. *The Last Phase of the East Asian World Order: Korea, Japan, and the Chinese Empire, 1860–1882.* Berkeley: University of California Press, 1980.

Kim, Richard. *Lost Names.* Berkeley: University of California Press, 1998.

Kim, Samuel S., ed. *Korea's Globalization.* Cambridge: Cambridge University Press, 2000.

Kim, Seong-nae. "Chronicle of Violence, Ritual of Mourning: Cheju Shamanism in Korea." Ph.D. diss. University of Michigan, 1989.

———, "Lamentations of the Dead: The Historical Imagery of Violence on Cheju Island, South Korea." *Journal of Ritual Studies* 3, no. 2 (1989): 251–285.

Kim, Seung-kyung. *Class Struggle or Family Struggle: The Lives of Women Factory Workers in South Korea.* Cambridge: Cambridge University Press, 1997.

Kirk, Donald. *Korean Dynasty: Hyundai and Chung Ju Yung.* Armonk, NY: M. E. Sharpe. 1994

Koo, Hagen. *Korean Workers: The Culture and Politics of Class Formation.* Ithaca, NY: Cornell University Press, 2001.

———, ed. *State and Society in Contemporary Korea.* Ithaca, NY: Cornell University Press, 1993.

Lancaster, Lewis, and Chai-shin Yu. *Buddhism in the Early Choson: Suppression and Transformation.* Berkeley: Institute of East Asian Studies, University of California, Center for Korean Studies, 1996.

Lee, Chang-soo, and George De Vos. *Koreans in Japan: Ethnic Conflict and Accommodation.* Berkeley: University of California Press, 1981.

Lee, Chong-Sik. *Korean Workers' Party: A Short History.* Stanford, CA: Hoover Institution Press, 1978.

———. *The Politics of Korean Nationalism.* Berkeley: University of California Press, 1964.

Lee, Doowon. "North Korean Economic Reform." In *Reforming Asian Socialism,* edited by John McMillan and Barry Naughton. Ann Arbor: University of Michigan Press, 1996.

———. "South Korea's Financial Crisis and Economic Restructuring." In *Korea Briefing: 1997–1999,* edited by Kongdan Oh. Armonk, NY: M. E. Sharpe, 2000.

Lee, Hi-seung. "Recollections of the Korean Language Society Incident." In *Listening to Korea,* edited by Marshall Pihl, pp. 19–42. New York: Praeger, 1973.

Lee, Hyung-Koo. *The Korean Economy.* Albany: The State University of New York Press, 1996.

Lee, Peter H., ed. *Sourcebook of Korean Civilization.* Vol. 1: *From Early Times to the Sixteenth Century.* New York: Columbia University Press, 1993.

———, ed. *Sourcebook of Korean Civilization.* Vol. 2: *From the Seventeenth Century to the Modern Period.* New York: Columbia University Press, 1996.

Lett, Denise Potrzeba. *In Pursuit of Status: The Making of South Korea's "New" Urban Middle Class.* Cambridge, MA: Harvard University Asia Center. Harvard-Hallym Series on Korea, 1998.

Lew, Young-ick. "The Conservative Character of the 1894 Tonghak Peasant Uprising: A Reappraisal with Emphasis on Chŏn Pong-jun's Background and Motivation." *Journal of Korean Studies* 7 (1990): 149–180.

Lewis, Linda. *Laying Claim to the Memory of May: A Look Back at the 1980 Kwangju Uprising.* Honolulu: University of Hawai'i Press, 2002.

Lie, John. *Han Unbound: The Political Economy of South Korea.* Stanford: Stanford University Press, 1998.

Lindauer, David L. et al. *The Strains of Economic Growth: Labor Unrest and Social Dissatis-*